D1528001

LABOUR AND PARASTATAL POLITICS IN SIERRA LEONE

A Study of African Working-Class Ambivalence

David Fashole Luke

Killam Fellow
Dalhousie University

General Editors of the Dalhousie African Studies Series
John E. Flint and Timothy M. Shaw

UNIVERSITY
PRESS OF
AMERICA

LANHAM • NEW YORK • LONDON

Centre of African Studies

Dalhousie University

The Dalhousie African Studies Series is co-published
by University Press of America, Inc. and Dalhousie University Press.

DEDICATION

FOR MY MOTHER, AND IN MEMORY OF MY FATHER

ACKNOWLEDGEMENTS

The research for this study, originally a University of London doctoral thesis, was carried out in Freetown (December 1979 - July 1980; February - June 1982); Oxford (November 1980); Liverpool (February 1981); and in London (at various times between October 1978 and January 1982), and has been assisted by several individuals.

I am sincerely grateful to the shop stewards and rank and file of the Sierra Leone Dock Workers' Union for accepting me as a 'brother' and for making both periods of field work at the docks so enjoyable and interesting. Thema Conteh, J. T. Kanu, Pa Karanke Limba, and Mark Luseni (who, it has been learnt with deep regret, recently lost his life in an air crash on his way home from a trade union course in Europe), David Sesay and Olu Vincent were among the shop stewards who introduced me to the rank and file of the union. Francis Brimah, the Union Secretary, initially introduced me to the shop stewards and allowed access to union records. His assistant, Aflred Conteh, was very helpful in locating the relevant files.

Ray Donker, General Manager of the Port Authority, kindly allowed me to study the corporation's archives, to interview workers and staff during working hours, and the use of a classroom in the corporation's training department to undertake a sample survey of the dockers. Ernest Williams, the Corporation Secretary, Moses Palmer of the Archives and Files Department, and Edrich Kandeh of the Operations Department were also very helpful.

I should like to thank several trade unionists who have discussed (and/or allowed access to records) the history and contemporary aspects of the labour movement in Sierra Leone with me. H. M. Barrie, Uriah Davies, Sahr Gbenda, H. N. Georgestone, Marcus Grant, F. B. Hamilton, James Kabia, E. T. Kamara, Tejan Kassim, Tony Rogers, Alhaji Savage, C. A. Wilton-During and T. E. Yambasu must be mentioned by name.

I received financial assistance from the British Council. A grant from the Institute of Public Administration and Management (IPAM) Educational Project facilitated the second trip to Freetown when I had the privilege of working at the Institute. Ted Cooper,

former Director of IPAM was instrumental in arranging
this award.

The original manscript was examined by Christopher
Clapham and Donal Cruise O'Brien and read by an anony-
mous reader appointed by University Press of America all
of whom made perceptive comments for its revision.
David Murray, former Editor of <u>Public Administration
and Development</u>, made some suggestions with regard to
Chapters 3 and 4.

The revision was carried out at Dalhousie University where I have been a Post-doctoral Fellow since the
autumn of 1982. I am deeply indebted to the Killam
Trustees for the award of the fellowship. Dalhousie
provided a congenial environment for further reflection
and a community of Africans and Africanists representing
a broad spectrum of political opinion who have commented
on several of the arguments advanced in this book. I
should like to mention especially, Tim Shaw, Director
of the University's Centre for African Studies. Marie
Riley brought her superb editing skills to the reading
of the proofs. My spouse, Rosamond, skillfully
prepared the camera ready copy via word processor in
record time.

This work has been supervised by Richard Jeffries.
In December 1977, while a student at the London School
of Economics (and a neophyte in matters relating to
academic research on African labour), I wrote to him to
explore the possibility of undertaking post-graduate
research at the School of Oriental and African Studies.
His reply that he would supervise the project and
urging that I make a formal application came quickly.
The relationship which developed between us (from
October 1978) may be said to be analogous to that
between a craftsman and an apprentice. A fine craftsman encourages and infects the apprentice with enthusiasm for the vocation. Richard Jeffries is a fine
craftsman. The research methods he encouraged me to
follow are in the best traditions of empiricism. If
this work achieves anything, it should be seen as a
tribute to the craftsman from whom this apprentice has
learnt the trade. Needless to say, I am wholly responsible for any difficulties with the arguments and the
defects which undoubtedly remain.

David Fashole Luke
Halifax, January 1984

of the University's Centre for African Studies. Marie

C O N T E N T S

LIST OF TABLES

ABBREVIATIONS AND A NOTE ON CURRENCY

AALC	African-American Labour Centre
APC	All People's Congress
DICOR	Diamond Corporation
DIMINCO	National Diamond Mining company
EEC	European Economic Community
ICFTU	International Confederation of Free Trade Unions
ILO	International Labour Organisation
IMF	International Monetary Fund
JIC	Joint Industrial Council
KPM	Kono Progressive Movement
NCSL	National Council of the Colony of Sierra Leone
NRC	National Reformation Council
PZ	Paterson Zochonis
SLBS	Sierra Leone Broadcasting Services
SLIM	Sierra Leone Independence Movement
SLPMB	Sierra Leone Produce Marketing Board
SLPP	Sierra Leone People's Party
SLTUC	Sierra Leone Trade Union Congress
TGNC	Trade Group Negotiating Council
TUC	Trade Union Congress (of United Kingdom)
UAC	United Africa Company
UDP	United Democratic Party
UNF	United National Front
UPP	United People's Party

In Section 1 of this study, monetary values are expressed in sterling. From Section 2, however, monetary values are expressed in sterling and in Leones and cents, the latter being Sierra Leone's national currency first introduced in August 1964. Le2 = £1 Sterling, a fixed rate of exchange until November 1978 when it was 'de-linked' from sterling and 'tied' to the IMF's unit of exchange, the SDR. Since that date the official rate against the £ has varied between £1 = Le2.10 and £1 = Le4.30.

INTRODUCTION

In most of the post-colonial states of sub-Saharan Africa, both the size and functions of the state bureaucracy have proliferated. This has allegedly (according to official rhetoric) been for the purpose of promoting economic development and social change. The centrality of the role of the state was, during the period of decolonisation and independence, lent intellectual respectability by fashionable 'progressive' economic thinking. This required that in order to transcend structural 'neo-colonial dependency', the direct participation of the state in the modern sector to the progressive exclusion of foreign capital was paramount. Much emphasis was therefore to be laid on developing import substitutive industry so as to increase national autonomy and lay the basis for 'independent' development. This strategy also involved the extension of state control over extractive industries and over rural economic activities so as to facilitate the appropriation of a large part of the value of the peasant farm produce. As a result of the pervasiveness of the role of the state in social and economic life, the majority of wage earners in most African countries, including Sierra Leone, are employed by government or parastatal organisations.

Whatever the economic rationale of these organisations, they do not exist and operate in a social and political vacuum. They are typically an integral part of a patron-clientelist political and economic system on which the very foundations of government sometimes depend.1 This is not simply or even necessarily to say that African governments preside over a 'spoils system' in which dictators give handouts to supporters and kinsmen from the treasury till. In the post-independence era of inter-communal competition and growing inter-class cleavage which constantly expose the institutional fragility of the new nation-states, political stability can greatly depend on the extent to which governments can underwrite the competing claims of different sections of the populace. More particularly, there has been (and there is) pressure for employment opportunities from a growing urban population which has generated the response from governments of providing jobs for political clients in public bureaucracies. It is against this background that government and parastatal organisations typically operate in the new African states.

In the now considerable literature on African labour studies, the problem of 'situating' lower-paid workers within the political economy when these are workers in a public corporation, which is in turn an integral part of a system of political clientelism, has not received sufficiently detailed attention. Most studies of African workers have tended either to focus on workers in capitalist industries, or to treat the situation of workers in the employ of public sector organisations as equivalent to employment in capitalist industries. In the latter case, there has been a tendency to apply a theoretical model which implies that such organisations are, like capitalist industries, geared to profit-making via surplus appropriation, and that the proper or ideal response of their employment is therefore one of anti-capitalist protest.2 On the other hand, there has also been a tendency to treat all employees of government and parastatals as 'parasitic' on the peasantry.3 It is far from clear that parastatals (even in societies developing in the direction of capitalism) operate in the manner or by the criteria of capitalist enter-prises. On the other hand, it is far from clear that all public sector employees are non-productive, unexploited, or purely parasitic on the peasantry and/or on the surplus appropriated from the extractive industries. Even less clear is it that, even if--by virtue of their employment--in a relatively favoured economic position, they are non-antagonistic towards the political and bureaucratic elite. The idea that as a 'labour aristocracy' all wage earners except the unskilled are closely allied to, or even part of, this elite has been effectively refuted by Peace for the case of Southern Nigerian industrial workers4 and by Jeffries for the case of Ghanaian railwaymen.5 This study is designed to examine the same question for the case of the Sierra Leone dock workers but also, hopefully, to make some theoretical advance.

The central concern is therefore to identify on the one hand the main features of the 'mode of appro-priation and distribution' in post-colonial Sierra Leone (the political and sociological processes which are involved as well as the pattern of income distri-bution which has emerged) and on the other, to show how these influence the attitudes and political behaviour of the dockers in the employ of the Port Authority. The first concern belongs to the realm of so-called 'ob-jective analysis of class relations' and largely follows Kitching.6 The second is sometimes denigratingly said by Marxists to belong to 'bourgeois stratification theory' but seems worth the effort as attitudes are crucial for the understanding of past and (probable) future political behaviour.7 Moreover, Marx's concept of the dialectic surely emphasises the immense useful-ness of understanding social and political change as the product of a continuous interplay between conscious-ness and 'objective' economic reality.

This study focuses, then, on the responses of one of the largest groups of wage earners in Sierra Leone to their employment by a parastatal organisation. Amongst the more important questions which are raised are the following: what are the economic and political dynamics, or rules of operation, of a public corporation such as the Port Authority? How have these been affected by the development of a system of political clientelism (and associated corruption) in post-colonial Sierra Leone? To the extent that these rules of operation are not those of efficiency in profit maximisation, such as characterises capitalist enterprises, can the employees in such a corporation (or certain sections of them) be said to be (in a Marxist sense) exploited, and by what criteria? If lower-paid workers, at least, can collectively be so described, what influence is exerted on their political perceptions and behaviour by the role of patron-clientelism in labour recruitment and managerial stra-tegies of labour control? More especially, what have been the most notable features of their trade union organisation and action? And to what degree has their trade union activity led them in a conscious (or unconscious) confrontation with government over major policy issues?

As already stated, it is an assumption of this study that the economic position and political behaviour of parastatal employees need to be seen in relation to the role and nature of the Sierra Leonean state. The latter issue has received inadequate and/or unsatisfactory treatment at the levels both of Sierra Leone politics specifically and of sub-Saharan politics generally. Despite a number of useful studies of various aspects of Sierra Leone politics, none of them has addressed itself directly to this question.8 At the more general level, the issue has tended to be dominated by Marxists or neo-Marxists, whose general conclusion has been that the post-colonial state is manned by a petty bourgeoisie and its role, in most instances, determined by metropolitan capital.

The weakness of this characterisation is not only that 'petty bourgeoisie' is here used in a very different sense from that of Marx's classic usage or even that it is used as a somewhat residual category to include the political and bureaucratic (and military) elite with local entrepreneurs and school teachers, whose interests are by no means obviously identical. It is also that it implies an economic rationale (the development of capitalism or whatever) to the treatment of various economic groups of classes by this ruling class when it is far from clear, judging from the post-colonial expression of most African states, that there is any such development rationale or dynamic to their actions and decisions. As this objection implies, it is equally far from clear that the interest of metropolitan (or international) capital has predominantly determined such actions and decisions. The position taken in this study is rather that firstly, the treatment of various economic groups (or the process of class formation and exploitation) needs to be understood as the product of relatively autonomous decision-making by the local state; and, secondly, that, to the degree to which there is a rationale to such decisions, it is political rather than economic.9

This is not to deny that it is of the greatest importance to understand the role of the state in a country such as Sierra Leone in terms of its favouring and disfavouring what might be broadly termed various 'classes', but it is to suggest that the political considerations influencing this process has not been very well understood in the neo-Marxist literature. It is also to draw attention to the fact that such political considerations, and indeed the political process as a whole, centrally involve the preferment of certain individuals and communal groups rather than (or as well as) economic classes. There would seem a great deal to be said, indeed, for characterising the Sierra Leonean state (as those of many other African countries) as a 'neo-patrimonal' regime, its derivation stemming from Max Weber's concept of patrimonal authority.10 In its application to contemporary African states, neo-patrimonalism captures the reality of the on-going struggle for power to control the appropriative mechanism of the state (and the consolidation of such power), a struggle in which the interests cemented by patron-clientelist relationships provide the foundations.

The resources of the neo-patrimonal regime are derived from control over external economic transactions

and the regulation of the economy. Political relationships and patterns of political behaviour are highly
personalised. Where loyalty to the dominant political
figure or ruler is not directly based on ethnic and
kinship ties, or piety to his person, they are based on
a network of patron-clientelist relationships in which
those involved agree to serve the ruler in exchange for
a variety of rewards. This network, within and across
communal groups, permeates all levels of society with
the ruler being the most prominent patron of all.
While recruitment in neo-patrimonal regimes is often
through ability and professional expertise, the highest
offices depend on the ability of the individual to gain
the confidence of the ruler.11

The post-colonial state's central role in development planning, making provisions for manpower training,
building infrastructures, administering commodity
exports, determining policy toward foreign businesses,
allocating mining licenses, import licenses, foreign
exchange, etc., has made access to its decision-making
machanisms a fundamental aspiration of the literate and
educated elite spearheaded by its more politically
committed members.12 Such people develop patron-clientelist followings in their competition for, and use of,
state power because they do generally (and perhaps
genuinely) feel a sense of obligation to their ethnic
commitments and original 'backers' both in the educational as well as in the political stakes and also
because of a need to consolidate support by making
available tangible 'rewards'. Moreover, where
different regions, areas, or locations (populated by
culturally distinct groups) are competing for the same
resources within the same nation-state (the availability of which does make a difference to the prospect of
individual life chances), competitive communalism is
likely to become the basis of political action. Thus
'tribalism', far from being an index of an African
state's fragility, may well be an index of its strength
precisely because what the state has to offer is so
important.13

An aspect of the operational logic of a neo-patrimonal regime is the use of the public sector to accommodate political clients. Not only does the state
finance the salaries, wages, and perquisites of public
sector personnel, over and above this, such personnel
might quite literally dip their hands into the till.
The diversion of resources from public and parastatal
organisations to private consumption and investment,

the deliberate overmanning of the corporation to
accommodate political clients or, the failure of such
organisations to operate like typical capitalist
enterprises, might more usefully be viewed as the
inherent operational logic of the neo-patrimonal
regime.14

One of the most thorny and inadequately answered
questions in the study of the political economy of
African societies is that of the relationship between
the patron-clientelist operations of government and the
process of class formation.15 To what degree does the
former necessarily inhibit the latter? There is
perhaps no adequate answer at a general level; but it
is the aim of this book to begin providing an answer at
the level of the relations between the state and lower-
paid workers in Sierra Leone.

A Note on the Organisation of the Study and Sources

This work falls into three sections and seven
chapters. The first section (and first two chapters)
provide an historical background essential for locating
the study in its proper perspective. Chapter 1
discusses the influence of laissez-faire economic
doctrines on British colonial public administration
and the consequent reluctance of the authorities to
take responsibility for the development of the port or
to bring the management of port services within the
scope of its bureaucratic apparatus. The historical
background to the development of a work force at the
port is narrated; the labour control strategies adopted
by the colonial authorities and the sociological effects
of changing labour market conditions are analysed.
Chapter 2 takes this analysis of labour in the colonial
state further, beginning with a narrative on the
origins of modern trade unionism. Developments during
decolonisation, and, in particular, the beginning of
party politics, the reliance of aspiring politicians on
kinship and clientelist relations to mobilise and
secure support, the 1955 strike and the failure of the
Labour Party are discussed and analysed.

The case study of the political economy of labour
in the Sierra Leone port organisation effectively begins
with the two chapters in the second section. A public
corporation such as the Port Authority, providing what
might be tenably construed as a 'public service',
should not perhaps be assessed as regards either its

'efficiency' or its 'exploitation' of its employees, by the strict capitalist criteria of relative profit. In the case of a quasi-monopolist organisation extracting fees and rent from commercial enterprises, however, the level of loss-making should obviously not be large, in the absence of strong countervailing economic arguments, in order to be regarded as permissible by either capitalist or 'socialist' criteria. It is extremely difficult in practice, and perhaps impossible even in theory, to decide precisely how to measure 'efficiency' or 'exploitation' in such a context. But some light might be gained from a comparative consideration of the performance of the Port Authority (and its equivalent) over various historical periods. It is partly with this in mind that these two chapters examine and contrast the administrative and economic operations of the port organisation between 1954 and 1965 (Chapter 3) and between 1965 and 1976 (Chapter 4). For much of the first period when the port organisation operated under the colonial state, the authorities continued to exhibit some reluctance to expand the public sector and create an autonomous public corporation. The commercial viability of the port enterprise was the most important aspect of managerial policy. In the face of these constraints, the port management deliberately adopted an illiberal employment policy. This created the conditions for the formation of the Dock Workers' Union in 1963 as the means to present an effective challenge to this aspect of managerial policy. During the second period, and in the post-colonial state, the Dock Workers' Union was not only able to reverse some aspects of the employment policy of the port management, but was also able (via the channels of political clientelism) to secure for its Secretary a seat on the Board of a new autonomous Port Authority public corporation. The commercial viability of the port enterprise, previously the cornerstone of managerial policy, increasingly assumed secondary importance resulting in the financial collapse of the corporation in 1976. The involvement of the management and lower-paid dockers in corruption and graft informs the argument that there is a strong element of parasitism in the collective operation of the corporation. This, of course, casts serious doubt on the extent to which the principles of capitalist organisation wwere maintained.

The third section (and last three chapters) attempt to resolve the theoretical problem. In developing a 'sociological profile' of the dockers, Chapter 5 follows Kitching in identifying the 'exploiting' and 'exploited' classes by indices of national income distribution. While it is not suggested that the involvement of the dockers in corrupt practices is sufficient to make them a part of the 'exploiters', the ambiguity reflected in their patron-clientelist relations and their attitudes to elite corruption (and hence their 'class consciousness') can be related to this. This involvement, however, is most accurately seen as merely mitigating their exploitation since they do largely perform the labour entailed in providing a genuine service for commerce (cargo-handling and related functions) at what are pretty low rates of remuneration (even when some graft is included). Moreover, there can be no doubt from socio-economic indices and from sociological observation of their way of life that they are very much a part of the urban poor. This helps to explain the vitality of their trade unionism (Chapter 6). They have not in the past engaged in frequent strike action primarily because of their awareness of their 'dependence' on a government much stronger than themselves alone. The pervasive tentacles of the political clientelist system has attempted to 'capture' their trade union leadership but with only limited success in the face of their solidarity over maintaining an accountable and responsive leadership. The union leadership of the dock workers, however, has inevitably been influenced and constrained in its strategy and decisions by the policy and orientation of the Sierra Leone trade union movement as a whole. It is therefore necessary to situate their trade union behaviour in the context and orientation of the trade union movement in post-colonial Sierra Leone (Chapter 7). An important aspect of this has been the use of the channels of political clientelism in order to secure and defend gains made through the formal processes of collective bargaining. However, it is also clear that the national trade union leadership has failed--as a result of their co-optation (in part at least) into the ruling elite--to consistently assert their right and duty to criticise government policy and performance publicly. More recently, however, the steady erosion in the real value of wages, coupled with an increasing trend in the scale and magnitude of elite corruption, created the conditions which made possible, in September 1981, the first general strike in the country's history in which dock workers played a leading part. The latter episode also illustrates the dynamising potential of a more truly expressive labour leadership as well as the limits of government tolerance. A conclusion summarises the main concerns of this work.

A variety of primary sources form the basis of this study. These include material from the archives of the London Chamber of Commerce; Ocean Transport Limited (the parent organisation of Elder Dempster Lines); the National Workshop Corporation (formerly the Sierra Leone Railway Administration); the Sierra Leone Port Authority; the Sierra Leone Dock Workers' Union; the Sierra Leone Labour Congress; the Sierra Leone Teachers' Union; the Artisans, Ministry of Works Employees' Union; and the Sierra Leone House of Representatives. Records of the Sierra Leone National Archives are also used. Newspapers, official reports, formal interviews, informal extended conversations with the dockers themselves and the results of a questionnaire survey of a sample of their number provide other sources.

SECTION 1

THE HISTORICAL BACKGROUND

CHAPTER 1

THE EARLY ORGANISATION OF THE PORT OF FREETOWN

AND THE EMERGENCE OF A WORK FORCE BEFORE 1954

The influence of laissez-faire economic doctrines
in the theory and practice of the administration of
British colonial possessions was as pervasive as it was
profound. The primary concern of colonial administrators was the establishment of seemingly reasonable
infrastructure and administrative services, and the
raising of sufficient revenue to maintain them. The
involvement of the colonial authorities in Sierra Leone
in large-scale ventures was therefore effectively
precluded. Even by the standards of adherence to this
policy, the colonial authorities were extremely
cautious. The modest Government Wharf, built between
1870 and 1873 in Freetown,1 is an example of such
fiscal caution. Several proposals to develop the port
to meet the requirements of the increasing trade in
produce failed to materialise as successive colonial
administrations felt unable either to put up a part of
the capital required or to guarantee loans. For
instance, a scheme to move the site of the port to its
present location remained on the drawing board of the
engineer who had been sent out from Britain to make the
preliminary surveys in the early part of 1911. 2

Early Organisation

This principle of restricting the colonial administration's involvement in the economic life of the
dependency to the minimum was reflected in the early
organisation of the port. Its functional areas were
separated between government departments and the local
representatives of the shipping companies, the most
important being Elder Dempster. This meant that the
work force at the port was for many years fragmented
between different employers. The Customs Department,
the main source of government revenue until it was
replaced by receipts from the mining industry in the
1930s, was responsible for the coordination of the
activities of the various port users. It maintained a
prominent presence and its warehouses became the
clearing centres for both imports and exports. The
Port and the Marine Department, also formerly an

3

important source of government revenue through harbour dues and fees collected for pilotage, was responsible for the regulation of shipping traffic in the harbour and the maintenance of navigational aids. The Railway Administration maintained the cranes and other cargo-handling equipment at the wharf which were first introduced in 1909. 3 The Public Works Department (formerly known as the Royal Engineers) undertook maintenance work on the sea wall and jetties. While the government department provided the services ancilliary to cargo handling, the shipping companies and the larger trading firms were directly involved in the latter activity.

In addition to cargo-handling, Elder Dempster, as part of its corporate strategy of establishing itself as the leading organisation in West African shipping, had since the early 1900s provided a 'feeder' and lighterage service in the more important trading areas along the West African Coast under British influence. A wholly owned Elder Dempster subsidiary, the West African Lighterage and Transport Company, was eventually formed in 1910 to manage this area of its activity.4 In Freetown, this company had virtual monopoly over the provision of a lighterage service between the jetties at Government Wharf and the ships anchored at mid-stream in the harbour, until the 1930s when the United Africa Company group (UAC) introduced their own fleet of lighters to service their own ships. Elder Dempster also owned and operated a dry dock at King Tom which was for many years the only site along the Freetown waterfront where repairs on lighters and small crafts could be undertaken. Another firm, the Sierra Leone Coaling Company, formerly a subsidiary of Elder Dempster, provided a bunkering service to ships calling at the port.5

Before the Second World War, therefore, the shipping companies and trading firms were directly involved in the movement of cargo at the wharf, while the government departments maintained the port infrastructure and collected the tariffs associated with the use of the port and the import and export trade. The private firms for the most part employed the labour required as and when needed. Of the government departments, only Customs and Port and Marine maintained a small number of permanent workers; the Railway Administration and the Public Works Department deployed workmen to the wharf to undertake specific projects. Developments during the war

4

fundamentally changed these arrangements. As will be shown later in this chapter, the system of recruitment of dock labour was formalised. The following section examines the emergence of a work force at the port during the years before the Second World War.

The Development of a Work Force at the Port Before 1939

It is clear that, before the development of the mining industry in the 1930s when the Sierra Leone economy took its present structure, the port, railway and public works were the only areas of relatively large-scale employment.6 The early produce trade did not provide much employment as 'middle men' traders bought directly from the peasant farmers in the interior in order to sell to the large trading firms established in Freetown and other main towns.7 No plantations were established. It did not even appear necessary to the colonial authorities to create a specialised agency for the regulation of labour. It was not until 1940, following two years of Youth League labour unrest and the enactment of war-time emergency legislation associated with the use of Freetown as a naval base, that a Labour Department was formed. The first figures it published on employment trends show that the demand for labour in Freetown amongst the larger employers hovered around a monthly avearage of 10,000 during the first few months of 1940. 8

The agents of the shipping companies and the larger firms have traditionally employed men from the Kroo tribe from the southern coast of Liberia in stevedoring, cargo handling and porterage. According to Fyfe, the Kroos, renowned for their ability in undertaking arduous tasks, first came to Freetown in 1793, a few years after its founding as a settlement for liberated slaves.9 Originally a transient people who only sought a few material possessions to take back to their villages, an area was reserved (by a special ordinance of 1816) to encourage them to settle in Freetown. This area, in central Freetown, has come to be known as Kroo Town. By 1819 an informal system of political and administrative leadership, the headman-ship, had developed among them. Over the years, Kroo labour was recruited through these headmen who trained, supervised, and regulated the men on behalf of the employers. Headmen also adjudicated disputes within the community. In 1905, at the time of the conso-lidation of colonial rule over the whole country,

the institution of headmanship, which had had a
parallel development among other ethnic groups in
Freetown, was given formal recognition by legisla-
tion.10 While headmen were not formally recognised as
labour contractors as such, it was intended that, in
addition to adjudicating disputes within their communities and acting as the general mouthpiece of the
government vis a vis their communities, they would also
act as a two-way channel of communication between
employers and workmen. Furthermore, under the Vagrancy
Ordinance of the same year, they had the power to
recommend the deportation of 'idle and disorderly'
persons back to the areas from which they came.11 The
position of 'tribal headmen' in Freetown was thus a
very powerful one; they effectively occupied an inter-
mediary position between the government, employers, and
their communities. These arrangements constituted a
classic case of the 'cheap government' practice and
'divide and rule' strategy of British colonial administration. In the absence of a specialised labour department, effective responsibility for labour administration was delegated to the headmen.

These arrangements may have also delayed a more
pervasive development of trade unionism until the Youth
League years. As a part of the colonial government,
the headmen had a vested interest in maintaining the
status quo. As a contemporary writer observed, "the
headmen had many opportunities of making money".12
Given the long association of the Kroos with the
shipping industry, these measures, and in particular,
the provision that headmen could assist in recruitment
and investigate disputes between workmen and their
employers, created the conditions for them to mono-
polise employment opportunities therein. The shipping
companies and large trading firms, with an overriding
interest in preventing delays in the loading and
unloading of ships at the port, preferred to deal with
the Kroos with whom they already had a long association. Indeed, as early as 1893, a Captain Walsh,
commander of the Matadi, (a ship belonging to the
British and African Steam Navigation Company, one of
the shipping companies out of which the Elder Dempster
group was formed), wrote to the Sierra Leone Weekly
News to suggest the formalisation of the recruitment of
Kroo labour by the formation of a "committee of
influential Kroo men with King Peter as president" to
fix hours and rates of work.13 The Kroos for their
part also had a vested interest in reaching some form
of arrangement with the shipping companies.

Employment opportunities in cargo-handling depended on
the number of ships calling at the port. It was casual
work. Casual work meant lower earnings and low
contributions to their community social insurance fund.
Whatever work was available at the port, therefore, the
Kroos strove to keep within their own community. This
they could only achieve by cooperating with the
employers. The tight grip which the Kroos maintained
on employment opportunities in the docks has been a
constant source of friction with labourers from other
ethnic groups. It was not until the Second World War,
when the demand for dock labour dramatically increased,
that labourers in the latter category were employed in
significant numbers.

It is difficult to estimate the number of Kroos
who have been employed in cargo handling. However, the
Kroo population in Freetown grew from 1,234 in 1891 to
4,460 in 1931. 14 Kroo workers maintain that
able-bodied men among them have worked almost exclusively in the shipping industry.15 This suggests that
about a third, about 1,100 Kroo men in 1931, might have
been available for casual work. Indeed, some contemporary travellers arriving at the port leave the
impression that stevedores, lightermen and other dock
labourers were almost exclusively Kroo.16

While the Kroos monopolised employment in cargo
handling at the port, the clerks, artisans and other
labourers employed by the shipping companies,
commercial firms, and government departments invariably
came from other ethnic groups. Again, it is difficult
to estimate the number of workers who were involved in
these functions. It is certain, however, that the
figure was well below the 10,000 estimated as the total
wage-earning population of Freetown by the Labour
Department in 1939 at a time of increasing opportunities for wage employment. It is also clear that the
Krios,17 who had ready access to the long-established
schools in Freetown and long experience as skilled
workmen, at first dominated the subordinate positions
in government departments and commercial firms. With
the introduction of modern education into the interior
of the country, and with more workmen of indigenous
origins acquiring skills over the years, this situation
had by the 1920s begun to change.18

Towards the Re-organisation of the Port

During the First World War, Freetown had been used as a naval base by the British colonial authorities. Given the uncertainties and anxieties surrounding the defence of the Suez Canal in time of war, Freetown, lying on the alternative route to the Cape, India, and the Far East, was chosen to provide water, provisions, bunkers and repairs for the Royal Navy. In his auto-biography, Kossoh Town Boy, Robert Wellesly Cole has described the contribution of Freetown to the war effort:

> Throughout the war, Freetown was an important watering station for the British Royal Navy, and an important station for the Atlantic Fleet. The water was obtained from the Freetown Water Works for which my father was responsible. It was about this time that I first heard the statement that this our Bay on which Freetown stands was large enough to contain the entire British fleet at anchor.19

Indeed, the use of Freetown as a naval base generated much economic activity and created severe problems after the reduction of the war-related public expenditure at the end of the hostilities. Freetown's ideal location also acquired it the status of "the headquarters of the African Station of His Majesty's Navy and a Defended Port".20

With the outbreak of hostilities again in 1939, measures were taken to secure the defence of the port and to provide facilities for visiting convoys engaged in the protection of British trade in the South Atlantic. This phenomenal increase in shipping and port activity during the war set in train a series of events which eventually led to the re-organisation of the port and the centralisation of the employment of dock labour. As an emergency measure, a Port Executive Committee was formed in May 1942 as the ultimate Port Authority. Under the chairmanship of the General Manager of the Railway Administration, its membership included the Comptroller of Customs, the Harbour Master, and representatives of the commercial firms, shipping companies, and the Admiralty.21 The committee was primarily a policy-making body, but it was also charged with the responsibility for administration of

8

the port for the duration of the war. The significance of the formation of this committee was that the existing decentralised system of port administration--stemming from the reluctance of the colonial authorities to extend the public sector--was greatly modified. With the formation of a Port Authority, official recognition of the status of the port as a public utility was implied, and the responsibility of the state for the port--beyond the collection of dues and tariffs--was affirmed.

As a result of the frequent congestion and delays to ships calling at the port, the war also demonstrated the impracticality of the long-standing practice of using lighters to load and unload ships lying at anchor in the Freetown estuary. Accordingly, one of the most important policy decisions reached by the Port Executive Committee was to recommend a deep-water quay, alongside which ships could be berthed, thus facilitating an easier and more modern method of taking supplies and of cargo handling. This was recognised as of vital importance for the speedy turn-around of ships and for the future development of the trade of the country. It was further recognised that, as a public utility, the colonial administration was best placed to make the necessary investments in quay construction at the port. The proposal was neither new nor novel, but it now had a much better chance of implementation. The evolution of colonial economic policy during the inter-war years and, in particular, the challenge to laissez-faire orthodoxy presented by Keynesian economic thought created a climate of thinking favourable to this kind of investment in capital formation.22

With the revocation of the emergency measures at the end of war, the Port Executive Committee was dissolved and the administration of the port re-organised. The concept of Port Authority was retained and vested in the office of the General Manager of the Railway Administration. A Wharf Superintendent was appointed as head of a specialised Port Department within the Railway organisation, to be responsible for the day-to-day management of the port; he reported directly to the General Manager.23 A new advisory body, the Port Advisory Committee largely made up of the same membership as the former Port Executive Committee, was appointed on 1st January 1946. 24 Its terms of reference were to advise the government "on matters relating to the future development of the port...on recommendations submitted for the improvement of its facilities...on the best use to which existing facilities may be put...and as to the best methods to be adopted for the sound and economic use of the port".25 Parallelling these developments, work had begun towards the end of 1946 on the construction of a deep-water quay and was scheduled for completion in 1954. 26

The re-organisation of the port stopped short of the creation of an autonomous public corporation with full responsibility for its management and organisation. The colonial government continued to utilise existing administrative machinery (in this case the Railway Administration) to manage the port. However, the principle of the responsibility of the state for the provision of port services had been recognised, and it was envisaged that the role of the Port Department would be enlarged after the opening of the new quay.

The Centralisation of the Employment of Dock Labour

Before the Second World War, Sierra Leone did not have a large wage-earning population. Until the development of the mining industry, the largest employers of labour had been the railway, public works, and the port. Even as late as 1940, when more comprehensive figures on employment trends became available (see Tables 1.1 and 1.2), the total wage-earning population excluding the security forces was only about 30,000. The population itself had been established in 1931 at just over 1.7 million, and that of Freetown at 96,422. 27 The 1931 census established that 66,962 persons (about 65 percent of the population of the city) living in Freetown were between the ages of 16 and 65 and may therefore be said to constitute the labour force. (The age composition of the population of the whole country was not provided but it can be reseasonably assumed that at least 60 percent of the population were between the ages of 16 and 65). The availability of this huge supply of labour had effectively weakened the bargaining power of wage labour. Indeed, the railwaymen, who were employed in a key sector of the economy and, had, in the years following the First World War, exhibited strong trade union consciousness, could not sustain their union organisation in the face of government hostility.

TABLE 1.1

The Wage Labour Force in Sierra Leone Circa 1940

SECTOR	NUMBER
RAILWAY	1,490
(a) Engineering	762
(b) Locomotive	411
(c) Traffic	317
PUBLIC WORKS	5,410
AGRICULTURE	445
POST OFFICE	92
MEDICAL	370
CIVIL SERVICE (CLERICAL)	495
MINING	11,567
TOTAL	20,869*

* Excludes workers employed by commercial firms, shipping companies, and the Security Forces.

SOURCE: British Parlimentary Papers, CMND 6277, G. St. J. Orde-Brown, Labour Conditions in West Africa, London, 1941, pp.136-139.

11

TABLE 1.2

Estimate of Wage Earners Employed by Commercial Firms

and Shipping Companies in Sierra Leone, Circa 1940

SECTOR	NUMBER
Commercial	8,000
Port	2,000
TOTAL	10,000

SOURCE: Estimate is based on size of the sectors.

By 1927, following several work stoppages, the union had been disbanded and its leaders dismissed or posted to the more remote parts of the country. The colonial authorities had become so confident in dealing with labour unrest that the need to create a separate Labour Department to secure the regulation and control of lower-paid workers was not perceived. It was not until after the triumphant return of Wallace-Johnson to Freetown in 1938, and the formation of the Youth League out of which modern trade unionism in Sierra Leone evolved, that the colonial authorities responded by creating institutions to channel labour grievances.

In adopting this strategy, the colonial administration implemented a host of labour policy measures which had been developed over the years by the Colonial Office at Whitehall. The measures themselves had been stimulated by the need to conform to International Labour Office (ILO) conventions, and by the experience of considerable and often violent labour protests in other parts of the empire during the inter-war years. Moreover, the Fabian Society, the intellectual conscience of the British Labour Party, had become a driving force for change in its criticisms of colonial

labour policies, and in its suggestions--often originating from detailed research--for reformist policy
measures. The Society often acted in close cooperation
with the British TUC, another important pressure group
in the colonial lobby. The colonial administration in
Freetown could therefore draw on the experience
available at Whitehall.28

In July 1939, legislation was passed giving legal
recognition to the trade unions, which had been
organised under the auspices of the Youth League, and
establishing procedures for the arbitration of
disputes. Two years later, on the recommendations of
Major Orde-Brown, the Labour Advisor at the Colonial
Office (following a visit to Sierra Leone to study
labour problems), the administration established a
fully-fledged Labour Department to implement its new
labour policy.29 The war itself, and the 'defended
port' status of Freetown initiated a phenomenal
increase in the labour force and added some urgency to
the development of a coherent labour policy. This
unprecedented demand for labour, both skilled and
unskilled, was due to the special work undertaken in
connection with the defence of Freetown and its
significance as a convoy port (see Tables 1.3 and 1.4).
Demand for unskilled labour was very easily met by
recruitment from the provinces, but a severe strain was
imposed on the available supply of skilled labour. The
newly established Labour Department in its first annual
report was critical:

> ...in normal times, facilities for
> training tradesmen in Sierra Leone
> were meagre, consisting only of
> those afforded by the Railway
> workshops, the Public Works
> Department, and the mining companies...
> there is no doubt that many of the
> so-called artisans now employed have
> really no claim to term themselves
> tradesmen as their qualifications are
> of the most amateurish kind. It is
> certain tha the ranks of the small
> number of competent artisans in
> Sierra Leone have been heavily diluted
> with ordinary labourers who profess to
> have technical knowledge, though in
> most cases, they have none at all.30

As the fortification works were completed,

retrenchments were made. The number of people in wage employment in Freetown fell by almost 50 percent between 1942 and 1945 (see Table 1.3). While the unemployment created was partly offset by the availability of jobs in road-building, construction, and other projects financed by the colonial administration at the end of the war, the competition, however, was extremely keen as the Labour Department reserved several of these vacancies for returning ex-servicemen.31 Freetown therefore acquired a legacy of unemployment from the war, a condition which it has since not been able to overcome. It was around this time that a class of destitute urban wage labourers became a permanent and visible strata of the Freetown social structure. Recent research has revealed a continuing increase in the ranks of the lumpen-proletariat in Freetown. For instance, a sociological survey of dock workers undertaken by this author in May 1980 provided details on migration to Freetown from the rural areas among their numbers, and revealed the existence of severe overcrowding in their households, most of which were without electricity or running water.32 Other researchers have drawn attention to the phenomenal increase in the size of the informal sector over the years as the unemployed and underemployed of the city have attempted to generate means of self-employment.33 However, the position of the authorities at the end of the war towards the growing urban misery was unequivocal:

> Sierra Leone had not a large wage
> earning population before the war,
> though the men engaged in subsistence
> farming constituted a potential supply
> of skilled and unskilled labour. This
> supply was prodigally tapped during
> the war, and when wholescale retrench-
> ments were made after the war, the
> larger centres of employment remained
> flooded with surplus labour not yet
> convinced that they should return to
> their former occupations.34

Freetown by the end of the war had become a remarkably transformed city. Its population had increased by a third from about 90,000 to just over 120,000. 35 The cost of living had soared as landlords inflated rents charged to the arriving wage earners. Following the withdrawal of peasant labour from the farms, rice, the staple food, was in short supply and

14

TABLE 1.3

Average Annual Employment, 1939-45, in Freetown

YEAR	NUMBER
1939	10,000
1940	14,833
1941	28,841
1942	45,041
1943	35,558
1944	26,091
1945	22,451

SOURCE: N. A. Cox-George, Finance and Development in West Africa: The Sierra Leone Experience, Oxford, 1959, p.223. (These figures have been compiled from Annual Labour Department Reports).

this was to become a perennial problem in the post-war years. More generally, the disorganisation brought about by the war resulted in a great increase in crime, delinquency, and other forms of anti-social behaviour. A report on penal administration and welfare services prepared just before the end of the war noted:

> There are in the colony a considerable number of boys and a certain number of girls who are either homeless or living in an undesirable environment...the great

TABLE 1.4

Monthly Averages During Peak Year 1942

MONTH	NUMBER
January	41,100
February	44,700
March	42,700
April	42,800
May	41,400
June	41,900
July	45,000
August	48,000
September	49,000
October	48,100
November	50,500
December	45,300

SOURCE: N. A. Cox-George, Finance and Development, p.224. (These figures have been compiled from the Annual Labour Department Report for 1942).

majority of boys and girls are not
receiving the education, recreation,
and employment essential to their
training as sound and stable citizens.
These conditions may rightly be said
to constitute a grave social problem.36

Many of the older dockers could recollect in informal
conversations held with the author (during the first
fieldwork in Freetown in 1979/80) that the area around
the port especially was one of a high crime rate. The
presence of visiting sailors in the vicinity attracted
prostitutes and pimps. Two additions were made to the
Krio language associated with war-time prostitution:
man o' war pickin, meaning a child born out of a
liaison between a prostitute and a visiting marine; and
longstep, meaning a brothel, after the old Portuguese
steps to the east of Government Wharf; but perhaps more
important was the fact that, as the older dock workers
could remember, Freetown before the war was a
relatively well laid-out city with few pockets of
ghettoes and shanty towns. During the war, Freetown
landlords, anxious to exploit the arriving labourers,
quickly put up tin shacks of various sizes,
particularly in the East End at the Kanike, Mountain
Cut, Ginger Hall, and Fula Town areas, and at
Grassfields in the west central part of the city. Over
the years, these ghettoes have been considerably
enlarged, have become more numerous, and are now a
permanent part of the Freetown scenario. This was the
background against which the centralisation of
employment at the port occurred.

One of the more pressing problems which faced the
new Port Department, which became responsible for the
coordination of the activities of port users following
the re-organisation at the end of the war, and the
newly appointed Port Advisory Committee, was cargo
pilferage. The attempts to get around the problem, and
the steps taken inter alia towards the creation of a
semi-autonomous port organisation, created the conditions that made possible the centralisation of the
employment of dock labour.

The problem of cargo pilferage first surfaced at
a meeting of the advisory committee in September 1946,
to which the Commissioner of Police was invited. The
meeting noted the presence of a large number of 'undesirables' within the vicinity of the port and concluded that security arrangements must be stepped up.

The police were invited to oversee workers engaged in cargo handling. A 24-hour watch was to be kept in the docks and a plan for the formation of a special unit of the police force, the Harbour Division, who were to use launches to patrol the seafront of the wharf was outlined. The docks were made a 'restricted access area', and the Customs Department assumed responsibility of issuing special security passes to individuals with legitimate business at the port.37

Two years later, it became clear that these measures were hopelessly inadequate. In May 1948, the representatives of the shipping companies on the advisory committee reported that "pilferage was on the increase, and in some cases, whole consignments were stolen".38 In the ensuing discussions, attention was drawn to the system of recruitment of dock labour which was felt to be too informal and subjected to many abuses. Under the decentralised system of port organisation—even then in transition—the shipping companies, the larger consignees and consignors provided their own stevedore and shore cargo-handling labour. They traditionally selected Kroo foremen or 'gang' leaders who were given a free hand to select other labourers to make up the gang. Kroo gang leaders invariably selected members of their own community or labourers from other ethnic groups who were prepared to pay a small bribe (or dash). The payment of a dash had the same effect as a tax on wages which some workers retrieved by stealing from cargo consignments. The cargo sheds were, moreover, a natural target for burglaries by the unemployed of Freetown, attracted to the vicinity of the port in search of casual work. This system of recruitment had been used for the employment of 'coastwise' and articled seamen, but had recently been reformed by the Labour Department, which brought into operation a Maritime Labour Pool at the beginning of 1948. The pool was essentially a labour exchange at which all persons available for work as coastwise or articled seamen were required to register. Foremen or headmen nominated by the shipping companies were still permitted to lead gangs, but the men were chosen in strict rotation from the register, thus giving everyone a fair chance of recruitment. The advisory committee meeting of May 1948 decided that a similar system should be introduced for the recruitment of stevedore and shore cargo-handlers.39 The pool eventually came into operation in 1952. The tone of the Labour Department in its report for that year was self-congratulatory:

A separate pool was opened early in
the year to recruit, on behalf of
shipping companies and commercial
firms, wharf and stevedoring labour.
The purpose of this additional pool
was primarily to control the entry
into Government Wharf of undesirables
who in the haphazard system of recruitment which prevailed, easily gained
entrance under the pretext of being
in search of employment. It is
gratifying to state that since the
establishment of this new pool not
only has recruitment been put on a
sound basis but the incidence of
pilfering which it was designed to
check has fallen considerably.40

When the new quay came into operation in 1954, the
employment of dock labour had therefore been central-
ised, parallelling the centralisation of the management
of the port. The latter was facilitated by the impact
of war and the gradual abandonment of laissez-faire
economic doctrines by the Colonial Office during the
inter-war years. The Port Department and the shipping
and commercial firms were assured, moreover, of a cheap
and reliable source of labour supply drawn from the
mass of the urban unemployed created by the upheavals
of the war. The chapter which follows examines the
organisation of lower-paid workers in Freetown into
trade unions and, more generally, the origins and
dynamics of modern trade unionism in Sierra Leone.

19

CHAPTER 2

THE DEVELOPMENT OF MODERN TRADE UNIONISM IN SIERRA LEONE

Origins and Dynamics of Labour Protest Action Before 1938

Before the development of the mining industry in
the 1930s the Sierra Leone economy was dependent on the
produce trade. Many Krios (and after they increasingly began to turn to the professions and to the lower
ranks of the civil service, the newly arriving 'Syrians'
or Lebanese) had made fortunes as middle-men in the
trade, opportunities for wage employment as such were
severely limited. While the 'labour question'--in its
very many guises--haunted metropolitan colonial secre-
tariats and local administrations in many parts of
Africa,1 it did not even appear necessary in Sierra
Leone to assign a labour brief to an official specifically appointed for that purpose.

The 'slack' demand for labour was reflected in
wage rates which greatly fluctuated with prevailing
economic conditions (see Table 2.1). The fluctuation
of wages also appear to have been a source of collective discontentment, of early stirrings of group
consciousness among sections of the small wage-earning
work force (which, until the thirties, was largely concentrated in Freetown), and the focus of collective
action. The "first systematic strike of the labouring
classes in the history of this colony took place in the
month of November, 1892" over one such reduction of
wage rates.2 During the 1880s skilled labour received
between 1s.6d. and 2s.6d. a day, while unskilled labour
received between 1s. and 1s.6d. 3 These rates, which
were reduced during the world depression of the 1880s,
remained at the reduced levels well into the 1890s even
though there had been an economic upturn. In November
1892, Freetown workers led by workmen at the Public
Works Department went on strike over demands for the
restoration of the pre-slump wages.4 In its leader on
the issue, The Sierra Leone Weekly News observed that
it was "not surprised that reduction of wages should
have been keenly felt by various classes of labourers
as to cause this universal general strike".5 The strike
appears to have brought the colony to a standstill.
The local administration, itself the largest employer,
was very clearly shaken by it.

The governor declared an emergency and constables were appointed from among 'loyal' citizens to help keep the peace.6 The strikers returned to work only after they had been assured that the falling wage rates would be stabilised.7

The action taken by Freetown workers in 1892 appears to have been a reaction to a specific situation. It was not so much a trial of strength between them and the agents of the colonial state (and of whatever little imperial and merchant capital there was) than an expression of discontentment. (Under the leadership of the railwaymen and, later, of the Youth League, trials of strength were yet to come). That no organisation of workers was sustained cannot really negate the political significance of this episode as an early manifestation among some sections of lower-paid workers of consciousness of perceived inequities in the colonial state. If this event became a part of the folklore of the "labouring classes", its success in meeting its limited objectives could have provided inspiration for later struggles. Divisions within Freetown society and, especially between those who could be relied upon to be 'loyal' and those who could not, were identified. In this regard, the failure of a specific attempt to organise Freetown workers into a trade union by the gifted, if demagogic S.H.A. Case (himself, at one point of his colourful career an artisan at the Royal Engineers' Department) is instructive. Fully aware of the low social esteem in which artisans were held in status-conscious Krio society,8 Case had in the 1880s formed a Mechanics Alliance which was in all essentials a craft union. Its stated objectives were to encourage the 'self-improvement' of its members in the quality of their work and to introduce them to the appreciation of music, literature, and art. Between 1884 and 1888, Case occasionally published and edited a newspaper, The Artisan, which he filled with platitudes and homilies urging the self-improvement of tradesmen. The paper and its editor were a fertile source of proposals for a programme of festivities to celebrate the centenary of the founding of Freetown in 1887 which coincided with Queen Victoria's Golden Jubilee. Membership of the Alliance grew from 176 at its inauguration in 1884 to reach a peak of 190. Thereafter it dwindled to 51, and was dissolved a few years later.9 The posture and objectives of the Alliance could not have been unrelated to its failure to be sufficiently attractive to the "labouring classes".

22

TABLE 2.1

Wage Rates 1880 to 1935

YEAR	SKILLED LABOUR	UNSKILLED LABOUR
1800 - 1885	1s.6d. - 2s.6d.(1)	1s. - 1s.6d.(1)
1886 - 1891	1s.0d. - 1s.6d.(2)	10d. - 1s.(2)
1892 - 1897	1s.6d. - 2s.0d.(2)	9d. - 1s.(2)
1898 - 1918	1s.0d. - 1s.6d.(2)	9d. - 1s.(2)
1919 - 1929	1s.3d. - 2s.0d.(3)	1s. - 1s.3d.(3)
1930 - 1935	9d. - 1s.0d.(4)	6d. - 9d.(4)

SOURCES: (1) The Artisan, 24 September 1884.

(2) N. A. Cox-George, Finance and
Development p.123.

(3) British Parliamentary Papers, CMND
2744, Report by the Hon.
W. G. A. Ormsby-Gore, (London, 1926),
p.58.

(4) M. H. Y. Kaniki, "Economic Change in
Sierra Leone During the 1930s",
TransAfrican Journal of History, 3,
1973, p.83.

In 1896 work began on the construction of a railway linking Freetown with the main market centres of the interior of the territory. By the end of 1906, some 227 miles of track had been laid, by which time the Railway Administration provided employment for just under 200 artisans and labourers.10 During the three decades that followed, railwaymen struggled with the railway management and the local administration to improve their lot, indicating a strong sense of group identity if, also, the existence of divisions within their ranks. Before the outbreak of the First World War, railwaymen took strike action on two occasions. The first, in 1898, during the war of resistance (and was perhaps encouraged by it) to the imposition of 'hut taxes' on the people of the interior by the colonial authorities following the declaration of a protectorate over the area two years earlier. At issue was a general dissatisfaction with working conditions and with existing wage rates.11 Again, in 1911, railwaymen took action for the same reasons. During the latter conflict, the local administration reacted with a heavy hand. According to Best, "when a riot seemed inevitable, firearms were discharged and two of the strikers were slightly wounded. The railwaymen resumed work the next day and no further trouble was experienced. A grant of 13/6d. was made to Thomas Hero and others as a reward for remaining loyal during the strike."12 After the war, railwaymen maintained this militant tradition and formed the first modern trade union in Sierra Leone. That various sections of the Freetown community rallied round them during periods of strike action suggest that these workers provided the wider community with opportunities for the venting of anti-colonial (as distinct from 'nationalist') sentiments. In view of the fact that nationalism in Sierra Leone never took the form of a coherent protest movement--given the strength of various cleavages within the society--action taken by the railwaymen provided (before the Youth League years) almost the only opportunity for a concentrated focus of such sentiments.

During the early years of the present century, some spectacular realignment of political interests became apparent. Following the accusations leveled at the Krios of complicity in the hut tax hostilities (the strike led by skilled railwaymen in 1898--many of whom, if not most, were of Freetown origin--does suggest that advantage was taken of the disorientation of the authorities), it became the policy of the colonial administration to exclude them from positions of trust. By the First World War, the practice of appointing members of the Krio elite to senior posts in the administration had been discontinued.13 At about the same time, the prosperity of Lebanese traders who had replaced them as middle-men in the produce trade had begun to become apparent.14 It had become increasingly clear that the main allies of the colonial administration were the traditional (and appointed) chiefs of the interior who facilitated the recently established system of indirect rule. In return for their cooperation they were allowed to keep 5 percent of hut taxes collected from their peasant subjects (also an incentive for them to collect the taxes) and paid a salary and other allowances.15 In the colony of Freetown itself, tribal headmen were appointed and paid by the authorities to maintain order within their respective communities.16 It was against this new trend of collaboration between the interior chiefs, tribal headmen, and the British authorities, increasing Lebanese prosperity, and Krio disaffection, that the 1919 railway strike and anti-Syrian riots occurred.

At the heart of the railway dispute lay the familiar problem of wages lagging behind the cost of living. During the war, the imperial War Office spent over £175,000 in strengthening the defence establishments in the colony. Naval and merchant vessels calling at the port to take bunkers added to the internal spending boom through purchases of food supplies and other necessities.17 The net effect of these developments was that the internal market failed to satisfy the growing demand and an inflationary spiral was set in motion. Between 1914 and 1919 prices rose by over 300 percent while wages generally remained at the pre-war levels. At the end of the war, imperial spending was sharply cut, retrenchment followed, leaving the workmen who had been temporarily employed, jobless.18 This combination of rising prices and unemployment together with the growing polarisation of the administration, the chiefs, the tribal headmen, and the Lebanese traders on the one hand, and the Krio elite on the other, created an explosive situation. The Freetown press owned by the elite thundered about the rising prices of food, the unemployment situation, and the growing prosperity of the Lebanese who were accused of profiteering. When daily-waged workers at the Railway Administration took strike action on 15th July to protest against the delay in the payment of the War Bonus, which had already been paid to European

officials (and even to other groups of lower-paid
workers in the colony), the press took up their case.19
The week-long strike soon turned into a populist
riot--which spread to parts of the protectorate--direct-
ted against the Lebanese. Within a few days, however,
the riot had been supressed and, as a punitive measure,
the colonial authorities ordered that £37,000 be paid
as compensation for damages inflicted on Lebanese
property during the riots. The Freetown press
vigourously opposed this order and the figure was
reduced to £5,000. 20 The railway and other workers
who had not received the bonus were paid in full.

The strike was evidently well organised and action
throughout the railway network properly coordinated. It
is clear from Best's account that the strike was a
calculated attempt--especially in view of the railway
department's precarious finances and the reluctance of
the colonial administration to increase subsidies--to
force the authorities to meet the workers' demands.
Those workmen who remained loyal were:

> prevented from working, engines
> under steam were stopped, the
> fires drawn by strikers, and two
> coaches and a wagon were derailed...
> attempts were made to stop Europeans
> attending the offices and to
> disorganise the railway as much as
> possible; in consequence all
> operations including the train service
> on the whole system were suspended
> from the 16th to the 22nd. The men
> resumed work on the 23rd of July on
> the understanding that the bonus
> would be paid as soon as possible.
> The loss of revenue...was approxi-
> mately £3,500. 21

The success of the strike drove home to the
railwaymen the advantages that could be derived from
proper organisation. In August, a group of workers
formed the Railway Skilled Artisans' Union declaring
their objectives to be "to act as a medium between the
employers and the employees and to protect its
members."22 Within a year the union had been able to
secure recognition from the railway management anxious
for good 'industrial relations'. In 1925, the union
was re-organised and the title Railway Workers' Union

adopted in order to emphasise that membership was open
to all grades of railwaymen.23 It was clearly the
case, however, that the artisans were the most militant
of the railwaymen and the driving force behind the
formation of the union. Union officials such as
A. E. Richards, W. D. Leigh, and J. B. Hington were
drawn from among their ranks. Members of the clerical
grades were "sleeping partners" while unskilled workers
and labourers (mostly of protectorate origin) were
regarded as no more than "infantry men".24

The support of the Krio elite for the strikers in
1919 was essentially opportunistic. Although a Civil
Service Association drawing its membership largely from
Krio officials had been formed in 1909, it adopted a
non-militant approach (sending 'memorials', as
memoranda were wrongly termed, to the Secretary of
State for the Colonies at Whitehall) in order not to
jeopardise their position even further.25 The 1919
strike therefore provided the opportunity for this
elite to vent anti-colonial sentiments reflecting their
increasing frustration at the colonial state.

During the 1920s Anglo-Krio elite relations
improved if also only temporarily.26 Following the
enactment of the 1924 constitution which provided for a
legislative council to which the Freetown community
could elect half the unofficial membership, its political organisation, the National Congress of British West
Africa (Sierra Leone Branch), adopted a more conservative posture vis-a-vis the authorities.27 The era of
'constructive criticism' and 'progress through
partnership' had begun. Nonetheless, this new era
was rudely shattered two years later when most sections
of the Freetown community felt obliged to support strik-
ing railwaymen subjected to high-handed treatment by the
railway management and the colonial administration. As
before, the action taken by the railwaymen reminded the
community of some of the most unsavoury aspects of
colonial domination and the day-to-day manifestation of
the supremacy of the jombul.28 The strike therefore
became a temporary but concentrated focus of anti-colonial sentiments. This episode was not over a wage
dispute as such. Wages during the 1920s remained at
post-war levels of between 1s.3d. and 2s. per diem for
skilled and 1s. and 1s.3d. for unskilled workers (Table
2.1) and may be said to have been relatively buoyant.29
The 1926 strike was a racial conflict between
lower-paid railway workers and the railway management
and involved "nearly the whole of the African

staff of the locomotive, engineering, and traffic branches, and practically all the telegraph operators"--1,000 railwaymen.30 The dispute embraced two separate issues, involving clerical workers of the traffic and operating sections on the one hand and, on the other, artisans of the locomotive and engineering sections. The former objected to, and refused to be subjected to the successful completion of examinations as a precondition for promotion. These examinations, from which European personnel were exempted, had been introduced the previous year by the management in the "interest of more efficient working".31 The artisans complained that their request for a grading system similar to those obtaining elsewhere had been refused and that in consequence their progress was being impeded.32 According to Best, "the strike was obviously pre-meditated and well organised with the intention of paralysing all telegraph and rail communication".33 The re-organisation of the union the previous year was apparently the first stage of the strategy, for "...it is evident from what transpired later that the expansion of membership and the renewal of union activity were the result of growing dissatisfaction on the part of the workmen at their conditions of service and had an obvious underlying motive"34. The railway management and the government were resolute in their determination to break the strike:

> It was considered that the men had
> ceased work in an authorised manner
> and they were made to understand that
> no discussion could take place until
> they returned to work...The
> railwaymen were repeatedly instruc-
> ted to return to work and this they
> refused even though some of their
> members were dismissed and replaced.35

The Freetown community were united in their support for the strikers. This "...deadlock was by no means eased by the clear expression of public opinion made in favour of the strikers and which culminated in a Strikers' Relief Fund being inaugurated".36 That the strike lasted a full six weeks is a testimony to the determination and solidarity of the railwaymen sustained by the support--fuelled by anti-colonial sentiments--of the local community and, indeed, branches of the National Congress of British West Africa in other territories in the region.

The British government was equally determined that the local administration should resist the demands of the railwaymen. The strike was viewed as nothing more than an attempt at blackmail.

> A number of telegrams were addressed
> to the Secretary of State by the
> strikers and certain public bodies in
> Freetown and questions were asked
> in the House of Commons, but to all
> approaches, the Secretary of State
> intimated that he saw no reason to
> intervene and he made it known that the
> Under Secretary (W. G. A. Ormsby-Gore),
> then about to make a visit to West
> Africa, would be instructed not to
> intervene.37

The colonial authorities simply bided time. As the weeks went by, the anti-colonial euphoria subsided. The hardship of a protacted struggle began to bite. The Railway Workers' Union reconsidered its position.

> Following a further unsuccessful
> appeal to the Secretary of State
> for the Colonies in which they
> asked that a special commissioner
> should be appointed (to inquire
> into the dispute), and that the
> status quo ante January 14th be
> restored--but with loss of pay
> for the strike period--the men
> returned to work on February 26th,
> 1926, on the conditions laid down
> by the government.38

Fully aware of the demoralised mood of the men at the end of the strike, the local administration lost no time in breaking the union. It was outlawed, and some of its influential leaders re-deployed to the more remote parts of the railway system. Following this experience, there was little trade union activity in Sierra Leone for more than a decade.39 Demoralised and dejected, railway and other lower-paid workers in the territory entered the depression years in a sullen mood. Living standards were shortly to drop dramatically. As the volume of freight carried by the railway decreased--following the reduction in the demand for Sierra Leonean produce in the world markets--retrenchments were made at the railway administration.40

When Wallace-Johnson returned to Freetown in 1938, he found lower-paid workers in the colony demoralised and forced to bear these hardships.

The Influence of Wallace-Johnson 1939-1950   41

Sierra Leone entered the depression years with the colonial authorities in firm control and receiving the cooperation of the Krio and chiefly elite. The depression years also coincided with the diversification of the economy and the beginnning of the exploitation of small deposits of gold, platinum and chromium, as well as the larger deposits of diamonds and iron ore.42 It was in general an era of rising expectations but hopes were quickly and cruelly dashed. Prevailing labour market conditions--the availability of a huge supply of labour--created a situation in which lower-paid workers were, in practice, in a weak bargaining position.43 Moreover, the politics of rivalry between the Krio and chiefly elite for influence in the local administration and the virtual exclusion of the 'masses' from the electorate in Freetown by property qualifications, created a situation in which the cultivation of a clientele by this elite among lower-paid workers brought the former no political benefits. Nonetheless, some of these workers in the mines and in establishments in Freetown took strike action on several occasions between 1932 and 1938 to register their discontentment with falling living standards.44 These strikes, like pre-1919 protest activity were sporadic and short-lived. The mines also became notorious for a high labour turnover as workers periodcally and seasonally--voting with their feet--moved in and out of peasant subsistence farming.45

There had emerged during the inter-war years a growing number of young locally and foreign educated professionals of upcountry and Krio origins. Although these men and women had kinship relations with individuals of the Freetown and rural elite, they were beginning (unlike the latter) to develop a solidly based nationalist consciousness. Newspapers of this period contain many letters signed by upcountry and Krio names drawing attention particularly to the exploitation of minerals by imperial and foreign capital--a very early precursor to the 'growth without development' debate. This group of doctors, lawyers, teachers, civil servants, etc., was, moreover, willing

and ready to create a clientele among the urban and
rural masses. What they needed was coherent political
organisation and the organisational skills of a leader
experienced in the art of demagoguery. Wallace-Johnson
perfectly fitted the bill, and arrived in Freetown at a
most opportune time. His biographers maintain that,
since his political activities in the Gold Coast had
ended badly, Wallace-Johnson was probably at the point
of withdrawal from active politics.46 The colonial
authorities unwittingly catapulated him into the
limelight by seizing some of his books, documents, and
papers at the customs examination centre on the day of
his arrival.

An indignant Wallace-Johnson gave this event the
widest and loudest publicity. His charismatic personality "drew people to him like pins to a magnet."47 He
wasted little time in denouncing the inter-war trends
in elitist politics and "large sections of the
community, the unemployed and employed, rich and poor,
the educated and the uneducated, men and women,
Muslims, Christians, and pagans, Creoles and
upcountrymen" were an enthusiastic audience for his
fiery rhetoric.48 Within weeks of his arrival,
Wallace-Johnson's strategy for handling the situation
quickly unfolded. First, he proposed to create a political organisation, the Youth League, to challenge the
elitism of the Freetown-based National Council of
British West Africa. Second, he proposed to organise
workers in the mines and in establishments throughout
the country into trade unions to provide the Youth
League with a strong grass roots base. By the end of
1938, Wallace-Johnson had achieved both objectives. An
adherent of the Leninist theory of revolution, he
believed in the use of strikes as a means of developing
the consciousness of workers and in forcing the end of
imperial rule. Overnight, Youth League activists, the
'verandah boys' of the Sierra Leone 'nationalist'
movement, became trade union leaders. Some were to use
these positions to launch careers for themselves in
national politics during the post-war years of decolonisation.

The months before the outbreak of war in Sierra
Leone were especially turbulent as strikes shook the
colonial state at its foundations. With the exception
of a handful of Youth League activists, however,
Wallace-Johnson's supporters among the 'middle-class'
professionals and among lower-paid workers were not
adherents of the Leninist theory of revolution.49

31

The former wished to bring about an end to the elitism in political representation and to hasten the devolution of power. The latter wished to effect improvements in living standards. With the outbreak of war, Wallace-Johnson was incarcerated at Bonthe Island off the coast of southern Sierra Leone, as the colonial authorities believed him to pose a security risk.

During the war, colonial labour policy was based on a strategy of guiding the trade union movement through the channels of 'industrial unionism'.50 Following the enactment of legislation giving legal recognition to trade unions in 1939, and the establishment of a Labour Department two years later, a Trade Union Advisor was sent out from Britain in 1942. He was Edgar Parry, himself a union official in the British trade union movement. Local unionists who knew and worked with Parry are all agreed he left an indelible mark on the practice of trade unionism in Sierra Leone.51 While Parry was without any doubt sympathetic to the aspirations of the fast-growing group of wage earners in the territory, he saw his role, quite unambiguously, as attempting to put into effect the policies on labour administration which had been developed over the years at the Colonial Office. Very simply, this meant turning the local trade union leadership away from the 'political unionism' of the Youth League and its destabilising tactics of agitation, to the institutionalised and more 'respectable' protest of 'industrial unionism'. It could not have been otherwise. Parry had himself obtained his industrial relations experience by working his way up through the ranks of the British trade union movement; the ideology of industrial unionism and institutionalised protest must have seemed only too natural. Indeed, writing in the Colonial Office journal, _Corona_, shortly after completing his tour in Sierra Leone, Parry maintained:

> The creation of trade unions is
> itself a fairly simple matter. To
> fit them into a comprehensive system
> of industrial relations is a much more
> exacting task...Since we have always
> encouraged the colonies to follow our
> example, we can only hope that workers
> there will eventually arrive at a more
> orderly method of running their affairs.52

It was to this 'exacting task' that Parry devoted

himself, but not before careful study of the pattern of
trade unionism that was emerging. He was aware of the
conditions obtaining in the territory when Wallace-
Johnson arrived. The seething discontent of workers in
the mines and in other establishments had swiftly been
given organisational expression in the formation of
trade unions. By 1942, the year of Parry's arrival,
eleven unions had been registered, claiming between
them a total membership of 5,000. The Labour
Department was quick to point out that a 'bare 15
percent' of this membership was fully paid up, while
the number of wage earners in the whole country had
risen to a figure between 70,000 and 80,000. 53 A
former Youth League activist and trade union leader has
pointed out that, in those early days of trade union
organisation, many of the activists leading the unions
"lacked the administrative skills to compile the type
of reports showing the returns demanded by the Labour
Department".54 The trade unions constituted a populist
movement. Membership was spontaneous and informal. The
movement grew out of the vacuum left by the orientation
of the elites in Freetown and the provinces towards
seeking greater representation for themselves in the
colonial administration. The momentum of the movement
was maintained by the particular conditions obtaining
during the war: a tight labour market, war-time
emergency, and considerable hardship caused by war-time
inflation.

    To exert some degree of control over the movement,
the Labour Department sponsored the formation of a
trade union centre, the Sierra Leone Trade Union
Congress (SLTUC), in 1942. During the war, however,
the unions were for the most part adversarial in
bargaining tactics, generally adopting a hostile
posture towards employers and officials of the Labour
Department. In its 1942 Report, the department
maintained:

            It is regrettable...that no progress has
            been made in the development of trade
            unionism during 1941-1942...This is due
            to the fact that real trade union leaders
            are conspicuous by their absence; that
            the so-called trade union leaders are
            very loath to take the advice of the
            Labour Department, including that of
            Mr. Parry who is an expert on trade
            unionism and even of the TUC at home.55

This was only to be expected. The colonial authorities had incarcerated Wallace-Johnson--in the eyes of the activists, a hero--while appointing two members of the Krio and upcountry elite, J. Fowel Boston (an eminent barrister) and Paramount Chief George Caulker, as members of the Executive Council in 1942. 56 In spite of the emergency measures in force, a total of thirty-four stoppages took place between 1940 and 1945. With the exception of two in 1945, which were over disputes relating to terms and conditions of redundancies, all were in respect of wage demands. This unprecedented increase in strike activity can be directly related to the internal condition of the economy during the war. 57 In most of these disputes, the Labour Department worked assiduously to effect negotiated settlements as was required under the 1939 Trade Union Ordinance. The government itself granted an annual cost of living allowance between 1940 and 1945, as its own statistics on the movement of prices had registered a persistent upward trend (see Table 2.2).

By the end of the war, Parry had developed a sound grasp of the pattern of trade unionism emerging in the country. He had not only seen instances of militant and aggressive wage bargaining, but also the strains in the solidarity of the labour movement. The union leaders, deprived of the inspiring leadership of Wallace-Johnson, were soon at odds with each other over demarcation disputes and personality rivalries. 58 Ethnic problems also surfaced. For instance, Kroo dock labourers, who had a virtual monopoly over the employment opportunities at the port, maintained a separate union organisation from that of non-Kroo dockers. Even after the two unions were merged in 1946, the system of recruitment of dock workers remained open to abuse until the centralisation of the employment of dock labour in 1952. Parry had also become acquainted with many of the union leaders and had developed a special affection for Siaka Stevens, Secretary of the Mining Employees' Union, who had by the end of the war emerged as a shrewd but moderate union negotiator. Parry singled out Stevens as a unionist of great promise and was instrumental in obtaining a scholarship for him to study industrial relations at Ruskin College, Oxford, and arranging a brief attachment for him with the British TUC at the end of his course in 1947-48. 59

Parry's strategy of re-organising the pattern of trade unionism in Sierra Leone involved three important phases. First, he aimed to reduce the number of trade

TABLE 2.2

Official Cost of Living Index 1939-45

YEAR	INDEX
1939	100
1940	N.A.
1941	175.6
1942	234
1943	242
1944	255
1945	233.7

SOURCE: Cox-George, Finance and Development, p.228. (N.B.: An estimation of rent paid on housing was excluded from the compilation of the index).

unions so that only one union could exist in any one industry or sector. Second, he wished to create institutions for collective bargaining at industry-wide level; and third, he hoped to encourage trade unionists to be more cooperative. When Parry left Freetown at the end of his tour in 1947, he had achieved all three of these objectives. The eleven unions in existence in 1942 were reduced to eight in the streamlining phase of the strategy (see table 2.3). The Maritime Workers' Union (Kroo stevedores) and the Waterfront Workers' Union (non-Kroo stevedores) became the Maritime and Waterfront Workers' Union.

TABLE 2.3

Registered Trade Unions 1942

1. The All Seamen's Union.

2. The Maritime Workers' Union.

3. The Mining Employees' Union.

4. The African Commercial Workers' Union.

5. The Yengema Diamond Workers' Union.

6. The Sierra Leone Building and Constructional Workers' Union.

7. The Sierra Leone Mason's Union.

8. The Sierra Leone Washerwomen's Union.

9. The Sierra Leone Waterfront Workers' Union.

10. The Railway Workers' Union.

11. The Mercantile Workers' Union.

SOURCES: Annual Labour Department Reports 1939-40, 1940-41

With the achievement of one union in each sector, Parry next turned his attention to the introduction of institutions for collective bargaining. Bargaining machinery of two types were introduced: Wages Boards and Joint Industrial Councils (JICs). The former, introduced in 1946, was a more paternalistic arrangement. A Board was formed in the cargo-handling, mining, and agricultural (plantations) sectors, each with representation from the unions and employers in these sectors, but under the chairmanship of a government appointee, who was only obliged to consult these representatives in fixing the minimum wage rates which were statutorily enforceable in each sector. If 'bargaining' was severely restricted at the Wages Boards, it was more openly permitted at the JICs. Two JICs were created in 1947 for the Artisan and Transport workers, each with an equal number of union and employer representatives, with the Labour Department providing administrative

services. It was envisaged that these would meet
periodically to review and agree on wage rates applicable throughout each of the sectors.

The third phase of Parry's strategy involved the
elimination of the aggressive posture of the trade
union leadership. This very simply meant seeking their
cooptation into the establishment. Parry resorted to
the use of a corporatist strategy, setting up a Joint
Consultative Committee of union leaders and government
officials, with terms of reference to advise government
on its economic, social, and labour policies. A block
of offices, Trade Union House, was provided in central
Freetown as the administrative headquarters of the
SLTUC and several individual unions. Trade union
leaders were promised scholarships to study in the
U.K., and invited to sit on the national institutions
of political power. J. Akinola Wright of the
reconstituted Railway Workers' Union was nominated by
the governor to sit on the Legislative Council and
represent labour interests in 1946, while Siaka Stevens
became a member of the Protectorate Assembly in 1949
and thus began a remarkable political career. The
speeches of the union leaders were relayed over the
rediffusion network, and reported in the press. In
this way, the trade union leaders, most of whom had
achieved prominence through being activists in the
Youth League, gradually became 'respectable' with a
corresponding obligation to be 'responsible' (see Table
2.4 for the occupational background of trade union
leaders in 1946). The union leaders welcomed these
arrangements, as the unions were given recognition and
security.60 Even Marcus Grant, one of the strongest
supporters of Wallace-Johnson in the Youth League,
appeared well pleased in a speech at the inauguration
of the JICs in March 1947:

> ...today marks one of the happiest days
> concerning workers...We can assure the
> the council of our cooperation and best
> relations to bring this our attempt
> to success.61

These reforms, nonetheless, had fundamental
implications for solidarity within the labour movement.
Towards the end of the war, Wallace-Johnson was
released from confinement at Bonthe Island and allowed
to return to Freetown. A clash with Parry, whose work
was directed at undermining his militant style of

TABLE 2.4

Registered Trade Unions 1946 (1) and Occupational
Background of Trade Union Leaders(2)

UNION	DATE REGISTERED	MEMBERSHIP	BACK-GROUND
United Mine Workers' Union	Amalgamated March 1945	5,000	Clerk
Sierra Leone Artisans' Union	Amalgamated March 1945	1,300	Artisan
Sierra Leone Maritime and Waterfront Workers' Union	Amalgamated November 1946	3,000	Clerk
Transport Workers' Union	Reorganised July 1945	480	Clerk
National Union of Seaman	Reorganised July 1945	1,200	Article Seaman
Clerical Mercantile Workers' Union	Reorganised October 1945	150	Clerk
Railway Workers' Union	Reorganised June 1941	500	Artisan
Washerwomens' Union	Registered 1942	300	Clerk

SOURCES: (1) Labour Department Annual Report 1946, p.26.
(2) Interview, with C. A. Wilton-During, veteran trade unionist, 13th April 1982.

leadership, was inevitable. The reforms were severely
criticised in the Youth League Press. Deeply resenting
Wallace-Johnson's influence, Parry's letters to his
friends in Britain were indicative of his increasing
exasperation. In a letter to Rita Hinden of the Fabian
Colonial Bureau (worth quoting at length, not least
for its entertainment value) Parry made it clear that
he had had enough:

> I consider him to be the most
> objectionable and unscrupulous
> person I have met in political
> life...All this I would abide if
> he did not interfere with my
> work...It is necessary for me to
> do a fair amount of reorganisation
> of the trade unions. They are in
> a sad state of health and require
> a lot of assistance. In spite of
> his loud protestations to the
> contrary, Wallace-Johnson seems to
> me as if he does not want them to
> be any different than they are. I
> believe this is because he meddles
> with the finances of one of them and
> also because he is a megalomaniac who
> cannot stand to see anyone trying
> to help his beloved 'toiling masses'.
> (He is full of pseudo-Marxist claptrap)...
> In the first place I think he ought not
> to be encouraged by anyone in the labour
> movement at home. It would be neither
> fair to the Africans here who want to do
> something decent nor to me...My job here
> is difficult enough without having to
> deal with a man of this sort...There is
> no doubt that this country would have made
> far more progress without him. There are
> a few enlightened men here who can easily
> fill his place with advantage, but will
> not make any effort while he is about.62

Wallace-Johnson, on the other hand, believed that
labour reform was only one aspect of the more important
question of imperial rule and that it was idle to argue
about the details of foreign domination while the
system itself remained unchanged. In a speech before
the World Federation of Labour in Paris in 1945 as the
delegate from Sierra Leone, he argued this thesis
forcefully:

> ...in countries where the people are
> ruled by a foreign race, whose economic
> exploitation is supported by the political
> forces of imperialism, politics and
> economics are inseparable.63

Parry, however, continued to work through the moderate
union leaders and, by so doing, was able to precipitate
a split between those leaders who subscribed to the
strategy of political unionism and those who subscribed
to the strategy of industrial unionism.   In 1946, two
moderates, Akinola Wright and Siaka Stevens, were
elected as President and General Secretary respectively
of the SLTUC, by virtue of the fact that the moderates,
having a greater proportion of the membership between
them, could muster more votes.   Marcus Grant and H. N.
Georgestone immediately disaffiliated their unions from
the SLTUC.   In a statement on the crisis signed by
Wright, Stevens, and several union leaders, the
moderates were unequivocal about their split with the
Youth League:

> Shorn of all its fanciful trimmings,
> the real reason for the conflict is
> that the Minority Section want to
> see the Trade Union Congress as
> part and parcel of the Youth League,
> and the Majority Section, whilst
> some of its members are Youth Leaguers
> and others have held prominent
> positions in the League in the past,
> maintain that it would be highly
> improper for the SLTUC to be hog-tied
> and controlled by the Youth League, a
> political organisation which is in no
> way accountable to the trade union
> movement.64

Delighted as it must have been with these
developments, the Labour Department nonetheless made
several attempts to bring the two factions back
together on terms compatible with its strategies of
labour administration.   Parry himself made several
approaches to Grant and Georgestone, who recall that he
painstakingly lectured them on the development of trade
unionism in Britain--drawing parallels with Sierra
Leone--and on the achievement of the pioneers of the
British labour movement.   "Parry often suggested that
the greatest service we could do to the nation would be

to cooperate with the department and the new JICs and Wages Boards. For this we would be remembered in history as the founding fathers of trade unionism in this country".65 By the time Parry left Freetown in November 1947, a new trade union centre had been formed with its membership drawn from the two factions.66 Increasingly isolated, Wallace-Johnson turned his energies and talents to the national political scene where arrangements for the devolution of power by the British were well underway.

Parry was therefore remarkably successful in achieving the objectives he set himself at the beginning of his tour. The effect of his reforms was that there was relative industrial peace for almost a decade. Between 1946 and 1955, there were no more than five stoppages and these were resolved by negotiated settlements. As Marcus Grant points out in his article on the recent history of the labour movement, "...up to the 1955 strike, industrial relations was presented as something of a model of close cooperation between unions, the Labour Department, and employers; the existence of the Wages Boards, and Joint Industrial Councils, and the national joint consultative advisory body on labour legislation and policy, and the mature role of the Council of Labour".67 One of the effects of union cooperation during this first post-war decade was that real wages soon lagged behind the cost of living. The gains which had been made during the years after the war had, by 1952, begun to be eroded. This era of 'corporatism' was perhaps not too surprisingly shattered by the 'general' strike of 1955 led by the two radicals in the 1946 dispute within the old SLTUC, Marcus Grant and H. N. Georgestone.68

The Responses of the Labour Movement to the Politics of Decolonisation

By the end of the Second World War, the social structure of Sierra Leone had altered noticeably. Not only had the number of wage earners increased significantly, but more and more peasants were being drawn into the market economy as the measures taken by the Agriculture Department to promote the cultivation of cash crops were beginning to mature. At the other end of the socio-economic scale, the educated professional Krios, while constituting an elite (but disunited over questions of constitutional reforms and, more

specifically, questions of the extension of the voting
franchise and the type of accommodation to be sought
with the provincial elite) had been witnessing the
enlargement of the latter elite. Several outstanding
professional people of provincial origins had emerged.
These included Dr. Milton Margai, Dr. John
Karefa-Smart, Siaka Stevens, Albert Margai, I. B.
Taylor-Kamara, and Dr. W. H. Fitzjohn. These elites,
taken together, were 'moderate' in their political
orientation. It was left to Wallace-Johnson and his
followers to keep 'nationalism' an issue on the
political agenda. But the support he had received
during these heady days of 1938 was on the decline by
the end of the war as the colonial authorities had
responded by creating institutions for collective
bargaining, and had committed themselves to the
introduction of constitutional reforms leading to the
transfer of power.69

These conditions made decolonisation in Sierra
Leone a smooth and gradual process of devolution. A
small degree of acrimony came from conservative Krio
opinion which resented the growing (and inevitable)
political influence of the provincial elite. By 1951,
two political parties had emerged, the National Council
of the Colony of Sierra Leone (NCSL), representing
conservative Krio opinion, and the Sierra Leone
People's Party (SLPP) representing a coalition of
liberal Krio, the provincial educated elite, and the
chiefs. Neither of these parties were 'mass' parties
sustained by 'nationalist' sentiments. Each relied on
kinship and patron-clientelist relationships to secure
support among a franchise limited by property qualifications. After elections in 1951, the SLPP, whose
network of support covered parts of Freetown and the
whole of the provinces, emerged as the winner. Some
of its leading members were appointed to the Executive
Council with Dr. Margai as Chief Minister and Leader of
Government Business. The leader of the NCSL, Dr.
Bankole-Bright, became head of the Opposition where
he was joined by Wallace-Johnson who had won a seat
on the legislative Council as an independent
candidate.70

The conduct of the affairs of state within this
Westminster-style institutional framework should not
obscure the broader sociological processes at work.
Milton Margai emerged as the dominant political figure
by mobilising the support of the chiefs in return for
the maintenance of their privileges at the local level.

This was facilitated in certain cases by communal and kinship ties, especially in the South and South-eastern areas of the country, and in others, by certain shared experiences such as originating from the protectorate, or belonging to the old boys' network of the Bo school (which had been established in 1906 by the colonial authorities to provide education for the sons and nominees of chiefs). Access to the state was required to help redress the historical imbalance in development resources expended in the colony vis a vis the provinces, and by so doing, to assist the improvement of life chances in the latter area. Leading members of the educated elite were represented in the SLPP including Krio politicians inclined towards national integration and reconciliation. These networks of support were based on informal clientelist relationships which were cemented by the location of schools, hospitals, and other projects of infrastructural development in particular areas, appointments to the civil service, the allocation of diamond mining licenses, produce and other purchasing contracts, etc. During these years of decolonisation, however, the African politicians in government were not given complete discretionary powers by the British colonial authorities to formulate the priorities for the appropriation of the resources of the state. The ethos of British colonial administration had been, and continued to be, strict bureaucratic accountability. Administrative procedures restrained and constrained the full manifestation of the characteristics of neo-patrimonal political leadership. Nonetheless, the African politicians had some room in which to manoeuvre. This was evidenced by the increasing prosperity of the politicians themselves, the award of substantial salary increases to senior civil servants following the publication of the Sinker Report in 1953--many of whom were Sierra Leoneans as the policy of Africanisation was pursued (see Table 2.5)--and the introduction of mortgages on very concessionary terms to this cadre of public servants.71 The re-negotiation of the terms of diamond-mining agreements between Selection Trust and the Margai administration in 1954/55 created other opportunities for the dispensation of patronage. In return for a £1.5 million 'compensation', Selection Trust was required to surrender its 99-year exclusive rights to mine diamonds throughout the country, with the exception of some 450 square miles--containing the most promising deposits--in Kenema and Kono. The rest of the country (in practice parts of the South and South-east) therefore became available to miners who

TABLE 2.5

Africanisation of the Senior Public Service

During the Period of Decolonisation

YEAR	OVERSEAS	AFRICAN	TOTAL	AFRICAN % OF TOTAL
1953	315	166	481	24
1959	297	381	678	56

SOURCE: Sierra Leone, Sessional Paper No. 4 of 1959, Government Statement on Africanisation, (Freetown, 1959).

were required to be licensed by government.72 The main beneficiaries of the increased access of Africans to the apparatuses of the colonial state in Sierra Leone were the politicians in government themselves, and their clientele among senior public servants, businessmen, and other members of citizenry. Lower-paid workers in the urban areas and the peasants in the countryside were not direct beneficiaries of the arrangements of the transfer to African political control. Moreover, the institutions of collective bargaining introduced just after the war, and the willingness of most trade union leaders (whose status had been significantly increased by the measures taken by Parry) created the conditions for effecting only very moderate wage settlements. Predictably, some sections of organised labour responded by taking strike action in 1955 in protest at the gradual decrease in real wages since the early fifties (see table 2.6).

On 9th February 1955, members of the Artisan and Allied Workers' Union and the Transport and General Workers' Union were called out on strike by their leaders, Marcus Grant and H. N. Georgestone respectively. This action was precipitated by deadlock in negotiations for periodic wage increases at the Artisan and Transport JICs. The workers' representatives at these JICs refused to refer

44

TABLE 2.6

Movement of Real Wages 1939-54

YEAR	COST OF LIVING INDEX	MINIMUM WAGE	INDEX OF REAL WAGES
1939	100	1s.0d.	100
1945	233.7	1s.6d.	64.2
1949	242	2s.6d.	103
1952	398	3s.9d.	94.2
1954	417	3s.9d.	90

SOURCE: Report of the Commission of Inquiry into the
          Strikes and Riots in Freetown During
          February 1955, (Freetown, 1955), p.7 (This
          document will henceforth be referred to as
          The Shaw Report).

the impasse to arbitration as was apparently required
under the Trades Disputes Ordinance. Hundreds of
workers in Freetown, and indeed in various parts of the
provinces, joined in the four-day strike--in most cases
in defiance of official union policy--which escalated
into riots, looting, and running street battles with
security personnel. The evident popularity of strike
action among the labour rank and file was suggestive of
widespread disillusionment with the formal procedures
of collective bargaining in effecting significant
increases in basic wage rates at a time of spiralling
inflation. It arguably reflected a certain envy, even
resentment, of the political and bureaucratic elite
following the appointment of the first African cabinet
in 1951 and the gradual Africanisation of the upper
echelons of the civil service. The strike also exposed
the existence of divisions among trade union

45

leaders. Following the departure of Wallace-Johnson to
national politics in 1947, Grant and Georgestone came
to regard themselves as the custodians of the militant
tradition of the labour movement. As such, they took
an uncompromising stand in fighting for what they
regarded as workers' rights and in stirring workers'
consciousness.73

The events which came to a head in February 1955
had begun three months earlier when Grant and
Georgestone--acting in close collaboration--submitted
an application for a general increase of 2/6 per diem
on behalf of the members of their respective unions to
the Artisans and Transport JICs on 2nd and 5th
November respectively.74 Neither Grant or Georgestone
had much faith in the formal institutions of bargaining
as a means of effecting 'fair' increases in wage rates
as it had become evident over the years that the JICs
and Wages Boards had been deliberately designed to
ensure that the government (through its officials at
the Department of Labour) was involved in wage settlements in both the private and public sectors. As an
employer of artisans and of transport workers, the
government was also directly represented on the
Artisans and Transport JICs. A cost-conscious government was obviously concerned to exploit these arrangements in order to effect moderate wage settlements
(Table 2.6).

The original claim for 2s.6d. per diem by Grant
and Georgestone was deliberately set so as to provide a
margin of bargaining.75 Indeed, at a meeting of the
Transport JIC on 2nd December 1953, Georgestone
indicated that he would be willing to settle for 1s.6d.
A week later, Marcus Grant also reduced his claim to
this amount.76 The employers, on the other hand,
initially offered 2d. at the Transport JIC and 3d. at
the Artisans JIC which was later increased to 4d. for
the Freetown area and 3d. elsewhere. The accuracy of
the cost of living index was challenged. Georgestone,
while conceding that the index was based on the
projections of the Labour Department and that no price
survey had been undertaken since 1942, argued that
"...their claim was a general one, and not based on
points, and took account of the rise in prices
generally."77 When the employers contended at the
Artisan JIC that they were willing to negotiate further
after a review of the index, Grant declared that
"...negotiations should be regarded as closed...
the workers would see how they would make their

presence felt."78 Following this impasse, pressure was brought to bear on the two union leaders to take their claims to arbitration. Grant has since explained that their refusal to go to arbitration was due to the fact that any award made by the tribunal was legally enforceable and they failed to see how a 'fair' settlement could be reached when the arbitrators were Labour Department officials.79 No less a person than the member of the Margai Cabinet with responsibility for the Labour Department, Siaka Stevens, himself a former moderate union leader, repeatedly urged Grant and Georgestone to allow a tribunal to review the impasse. His exhortations and perorations were ignored.80 A joint mass meeting of the Artisan and Transport unions voted overwhelmingly for strike action, and accordingly, a fourteen-day strike notice was served on employers on the 21st of January. Once this decision had become official, more pressure was put on the two union leaders to go to arbitration. The President of the national trade union centre--the old SLTUC had been reconstituted--the Sierra Leone Council of Labour, J. Akinola Wright, wrote to Grant and Georgestone urging them to call off the strike:

> ...It is the usual course for such
> matters to be referred to a tribunal;
> this is the usual procedure even in the
> United Kingdom...I must express my
> disappointment and disapproval of the
> method you are adopting at the present
> time and therefore consider it my duty
> to implore you to stop and think the
> matter all over again as it seems to
> me that up to the present time there
> is nothing to justify going on strike.81

Officials of the Maritime and Waterfront Workers' Union and of the Railway Workers' Union also dissociated themselves from the dispute.

By the end of January, it became clear that Wallace-Johnson was a key adviser to the two unions and that he had done much work behind the scenes regarding the strategy to be adopted.82 A week before the strike notice was due to expire, Siaka Stevens appointed a Board of Inquiry under the charmanship of R. B. Marke, a Freetown barrister, to examine the causes and circumstances of the deadlock in the negotiations at the JICs. The other members of the Board were Rev. Solomon Caulker, a philosophy lecturer at Fourah

Bay College, and H. E. T. Hodgson, a retired civil servant.83 The Board began to consider the evidence almost immediately, while Stevens and his officials at the Labour Department made frantic efforts to persuade the two union leaders to have the matter decided by a tribunal or to reduce their claim. Following consultations with the membership of their unions, Grant and Georgestone agreed to reduce their claim. At a joint meeting of the two JICs on 2nd February, the notice was withdrawn and the two leaders indicated that they would be prepared to settle at 10d. per diem. The employers felt only able to increase their offer to 6d., resulting in yet another deadlock.84 Two days later, a joint mass meeting of the two unions was held and the rank and file informed of these developments. Workers again came out in favour of a stoppage. Accordingly, a three-day notice was served on employers on 6th February. The government responded by putting out a statement declaring that any action by government employees would be regarded as a 'break in service' and that long-service employees would stand to lose gratuity, pension rights, and other benefits.85

The 6,353 members of the Artisans Union and the 1,160 members of the Transport Union came out on strike as planned on 9th February and were joined unofficially by workers in Freetown and other parts of the provinces. Working behind the scenes and apparently anxious to prove to British officials supervising the devolution arrangements that they were in control of the situation, leading politicians made desperate efforts to undermine the protest action. On the second day of the strike, Grant wrote to Siaka Stevens that "certain Ministers had been trying to undermine the strike through tribal rulers."86 On the third day, however, riots, looting and running street battles with security personnel occurred. There were several casualties among civilians and the security forces. The homes of three Cabinet Ministers, Siaka Stevens, M. S. Mustapha and Albert Margai were ransacked and looted.87 Shaken by the violence and stunned by the determination and vehemence of the strikers, Grant and Georgestone agreed to call off the action.88 Stevens immediately announced the setting up of a conciliation committee to resolve the deadlock.89

Meanwhile, the Board of Inquiry under R. B. Marke had reported to the Ministry of Labour. The Board concluded that there were three reasons for the initial deadlock. It agreed that there was a necessity for a substantial increase in wage rates to make up for the fall in the value of real wages. It criticised the Labour Department for having failed to undertake a cost of living survey in recent years. It pointed out that under existing legislation, the decision to go to arbitration was, contrary to the widespread supposition, a voluntary one and not a legal requirement.90 The Marke Report has never been published. In a press statement of 18th February, the government explained that since a commission of inquiry was being appointed which would include within its terms of reference the same questions as the Board of Inquiry had considered, its report would not be published "since to do so would prejudge part of the report of the major commission".91

At the conciliation committee, agreement could not be reached. Grant and Georgestone therefore opted not to pursue their claims but to wait until the cost of living survey had been undertaken. The employers, however, agreed to pay an ex gratia award of 6d. per diem, "which will continue to be paid unless or until superceded by a larger increase following the review of the cost of living".92

A Cambridge University economist, Brian Reddaway, was flown out to Freetown to carry out the survey which was published as a 'movement of retail prices'. A joint session of the two JICs was convened on 17th June 1955 at which agreement was reached for an award of 1s. per diem to be back-dated to 1st February.93 The government had earlier rescinded its decisions that all strikers in its employ were to lose their gratuity, pensions, and other benefits.94

The commission of inquiry under Sir John Shaw, a senior official at Whitehall, began its sittings in March 1955 and reported in May. The commission acknowledged that "there is no question that there had been an increase in the cost of living", and noted the "widespread dissatisfaction with the official cost of living index".95 Nevertheless, dismissing the arguments of Grant and Georgestone against going to arbitration, the commission blamed them for intransigence and lack of good faith:

> ...it is tragic that within the
> youthful trade union movement in
> Sierra Leone, so much authority
> should be concentrated in the hands

of a man as ambitious, unscrupulous,
and worthless as Marcus Grant. So
long as he remains where he is, the
interests of the community at large
will not be well served. No doubt
there are good...union leaders in
Sierra Leone. Some of them we saw
and heard...While we do not exonerate
Georgestone altogether, we do not
attribute to him a major share of
the responsibility for the strike and
its consequences. Indeed, we do not
exclude him from the number of potentially good trade union leaders.96

Both Grant and Georgestone have said that the report
was a 'whitewash' of the real facts of the situation.97
There is little doubt that the rank and file of both
unions were solidly behind the leaderships, and indeed
precipitated the crisis. Representatives of the Labour
Department were invited to a meeting of the Artisan
Union at which the report was discussed, and, according
to the Department, "no doubt should be left in
anybody's mind that the report was very bitterly
received, and the workers strongly resented its
contents and recommendations. The overcrowded and
excited audience would not accept the adverse criticism contained in the report of their leader,
Mr. Marcus Grant, and enthusiastically moved a
unanimous vote of confidence in him".98

    The strike was significant for several reasons.
As an essentially economistic response to declining
real wages, it demonstrated the determination of
lower-paid workers to defend their standard of living.
It served notice to the African heirs of state power
from the British that workers reserved the right to
defend their interest as they perceived them. Unlike
the railway strikes of 1919 and 1926 and the crisis
associated with the activities of the Youth League in
which anti-colonial sentiments played some considerable
part in fuelling the furore, the 1955 strike was
primarily a protest against the straight-jacket into
which the new institutions of collective bargaining had
constrained wage negotiations. After the introduction
of Wages Boards and the JICs, it had become the custom
and practice for wage settlements reached at the two
JICs for artisans and transport workers to be taken as
the minimum wage rates for skilled and unskilled
workers throughout the country. The JICs being

'wage leaders' in this respect, explains the profound
interest of lower-paid workers not employed as artisans
or in the transport industry in the negotiations
preceding the strike, and the spontaneity with which
they joined (against the advice of the leaders of their
unions) in the action.99 The events of February 1955
therefore exposed the conservatism and detachment of
the majority of union leaders whose cooperative posture
had been responsible for the failure of wages to keep
pace with the cost of living.100 Anxious to preserve
their newly found 'respectability', the trade union
leadership (most of whom had come to prominence by
being Youth League activists) had worked assiduously to
maintain industrial peace during the decade following
the end of the war.

Arguably, the strike was also a demonstration of
resentment at the evident and increasing prosperity of
the politicians and senior civil servants. It is
significant that the homes of three Ministers were
singled out for attack during the disturbances:

> An ugly feature of the events on the
> 11th of February was the attack on
> the houses of certain Ministers
> which took place in the early
> evening of that day. In point of
> time, the first house to be attacked
> was that of the Hon. Siaka Stevens
> the Minister of Land, Mines, and
> Labour...a large crowd of about 100
> attacked the house in Third Street
> of the Hon. Sanusi Mustapha, the
> Minister of Works and Transport, with
> sticks and stones. On their way to
> the house they were overheard that
> they would kill the Minister if he
> could be got at...Later, a crowd
> proceeded to stone the house of the
> Hon. A. M. Margai, the Minister of
> Education, in Westmoreland Street.
> All the windows were broken.101

That lower-paid workers resented the prosperity of
prominent politicians, some of whom had been known only
a few years before to be men of very moderate means but
could now be distinguished by conspicuous display of
the symbols and paraphernalia of increased wealth and
status should be evident. Nonetheless, the sociological processes (even then only gradually unfolding)

underlying the articulation of political interest at
the national level during this period of decolonisation
(and also indeed in the post-colonial state), suggest
that lower-paid workers (and the poorer peasantry)
would take action to defend their economic interest and,
at the same time, identify with their respective
communal groups in political (or electoral) competition.
Herein lies an apparent contradiction between the manifestation by lower-paid workers of resentment at the
inequities of the mode of appropriation and distribution
and their contribution to the maintenance, even rein-
forcement, of the conditions upon which neo-patrimonal
political leadership thrives, and from which they (as a
group) are not even significant beneficiaries. This
is evident from analysis of the 1957 general election.

The Labour Movement and the 1957 Elections

Six political parties contested the 1957 elections
from which the ruling SLPP emerged the winner. While
the unrest in Freetown and other centres of relatively
large-scale wage employment, and in the countryside
during the last two years of Dr. Margai's first
administration of 1951-1957, might have suggested that
the ruling party would receive a battering at the
polls, the SLPP was in fact able to increase its
majority.102 The SLPP fielded candidates in thirty-
eight of the thirty-nine constituencies, winning
twenty-five seats including nine in the Freetown area.
The opposition NCSL which did not in any event stand a
chance in the provinces, fielded only ten candidates in
the Freetown area, all of whom were unsuccessful. The
United People's Party (UPP) which drew its leadership
from Krio and provincial elites, but of a more
'radical' persuasion especially on the question of
imperialism, and included Wallace-Johnson among its
leadership, fielded eighteen candidates in Freetown and
the provinces, five of whom were successful including
two in provincial constituencies. The Kono Progressive
Movement KPM), a party confined to the diamond-rich
Kono district, and whose leadership resented the collaboration of some members of the Kono elite in the exploitation of this resource from which ordinary Konos had
not derived much benefit, won one of the two Kono seats
it contested.103 The Sierra Leone Independence Movement
(SLIM), under the leadership of Edward Blyden III (a
descendant of the nineteenth-century luminary bearing
the same name) which purported to be a nationalist
party, lost all four of the Freetown seats it contested.

The Labour Party, which had Marcus Grant among a
leadership, mainly of Krio lawyers and intellectuals,
and which professed a reformist socialist ideology,
lost all six Freetown seats contested. Eight
'independent' candidates won seats in various parts
of the country. In nearly all the cases, these
candidates were members of local influential families.

There are several reasons for the SLPP's
success.104 Exploiting its advantage of incumbency to
the full, the SLPP was able to present a convincing
image of its own inevitable victory to an enlarged but
still restricted franchise.105 Only this party had the
resources to field candidates in a majority of the
constituencies. By drawing upon its patronage
relations with a network of local 'big men' in various
parts of the country, the SLPP was able to mobilise
support as the party which had a truly national
following, and could therefore contribute to 'nation-
building'. It campaigned on the theme of 'one country,
one people', this slogan--easily translated into other
Sierra Leonean languages--having been adopted as its
motto. This impressed the British administrators supervising the devolution of power. The SLPP, however, was
neither a mass party, nor did its leadership espouse
populist causes. It presented itself as the party
which could maintain law and order. "Dr. Margai made
speeches saying that his government had taken a tough
stance during the strike and provincial riots and that
he has shown the British that the black man can rule
himself".106. During the campaign, SLPP leaders
dismissed the other parties as not having a comparable
wide base of support.107 The NCSL was derided as the
'Krio man party'; the UPP as the party of agitators;
and the Labour Party as a party with an irresponsible
leadership. SLIM and the KPM were thought to be too
small to warrant much attention.108 At the constituencies, SLPP candidates, in most cases 'sons of the
soil', openly appealed to ethnic loyalities and at the
same time presented an image of the party as being best
placed to look after the 'national interest'. Thus the
SLPP won the 1957 elections by being able to demonstrate
convincingly that it could win, and by mobilising
communal support through its network of clientele at
the local level. The mobilisation of support along such
lines cuts across what might be termed 'objective class
interest'. Marcus Grant correctly perceives this as the
reason for the rapid evaporation of the idealism behind
the formation of the Labour Party and its subsequent
demise (and the lost deposits) at the elections.109

53

The Development of Modern Trade Unionism: Some Conclusions

In spite of the manifestations of a fairly developed proletarian consciousness by Freetown and other wage earners in Sierra Leone in 1955, this could not find expression in support of a party which stood little chance of winning. Thus the post-colonial pattern of political competition which is quite literally a struggle (and more often than not, a violent struggle) for access to the resources of the state and the institutions of state power, which, in turn, are used to maintain the system of patron-client-elism, became established during the period of decolonisation.110 In the years that lay ahead, the resilience of neo-patrimonal leadership--in particular its ability to survive periodical manifestations of factionalism by cliques close to the leaders, and its ability to renew and extend the network of clientele--was to have severe repercussions on the efficiency of management of the public sector, and on efforts at economic development. For lower-paid workers in the urban areas in general, and the para-statal sector in particular, patron-clientelism has become one of two channels that could be used to effect improvement in their living standards. The other has been aggressive bargaining at the work place through their trade union organisations. These two strategies are ambiguous but not mutually exclusive. Indeed, they will be shown to have been complementary in this study. Modern trade unionism in Sierra Leone has, therefore, evolved over the years to be accommodated within a political context of neo-patrimonal leadership.

SECTION 2

THE ADMINISTRATIVE AND ECONOMIC OPERATIONS OF

THE PORT ORGANISATION IN THE COLONIAL AND

POST-COLONIAL STATES

CHAPTER 3

THE DEVELOPMENT OF A SMALL-SIZED MODERN PORT IN

FREETOWN: THE PORT ORGANISATION AS A

SEMI-AUTONOMOUS PUBLIC ENTERPRISE 1954-65

In May 1954, Deep Water Quay, providing berthing facilities for ocean-going vessels and modern cargo-handling installations, was officially opened. The provision of modern port facilities had been made possible by the gradual change in policy at the Colonial Office at Whitehall towards investment in capital formation in the colonies which began in the late twenties, and received added stimulus from the Keynesian revolution in economic thought during the inter-war years. The colonial authorities, however, still cautious, and still reluctant to extend the public sector, continued to utilise existing administrative apparatus--the Railway Administration--to supervise the management of the new port. The ethos of bureaucratic accountability in the practice of British colonial administration was maintained. A report commissioned by the authorities on the organi-sation of the quay had recommended that:

> ...the quay and its ancilliary
> facilities should be placed under
> and operated by one centrally
> controlled organisation...It must
> be managed on business lines...1

This chapter examines the performance of the port organisation as a semi-autonomous public enterprise between 1954 and 1965, when a fully autonomous public corporation was created by an indigenous government. It begins by discussing the administrative and organ-isational structure that emerged to provide modern port services before going on to discuss the economic and commercial policy adopted by the port management. A third section examines the responses of lower-paid workers to their employment by the port organisation.

The Provision of Modern Port Services

Shortly before the opening of the new quay, a Port

Manager was appointed to head the new Port Management
Department created at the end of the war as a branch of
the Railway Administration. He was E. P. C. Gillespie,
who arrived in Freetown in March 1953. Some of the
longer serving dock workers remember Gillespie as a
cherry-red-faced Englishman who, during a tour lasting
seven years, master-minded the transition of the port
from little more than a river roadstead to a
small-sized modern organisation. A retired official of
the Port Authority who had worked with Gillespie as a
clerical assistant remembered him as personable,
eloquent, versed in matters pertaining to port
economics, and a competent administrator.2 The department was to be responsible for a system of master-port-
erage (receiving cargo at ship's tackle and delivery to
consignees, and vice versa), while the shipping
companies and agents continued to be responsible for
stevedoring (or the handling of cargo on board the ship
itself) and lighterage (the removal of cargo from ship
anchored at mid-stream to shore). The Railway Administration provided maintenance and managerial services.
Ministerial responsibility for the port resided in the
Department of Works and Transport which was first
created in 1951 at the beginning of the Margai Ministry
of 1951-57. The labour used in cargo handling was
provided by the port labour pool administered by the
Labour Department (see Chapter 1).

Gillespie recognised that the provision of
berthing facilities at the new quay should be matched
by an efficient system of cargo-handling which would
facilitate the speedy turn around of ship. The easy
approach to the harbour provided by the estuary of the
Rokel could be exploited if shipping traffic along the
coast was encouraged to call at Freetown to take
bunkers, water and other provisions, in much the same
way as Las Palmas in the Canaries had become a major
fuelling station for shipping traffic on the Atlantic
side of the African coast.3 He aimed therefore, to
provide varied and efficient services at the port,
while adopting a commercial policy that would enable
the Port Management Department to cover its operating
costs.

The evidence at the port archives suggests that the
administration of the port during these early years was
based on three principles, viz: first, the formulation
of port policy was to be the preserve of the department; second, in a labour intensive industry such as
cargo handling, effective control was to be maintained

58

over the labour force; and third, a variety of services were to be offered at the port.

One of the first decisions taken by Gillespie was to recommend the 'watering down' of the status of the Port Advisory Committee (see Chapter 1) which had since the war-time emergency become the main forum for the formulation of port policy. While the need for a forum at which port users could make representations vis a vis port services was evident, it was also obvious that the interest of port users and the department were not congruent. Hence, the Port Manager sought to reduce its influence on policy matters. In a memorandum to the General Manager of the Railway Administration, the case was forcefully argued:

> Now that the quay is nearing
> completion and the organisation
> required for its operation and the
> master porterage system is being
> finalised, it is considered that
> the status and functions of the
> Port Advisory Committee should be
> reviewed...Much of the time of the
> committee had been taken up in the
> past with...operating and mainten-
> ance matters as the inevitable
> result of the lack of central manage-
> ment of port operations and in conse-
> quence as the only coordinating body
> concerned, the Committee has appeared,
> perhaps, to have ben usurping normal
> departmental functions. This situation
> will not obtain with the establishment
> of the Port Management organisation at
> the Queen Elizabeth II Quay, when all
> such matters can be resolved directly
> with the Port Manager with consultation
> as necessary with General Manager,
> Railway as Port Authority.4

In the same memorandum, a new role for the committee as a 'consumer association' was outlined:

> It is however essential that the port
> advisory body should assist in the
> framing of port regulations and charges,
> review port estimates and expenditure,
> and generally advise on matters
> concerning the effiency of the port.5

Shortly before the opening of the quay, the terms of reference of the committee were redefined and the Port Management Department assumed full responsibility for the formulation of port policy. Gillespie's decision to reduce the influence of the committee was timely. Within a few years, port users had begun to protest against the increases in tariffs and other charges arising out of the department's periodic review. Nonetheless, a distinctive feature of the port organisation prior to the formation of a fully autonomous public corporation was that it was associated with the major consumers of port services and accountable to the General Manager Railway, as Port Authority, and through that office, the Ministry of Works and Communications. These separate channels of accountability to consumers and to the civil bureaucracy were not, as we shall see, maintained in the post-1965 port organisation.

A second principle evident in the early years of the Port Management Department was concerned with the measures taken to secure the effective regulation and control of the work force. Gillespie recognised that in a labour intensive industry such as cargo-handling, a considerable proportion of operating costs could be constituted by wages and other benefits. Accordingly, he chose to make extensive use of the casual labour system under which stevedore and shore cargo handling labourers were drawn from the labour pool administered by the Labour Department. These labourers received no benefits and were paid only for the number of hours worked. This same principle was extended to the 'white collar' workers, that is to say, the large number of clerks engaged in the processing of documents related to the movement of cargo. They were paid on a daily basis and denied the benefits associated with security of employment:

> The Port Manager pointed out that
> government did not favour the use
> of directly employed labour as such
> employees might well come to regard
> themselves as permanently government
> employed and press for leave, pension,
> and other benefits in line with other
> government departments.6

Furthermore, Gillespie sought to introduce the partial mechanisation of cargo-handling. This involved the palletisation of cargo and the use of fork-lift and electric platform trucks to move relatively large

quantities. He recognised that the introduction of
mechanisation would reduce the number of labourers
required, but argued that economy and efficiency
will be achieved:

> It may perhaps be argued that the
> introduction of mechanised handling
> will result in unemployment consequent
> upon the reduced labour force required,
> but it is submitted that in view of the
> general economic situation in Sierra
> Leone, it is imperative that maximum
> efficiency is achieved with lowest
> possible costs...the introduction
> of mechanical appliances will
> enable a smaller force of
> relatively skilled technicians to
> be created, trained in modern
> operating methods, to replace the
> present large numbers of casual
> labourers with only very limited
> knowledge of safe working methods.
> Redundant labour can in any case
> be more usefully diverted to
> productive employment in the
> provinces and the various
> development projects.7

In the event mechanised handling was introduced; road
building and other developing projects never absorbed
dock workers since competition for jobs in these
sectors was extremely keen. The hardship that resulted
was however mitigated by an increasing tonnage of cargo
handled at the port, so that the number of placings
made by the labour pool increased over this period (see
Tables 3.1 and 3.2). The net effect of the strategies
of labour control adopted by the department and the
widespread use of the casual and daily wage systems was
to create the conditions for the manifestation of
solidarity by dock workers. It was during this period,
that the 'white collar' workers among them, denied
benefits enjoyed by their counterparts in other
departments, became radicalised. It was this group of
workers that spear-headed the formation of the Dock
Workers' Union in 1963. These developments are
discussed in Chapter 6.

The third principle which characterised these
early years was the provision of a variety of port
services. Facilities for ships to take oil bunkers

TABLE 3.1

Dock Workers Registered and Total Number of

Vacancies Filled, Port Harbour Pool*

YEAR	NUMBER REGISTERED	NO. OF VACANCIES FILLED
1953	1630	61,986
1954	1628	151,545
1955	2188	208,000
1956	2180	319,300
1957	2192	336,480
1958	N.A.	N.A.
1959	2234	182,721
1960	2278	149,141

*Excludes stevedore labourers who were not in the employ of the Port Management Department.

N.A. = Not available (it has not been possible to locate a copy of the 1958 Labour Report).

SOURCES: Annual Reports of the Labour Department 1953-1957; 1959-1960.

and water and for limited repair were created. During the Suez Canal crisis of 1957, these services provided at Freetown were greatly in demand by ships forced to take the longer route round the West African Coast to

TABLE 3.2

Total Freight Tonnage Handled at the Quay 1955-1964

YEAR	FREIGHT TONNAGE
1955	326,626
1956	393,933
1957	422,579
1958	495,739
1959-60	371,067
1960-61	403,455
1962	496,393
1963	473,624
1964	487,632

SOURCE: Port Authority Archives, Annual Returns of Tonnage of Cargo Handled.

the Cape, the Near East, and the Far East:

> The installation of oil bunkering facilities...in addition to being of considerable advantage to existing port users, in view of the closure of the Suez Canal it is proved of inestimable value to international shipping...

Considerable additional revenue has
naturally also accrued from these
extra bunkering operations.8

By this time, the port of Freetown had come a long
way from the laissez-faire years before the Second World
War. One of the effects of this modernisation was that
the Port Authority had full control over port services
and the opportunity of adopting a commercial policy to
fully exploit the new facilities. The role of the
shipping companies was transformed from being providers
of port services to being consumers. This was the
expectation of a committee which reported in 1946:

> The central operation (of the port)...
> ensures that a shipping firm does not
> obtain a monopoly in handling cargo and
> is thus able to charge high handling
> rates which discourage ships other than
> those owned by the firm in question,
> thus leading to a monopoly of shipping
> using the port, and consequently leading
> to high freight charges on Sierra Leone
> exports to the detriment of the trade
> of the country. Only by all operations
> being conducted by the (port) manage-
> ment can rates on charges be kept to a
> minimum and the maximum encouragement
> be given to shipping to use the port.9

With the provision of port services in the public
sector, the shore operations of foreign shipping firms
operating in West Africa were significantly reduced and
their company structures rationalised. In the case of
Elder Dempster, Davies has written:

> The net effect of these changes is that
> Elder Dempster now has little direct
> business within West Africa, and even
> its subsidiary companies play a much
> smaller role than in the pre-war days.10

The Commercial Policy of the Port Management Department

The commercial policy set out by the authorities
for the department was that it must operate as a
'quasi-commercial' organisation with the port being
expected to pay its way. As a 'quasi-commercial'
organisation, the Port Management Department was

expected to meet its operational costs (including
depreciation of capital, both the physical port entity
as well as mechanical installations). The department
was not expected to make a return to the government on
the capital originally invested. Policy was not
geared towards obtaining adequate returns on the total
cost of port operations (i.e. original investment plus
depreciation plus operating costs), but to cover the
long-term average cost of port operations (i.e.
depreciation plus operating costs). This was officially
stated as:

> ...Government has accepted in
> principle the need for the port
> to be self-accounting with
> appropriate renewal and betterment
> funds...11

During these early years the principle was fully
applied and the expenditure borne by the port in the
course of its operations was covered by its revenue.
However, two problems soon emerged with the policy.
First, the authorities began to use the profits from
the port to subsidise the Railway Administration of
which the department was a branch:

> ...to date, earnings in excess of
> ordinary working expenditure have
> actually been credited to general
> revenue and used to reduce the
> amount of subvention payable
> annually from general revenue to
> meet the working expenditure of the
> Railway.12

Second, while the whole range of port services actually
included the regulation of shipping traffic provided by
the Port and Marine Department under the Harbour
Master, stevedoring provided by the shipping companies,
and storage accommodation in warehouses for which
rent was paid to the Customs Department, the Port
Management Department had jurisdiction only over shore
cargo-handling operations and lighterage:

> As I feel sure you will agree,
> comparison of merely Port Management
> revenue and expenditure figures fails
> of course to give a complete picture
> of the economics of port working
> here and it is essential that both

>the marine and shore working be
>included in one single port account
>if a properly balanced statement of
>overall working is to be seen.
>Similarly, items such as Queens
>Warehouse rent at present credited
>to Customs revenue should properly
>accrue to port revenue...13

Since port operations were not fully integrated,
there was a 'leakage' of revenue away from the
department, quite apart from the deliberate policy of
the authorities of subsidising the railway out of
revenue accrued by the department. On the other hand,
management and maintenance services were provided by
the Railway Administration and no direct change made to
the department. On the formation of a public
corporation in 1965, all these services were integrated
(with the exception of stevedoring which continued to
be provided by the shipping companies until it was
nationalised in 1971). The decisions thus taken by
the department to provide a lighterage service (to
reduce the possibility of congestion at the relatively
short 1200 foot quay) and to mechanise cargo-handling,
imposed a considerable burden on its finances.14   In
addition, the department, like all other employers, had
been forced to grant wage increases following the 1955
strike and salaries of more senior government officials
were increased in 1957. These additional items of
expenditure were passed on to the consumers of port
services through increased tariffs and a special levy,
known as Quay Dues:

>He (the Port Manager) realised of
>course that the imposition of
>additional dues at the present
>juncture would hardly be welcomed
>by the shipping companies, but it
>was imperative that the port should
>be economically self-supporting if
>it was to retain its present virtual
>autonomy which was to the overall
>benefit of all port users. The Port
>Manager went on to explain the
>necessity for increasing the revenue
>of the port...the necessity for the
>port to operate as a self-supporting
>economic venture on strictly commercial
>lines, i.e., earnings needing to cover
>loan interest and redemption charges

in addition to working expenditure
including renewal contributions
together with some provision for
betterment, were such as to demand a
complete reassessment of existing rates.15

During these years of its operation as a
semi-autonomous public enterprise, the Port Management
Department successfully introduced modern port services
while operating along 'quasi-commercial' lines. The
rather limited integration of these services and the
policy of subsidising the railway made port revenues
much lower than they otherwise would have been. Faced
with these constraints, the department adopted an
illiberal policy regarding wages and benefits of its
employees, the majority of whom were employed on a
daily wage and casual basis (see Table 3.2).

The Responses of Dock Workers to Their Employment by
the Port Management Department: The Failure of the
Works Committee

Between 1959 and 1963, a Works Committee
functioned at the department. A creation of the
management, it was an attempt to provide a forum for
continuous dialogue with workers on routine issues
relating to the performance of any large organisation
(e.g. time-keeping, grievances, or productivity).
Given the chequered history of the organisational
evolution of the port (see Chapter 1), there had not
been a central trade union into which dock workers in
the employ of the department were organised. A small
proportion of workers among the artisan grades
(deployed to the port to undertake civil and mechanical
maintenance work by the Railway Administration), had
been members of the Railway Workers' Union, but these
withdrew their membership in protest at the failure of
the leadership of the union to support the 1955
strike.16 Another small group were members of the
Artisans' Union.17 Since stevedoring had not been
integrated with the other functions of the department
and continued to be undertaken by the shipping
companies, the Maritime and Waterfront Workers' Union,
into which these workers were organised, operated
outside the jurisdiction of the port management. Thus
the 1,948 lower-paid workers in the employ of the
department or deployed by the Railway Administration in
1954 (see Table 3.3) were not organised into a central
trade union. The Works Committee was therefore

TABLE 3.3

Port Management Department Work Force 1954 and 1962

CATEGORY	1954	1962
Salaried	40(1)	76(3)
Daily Wage	320(1)	629(3)
Casual	1628(2)	6052(4)
Total Lower Paid	1948	6681

SOURCES: 1. Port Authority Archives, Governor's Annual Address, 8th October 1954. (Notes prepared by the Port Manager on the activities of the port for the Governor's annual review of the work of the administration at the Legislative Council).

2. Annual Report of the Labour Department 1954 (excludes stevedores).

3. Port Authority Archives, Work Force, March 1962.

4. Annual Report of the Labour Department 1962 (this figure is the total number of the dock labourers and stevedores registered at the labour pool).

designed to fill the vacuum left by the absence of a trade union organisation to represent the dockers. Before examining the working of the committee and its subsequent failure, the impact of the 1955 strike will be discussed.

Wages of shore cargo-handlers in the employ of the Port Management Department and of stevedores in the employ of the shipping companies were fixed by a statutory Maritime Wages Board. It was the custom for wage settlements reached at the Transport and Artisan JICs to be taken as the minimum rates for skilled workers (and adjusted accordingly for unskilled workers such as port labourers). The fact that these bargaining bodies were 'wage leaders' explains the profound interest of workers theoughout the country in the negotiations preceding the 1955 strike. At the port, officials of the Railway Workers' Union and the Maritime and Waterfront Workers' Union dissociated themselves from the strike (see Chapter 2) and in view of the widespread use of casual labour (and job insecurity among the workers) sufficient dockers remained at work to enable the port to continue to function. Nonetheless, a significant number of dockers picketed the docks, causing much harassment and irritation to the port management:

> ...all staff were warned of the
> consequence of strike action by
> government employees. Damage to
> port property consisted of broken
> windows at the labour recruiting
> centre and in the police box at
> the Main Gate...There was some
> loss of revenue...as a result
> of reduced output owing to the
> state of tension but it is
> impossible to calculate the amount
> of loss involved.18

This experience left some lessons for both the port management and the dockers. The strike demonstrated to the management the damage to the reputation of the port that might result from such action among international shipping companies. This was seen to be critical in view of recent attempts at modernisation and reorganisation, and for the success of the strategy to make Freetown an attractive port of call to shipping traffic on the West African coast.19 For the dockers, confidence in the leadership of the Railway and Maritime Unions was shaken and the necessity of a trade union to represent their interest was demonstrated.20 The formation of an independent dock works' union has been said to lie in the lessons learnt from the strike.21 The management for its part responded by seeking amendment to the existing labour legislation to allow the creation of an independent JIC for the port industry at which negotiations on wages and working conditions could be undertaken. The introduction of a

Works Committee within the department, where representatives of management and of the work force could deliberate issues relating to the work process, was also planned:

> Arrangements are well advanced for the establishment of a Works Committee to facilitate consultation between management and employees and for the setting up of a single Joint Industrial Council to embrace the whole port industry...I am confident that by continuing to work together as a team, we shall succeed in establishing a truly efficient port...22

The Works Committee held its first meeting on 27th January 1959. 23 Its elaborate constitution had been drawn to give management much control over its deliberations. One clause made this provision:

> No other business than that appearing on the agenda shall be transacted at any meeting unless both sides agree to its introduction.24

Another clause asserted that:

> Workers' representatives shall hold office for a period of one year. At the end of the period, there shall be an election of workers' representatives for the ensuing year. Any representatives leaving the employ of the department or resigning his position shall be replaced by a representative of the section concerned. A member of the committee who is unable to attend any meeting is authorised to appoint a deputy from the section he represents.25

The port management apparently believed that by subjecting workers' representatives to frequent elections, 'agitators' would be weeded out.26 This requirement, however, was later to have the unintended consequence of nurturing and fostering a democratic shop stewards' movement after a dock workers' union had been formed.

The chairmanship of the committee was to be the

70

preserve of the Assistant Port Manager, as the Port
Manager himself was to be seen to be above bargaining
between management and workers. At a rare appearance
at the committee, Gillespie made this quite clear:

> They would appreciate that it would be
> only on rare occasions such as at present
> that he would attend such meetings and
> would normally be represented by the
> Assistant Port Manager in order that he
> could deal with points raised by the commi-
> ttee as impartially as possible when they
> were ultimately referred to him in his
> official capacity as Port Manager without
> being prejudiced by participating in the
> discussions.27

A careful study of the minutes of the committee
reveals that the workers' side was most concerned with
reversing the illiberal employment policies of the port
management and, in particular, the widespread use of
casual and daily-paid labour. At the second meeting of
the committee, the question of the absorption of casual
workers was raised:

> The Chairman said that employment of
> tally clerks depends on the work
> available and it was normal practice
> all over the world to have casual
> employees in the shipping industry.28

Such demands persisted at meetings of the committee:

> Alimamy Kamara complained that the
> platform truck drivers operate expensive
> equipment, the operation and maintenance
> of which required some techniques and
> that it was felt that such drivers should
> be offered regular employment instead of
> casual.29

The management for its part was keen to use the
committee to reach a consensus on issues relating to
punctuality and productivity. At one meeting:

> The Chairman asked representatives to
> impress upon all members of their sections
> that they must come to work on time and
> not to absent themselves without leave
> during working hours.30

By the end of 1962, however, when the committee had been in existence for four years, the workers' representatives had lost their initial interest, since many issues which they regarded as important were being ruled outside the competence of the committee. Many of these representatives were beginning to warm to the idea of the formation of an independent dock workers' union which was being canvassed by Jack Sandy, Moses Fatoma, and Amadu Jalloh (clerks in the operations section of the department), Alimamy Kamara who had represented drivers and maintenance workers on the committee, and by Pa Karanke.[31] Another view which was widely held was that dock workers in the employ of the department were not effectively represented at the port JIC.[32] Given the impending expansion of the Port Management Department into a fully autonomous public corporation, it was felt that a strong union organisation ought to complement that development.[33] By the end of 1962, Sandy, Fatoma, and others had persuaded most workers at the department of the potential of a dock workers' union. An application for registration and a bargaining certificate was made at the Labour Department. These were granted in May 1963. [34]

The Port Organisation in the Colonial State: Some Conclusions

During the early years of its operation as a semi-autonomous public enterprise, the Port Management Department successfully introduced modern port services while operating along the rules set out for it by the colonial authorities. The narrower range of services over which it had jurisdiction, as a result of the limited integration of these services, and the policy of subsidising the railway, made port revenue much lower than it otherwise would have been. Hence, the management adopted an illiberal policy with regard to wages and benefits of its employees, the majority of whom were employed on a casual or daily paid basis. This 'exploitation' was facilitated by the state of the labour market in Freetown at the end of the war (see Chapters 1 and 2), and raises serious questions for theorists who have argued that lower-paid workers in the public sector 'live off the fat' created by the peasants and other revenue appropriated by the state. The department, however, was associated with its consumers and was responsible through the Railway Administration to the colonial government. The evidence in the port archive suggests that the department operated

as a 'quasi-commercial' organisation as it was formally
required to do. There was no suggestion of overmanning
or of consumers of port services being allowed extended
credit on the strength of their 'connections' with
important politicians and civil servants. There was no
suggestion of corrupt practices among the management.
The phenomenon of corruption in the post-colonial state
is, as we shall see, related to a political culture and
to political norms which place a lower premium on the
accountability of public officials than to the loyalty
and continued support of such officials to the regime
in power. The Port Management Department operated in a
colonial state in which the rules were made by the
colonial authorities and behaviour accorded with the
rules.

CHAPTER 4

THE PORT ORGANISATION 1965-76: THE DYNAMICS

OF POST-COLONIAL PARASTATAL POLITICS

On 1st January 1965, the Sierra Leone Port Autho-
ority was constituted as a statutory public corporation
with responsibility for the management of the port.
The need for an autonomous port organisation had been
apparent for several years. It had been the view of
Port Management Department officials that the
loss-making Railway Administration was 'dragging down'
the port, and the lack of integration of port services
was thought to have denied the organisation of
much-needed revenue. As the government began to con-
template the future of the railway, the department was
made independent in April 1962. 1 The Harbour Master's
Department was linked to it and new sections--accounts,
purchasing and stores, civil and mechanical mainten-
ance--were created within the new organisation to
provide services previously provided by the Railway.
Although the Port Act under which the corporation was
created stipulated that responsibility for stevedoring
was to become one of its functions, the shipping companies which had provided this service successfully
lobbied to retain it.

This chapter discusses the economic and administrative operations of the Port Authority between 1965 and
1976. It begins by reviewing the performance of the
parastatal sector in post-colonial Sierra Leone, and
assessing its impact on the national economy. The case
study of the Authority is then taken up in the second
section, beginning with an examination of the organisation of the new corporation, its economic performance
and its procedures for accountability. A third section
examines the factors leading to the financial collapse
of the corporation in 1976.

The Parastatal Sector in Post-colonial Sierra Leone:
An Overview

The expansion of the economic activities of the
state in many African countries have been encouraged by
the need to facilitate development and by the important
role accorded to state intervention in this task by

75

fashionable economic theory (Nkrumah's Ghana being the
most notable example). In Sierra Leone, on the other
hand, there was no dramatic expansion in the economic
activities of the state immediately after independence.
This was partly because the financial resources
available were much more modest, but also because the
government of Sir Milton Margai adopted a 'gradualist'
market orientated strategy of economic growth
manifested in the so-called 'open door policy'.2
Nonetheless, the importance which the state had assumed
(not least by being the largest employer) in social and
economic life, put into the hands of the politicians
considerable resources (from mining, agriculture, etc.)
for appropriation and selective distribution. When
Sir Milton died in April 1964, the frontiers of the
parastatal sector were confined to the marketing of
commodities (by the Produce Marketing Board, the
SLPMB), the marketing of the staple food (by the Rice
Corporation), the buying of diamonds from licensed
alluvial 'diggers' for polishing and marketing locally
and overseas (by the Diamond Corporation, DICOR), the
broadcasting service (SLBS), one national newspaper,
and the public utilities (Railway Administration, Port
Management Department, Guma Valley Water Company, Electricity Corporation, Road Transport Corporation, Post
and Telecommunications, Cable and Wireless, and Sierra
Leone Airways). On the drawing board were plans for
the creation of an autonmous Port Authority and a Forest
Industries Corporation for the manufacture of funiture
from local timber resource. Both corporations came
into operation in January 1965. The SLPMB had since
the early sixties ventured cautiously into plantation
agriculture and the processing of produce. Import
substitutive industries were encouraged in the private
sector where overheads were kept low by the generous
provisions of the open door policy. Notice of Sierra
Leone's withdrawal from participation in the West
African Currency Board had been given and the necessary
legislation for the creation of a national central bank
had been passed the previous year. (Ghana and Nigeria
withdrew their participation in 1957 and the 1960
respectively, leaving Sierra Leone and The Gambia as
members of the Board). The Bank of Sierra Leone began
operations in August 1964. The significance of the
formation of a national central bank was that decisions
relating to the regulation of money supply could be
made locally. Under the regime of the Currency Board,
changes in the level of money supply depended on
changes in the level of income generated by foreign
trade. Under the regime of a national central

bank, a whole range of fiscal and monetary policies
could be employed in deficit financing.3

Since its first intervention in 1966, the International Monetary Fund (IMF) has been a major
influence--though it must be emphasised, only one among
others--on the settting of objectives and criteria of
performance of the parastatal sector in Sierra Leone.
This influence has been particularly evident since the
mid-seventies when the spiralling cost of imported
energy became the source of a now chronic trade
imbalance. The first intervention of the IMF was necessitated by the rapid expansion of some areas of the
parastatal sector after the death of Sir Milton, when
his more 'radical' brother, Albert, became Prime
Minister.4 The rationale of this expansion was ostensibly to diversify the economy and reduce the dependence
on the mining sector whose share of the value of income
generated by foreign trade had never fallen below 65
percent during the early sixties.5 But it was also an
attempt by the new Prime Minister to consolidate his
political base (via the patron-clientelist network of
the SLPP) by opening up new areas for the award of
contracts and for appointments to positions in the new
or expanded organisations. Consequently, the subsidiary activities of the SLPMB in agricultural planata-
tions and processing industries were expanded, and
investment made in tourist infrastructure, the expansion
of the internal services of Sierra Leone Airways, and
other industrial ventures, necessitating considerable
expenditure on imported technology and building
materials. With export earnings in 1965 falling below
the 1964 record level, the expansion of the SLPMB was
financed by its accumulated trading surpluses and the
more direct investments by the government were financed
partly by external short-term contractors' credit and
partly by the increased use of accumulated cash balances
and bank credit. The result, however, was a substantial
rise in the trade deficit from Le0.6 million at the end
of 1964 to a record Le11.6 million at the end of 1965. 6
The total foreign exchange reserves, including those of
the Bank of Sierra Leone, declined from Le29.2 million
at the end of 1964 to Le17.6 million at the end of
1965--the equivalent of three months' imports. For the
1966-67 fiscal year, the budget estimates showed a
deficit of Le19.3 million. In these estimates, the
government budgeted for an increase of almost 100
percent in its 'development' expenditures.7 By this
time, the SLPMB, which had committed its liquid assets
to long-term projects in agricultural production and

processing, was unable to meet its current liabilities
to the buying agents. Farmers were issued with 'I owe
you' chits for their produce. Moreover, large repay-
ments were falling due and it was anticipated that the
trade deficit would deteriorate further. Given the
skillful exploitation of the crisis by the Opposition
APC (which claimed that the government had 'eaten' all
the country's money), and with a general election due
by May 1967, Sir Albert called in the IMF in mid-1966.

        The SLPP, quite understandably perhaps, lacked the
political will to implement a policy of economic
austerity on the eve of the general election. It was
left to the National Reformation Council (NRC), which
came to power following the intervention of the
military after the election, to implement the stabili-
tion programme. As a study of the NRC argues, it was
in its interest to do so, being "faced with the harsh
economic realities and with a need to strengthen its
initial flimsy arguments for intervening".8 In return
for credits totalling some Le9 million over a
three-year period to help meet the trade deficit, the
NRC agreed to undertake significant reforms not only in
fiscal and monetary policy, but also in policy relating
to the management and organisation of the public
sector.9 Accordingly, measures to reduce the budget
deficit, to increase personal taxation and improve the
efficiency of tax collection were implemented. The
rate of domestic monetary expansion was made consistent
with the realisation of targets relating to the
building up of foreign reserves.10 Organisations in
the parastatal sector were required to make economies
which were closely monitored by the IMF representatives
and their local counterparts at the Department of
Finance. The SLPMB was reorganised and its activities
confined to the marketing of produce. Plantations
which were assessed not to be viable were closed down
resulting in over 2,000 redundancies. A loan of Le4
million was negotiated with a London-based bank to help
the Board with its liquidity problems.

        When the NRC was ejected from office in April
1968, these measures had begun to make an impact on the
economy. The APC which then assumed office had
campaigned on a 'radical' programme of economic nationalism aimed at assuming control of the 'commanding
heights' of the national economy. While Siaka Stevens
and his new government felt committed to the continued
implementation of the IMF programme for the remaining
year, a state-led programme of economic expansion was

very much expected. Nonetheless, in his first budget, the APC Minister of Finance was critical of the forays of the SLPP regime into industrial and tourist ventures:

> ...under the slogan of industrialisation abuses can flourish...We shall make it our guiding principle that industrial ventures which have government support shall be undertaken only if it can be demonstrated beyond doubt that they will bring benefits not for a group of unpatriotic politicians, but for the common people of our country.11

One of the first measures taken by the APC on assuming office was to begin negotiations for the acquisition of a 51 percent share of the equity in Selection Trust (in return for commensurate compensation) the largest diamond mining concern in the country. A new company, Diamond Mining Company of Sierra Leone was formed in October 1970. The APC was also committed to the reform of banking and insurance practices and to the formation of state-owned financial institutions. Accordingly, legislation was passed requiring the (mainly British) commercial banks and insurance companies to be incorporated in Sierra Leone and to maintain large deposits at the Bank of Sierra Leone.12 In 1968, a National Development Bank had been formed to extend credit facilities to indigenous businessmen, and this was followed by the formation of a National Cooperative Development Bank and the Sierra Leone Commercial Bank in 1971 and 1973 respectively.13 In 1972, a state-owned insurance business, the National Insurance Company, was formed. The rationale for the reform and the establishment of these financial institutions was to increase the sources of credit available to indigenous entrepreneurs, the APC having rejected the whole-scale nationalisation of foreign financial institutions. Needless to say, these developments (and the passing of the Non-Citizens Trade and Business Act in 1969) have also had the effect of increasing the scope of patronage of the regime. Partly because of the competitive market situation in which these state-owned financial institutions operate, partly because the confidence of the public is an essential ingredient for their continued viability, and given the supervisory role of the Bank of Sierra Leone in cooperation with the African Development Bank and other international financial institutions

(which have either provided technical expertise or
have provided loans to meet the capital required)
each of these businesses have performed relatively
satisfactorily.14

Two other parastatal organisations, the National
Shipping Company and the National Trading Company,
created by the APC in 1971 have not shared the success
of the financial institutions. The shipping company
was established to give the government a foothold in
the provision of shipping services to and from Sierra
Leone. Being unable to meet the financial commitment
required in the purchase nd maintenance of vessels and
the hiring of experienced manpower, this ambitious
project has consequently been modified. Since 1976,
the shipping company has operated as a clearing and
forwarding agency (in competition with other shipping
agencies operating in the private sector). The
monopoly over the provision of stevedore services which
it assumed at its formation was transferred to the Port
Authority in November 1979 to enable the latter
organisation to provide a fully integrated system of
cargo-handling. The trading company was established to
centralise the purchase of imported merchandise and
thereby cut out the middle-man role of foreign
companies such as Paterson Zochonis (PZ) and the United
Africa Company (UAC) group. After only two years of
operation, the company faced a cash crisis, having
provided extended credit facilities to retailers
typically on the strength of their connections with the
ruling party, rather than by traditonal business
criteria of the assessment of risks. The company was
forced to increase mark-ups on its merchandise over
which it held monopoly import rights. This contributed
to the rising trend in prices (following the substantial
increase in the price of imported energy in 1973) and
brought protests from the labour movement (see Chapter
7). The government responded by decentralising the
importation of merchandise.15

Under the APC, the performance of the SLPMB has
been, superficially at least, very satisfactory. This
of course means, however, that the export agricultural
sector has been subjected to considerable exploitation.
The Bank of Sierra Leone reported in 1979 that during
the previous year the Board purchased 48,943 tons of
produce valued at Le46.2 million. Resales by the Board
amounted to Le61.9 million suggesting a profit of
Le15.7 million.16 After the fiasco of 1966-67 when
farmers were issued with chits for their produce, the

APC has apparently been very cautious with regard to
its management of the Board, though the relatively high
profit margin suggests that producer prices could be
increased. Indeed a recent study of incomes in Sierra
Leone suggests that between 1968 and 1977, agricultural
taxation on coffee and cocoa has, on an average, been
45.6 percent and 40 percent respectively. Taxation on
palm kernel during the same period has on an average
been 6.3 percent, this lower figure being due to lower
receipts in the export markets in 1972-3 and in 1975-6.
As the study concludes, no one in Sierra Leone had
one-half, or even one-quarter of his income deducted
through any form of taxes.17

Following several years of relatively unsatisfactory performance, the Port Authority, the Electricity
Corporation, Post and Telecommunications, and the
state-owned hotels were reorganised in the late 70s.
With the exception of Post and Telecommunications and
some of the hotels, the management of these corporations
were subcontracted to foreign consultants. The
Minister of Finance in his 1978 budget speech failed to
locate this poor performance in prevailing political
practices, bitterly criticising, instead, the management of these corporations:

> ...the financial performance of our
> public corporations has been dismally
> poor...Obviously such a state of
> affairs adds to our budgetary
> difficulties...I should underline the
> point that public corporations are
> meant to be revenue earners for the
> central government, not revenue
> devourers. A large degree of
> independence is accorded them which,
> if it were exploited advantageously,
> should make it much easier to adopt
> sound business principles and thereby
> create the conditions necessary for
> effective performance...Of course...we
> do not judge their financial performance
> by the demanding standards of private
> business...the bitter truth revealed
> by the evidence gathered so far is
> that the vital resources entrusted to
> public corporations are woefully
> misued, mismanaged, and misdirected...
> the chilling revelations of the Report
> of the Forster Commission of Inquiry

into the Sierra Leone Port Authority
have forcibly brought home to us the
need for stricter measures of control...
I would sound a warning here that
inefficient managers and those found
to misuse resources will have to go.
I would hope, however, that the swift
action of government in dismissing the
top management of the...Port Authority
would serve as a corrective measure...18

It should be clear from this review of the impact
of the parastatal sector on the national economy, that
Sierra Leone's modest resources can hardly afford to
absorb inefficient and unprofitable public corporations
riddled with graft and corruption. Consequently there
is pressure for reform from international institutions
of development and other creditors. In this respect,
the parastatal sector in Sierra Leone has been more
amenable to reform than their counterparts in Ghana
under Nkrumah and elsewhere in post-colonial Africa.
Nonetheless, state-led economic expansion primarily to
'accommodate' political clients (but ostensibly for
other reasons such as to control the 'commanding
heights' of the national economy) is the inherent logic
of a neo-patrimonal political system. Not only does
the state finance the salaries, wages, and perquisites
of public sector personnel, over and above this, (and
since loyalty to the regime is of greater importance
than the accountability of public officials), such
personnel might quite literally dip their hands into
the public corporation till. The diversion of
resources from public and parastatal organisations to
private consumption and investment, the deliberate
overmanning of these organisations to accommodate
political clients or, the failure of such organisations
to operate like typical capitalist organisations, might
more usefully be viewed as the operational logic of a
patron-clientelist political system. This approach
also encapsulates the broader sociological processes
underlying actions of political corruption. Even as
Sierra Leone enters the latter years of the 1980s, the
public sector is locked in a vicious circle of unsatisfactory performance and international pressure for
reform. This is very clearly illustrated by the case
study of the Port Authority.

The Port Authority 1965-70:   Organisation, Accountability, and Economic Performance

The appointment of a Board of Directors accompanied
the vesting of responsibility for the management of the
port in a fully autonomous public corporation. Under
the Port Act, a total of seventeen part-time Directors,
including a Chairman, could be appointed.19 The Act
also stipulated that the Board members must include
representatives of the Ministry of Transport and Communications and of the Ministry of Finance, the Managing
Director of the Produce Marketing Board (the largest
consumer of port services) the General Manager of the
Railway Administration, and the head of personnel
administration in the civil service (the Establishment
Secretary). The Board was to be the main forum for the
formulation of port policy. The General Manager of
the Authority, an ex-officio member of the Board, was
to be responsible for the implementation of policies
decided upon by the Board to which he was accountable.

The initial structure of the corporation and the
designated composition of the Board were intended to
safeguard the Authority as a quasi-commerical organisation. However, manifestations of political patronage
were evident in the composition of the Board and of
subsequent Boards. The Chairman had been a defeated
SLPP candidate for the Waterloo constituency at the
1962 general elections, and had been an associate of
the late Prime Minister, Sir Milton Margai. The
Establishment Secretary, the Managing Director of the
Produce Marketing Board, the General Manager of the
Railway, and the Financial Secretary who represented
the Ministry of Finance were, apparently, proteges of
the new Prime Minister, Sir Albert Margai. While they
were all fully qualified for the positions they held,
Gaffney has argued that the careers of the incumbents
of certain of these offices were 'helped along' by the
pervasive system of political clientelism.20 The other
Directors appointed in 1965 were the Permanent
Secretary at the Ministry of Transport and Communication, the Comptroller of Customs, three representatives
each of the shipping companies and of commercial
interests, and the Secretary of the Dock Workers' Union,
who with origins in the southern province was reputed
to have kinship connections in the hierarchy of the
SLPP (see Chapter 5). All received Directors' fees.

Scrutiny of the port archives leaves the impression
that the Directors worked through specialist

sub-committees where policy was discussed and agreed upon before being ratified by the whole Board. Although the Board was supposed to be formally account-able to the Minister of Transport and Communications, the procedures for such accountability were never made clear—the Permanent Secretary being only a represent-ative of the Ministry on the Board. Neither were there clear procedures for the Minister's own accountability to parliament. Indeed, the Minister was never questioned in parliament about the Authority even though its economic performance during its early years should have been a cause for concern. From reports on the proceedings and debates in parliament, it appears that the Produce Marketing Board was the main target of criticisms by the APC Opposition as regards the govern ment's management of the parastatal sector. There is also evidence in the port archives that important poli-ticians exerted influence on the management of the Authority to provide jobs or credit facilities to their clienteles. For instance, a letter signed by the then Minister of Transport and Communications asks specifically that the bearer of the letter, described as "one of the strongest supporters in my constituency" be given a job as a labourer.21 The Minister also intervened to modify penalties imposed by the Board on one of its largest debtors.22

If procedures for accountability between the Board and the Minister and between the Minister and parliament were ill defined, there were some 'external' considera-tions which exerted an influence on the maintainance of the bureaucratic chain of accountability between the management and the Board, and which influenced the decisions of the latter. These consisted of the IMF package negotiated with the government in 1966 and effectively implemented by a resident team of officials from Washington working with counterparts in the Ministry of Finance over a three-year period to 1969. The package consisted of stand-by arrangements to save the government from further financial embarrassment and, at the same time, ceilings were set for government borrowing from the banking system and for contracting new short- and medium-term foreign credits. The growth of public expenditure was to be restrained through tightened controls over budgetary disbursements, the credit policy of the central bank, curtailment of development expenditure, and the monitoring of all public corporations.

This deflationary package and the glare of the IMF

spotlight to which the parastatal sector became
subjected had much influence on procedures for accountability at the Port Authority. While SLPP politicians
continued to make demands on the parastatal
sector--understandable enough in view of the approaching
general elections in March 1967; Sir Albert himself had
resisted pressure for the devaluation of the
Leone--guidelines were introduced which public corporations were expected to implement. In mid-1966, the
Board of the Authority was advised to make cuts on its
overtime payments, and to make efforts to recover debts
owed by port users.23 These instructions duly received
the attention of the finance and staff sub-committees
of the Board. Regarding the overtime bill, which
amounted to Le250,661, being almost a third of the
total wages and salary bill of Le701,298 for the first
eleven months of 1966, 24 it was decided that a system
of shift working should be introduced.25 This had the
advantage of avoiding redundancies which would have
been politically unacceptable. Militant action by the
Dock Workers' Union delayed the effective implementation
of these plans until they had been properly negotiated
with the union (see Chapter 6). The Board also directed
that vigilance on corruption and graft particularly
among senior managerial personnel should be stepped up.
This resulted in the dismissal of the corporation's
chief accountant in November 1966 following allegations
of corrupt practices.26 The incident contrasts sharply
with the more flexible standards of managerial behaviour
accepted at the Authority after 1970, following the
withdrawal of the IMF at the end of the stabilisation
programme, when senior management openly plundered the
property of the Authority with little fear of discipli-
nary action.

    Effective accountability within the port bureau-
cracy continued to be maintained under the military
junta of 1967-68. Indeed, Colonel Juxon-Smith, the NRC
Chairman, evidently required a sense of messianic
purpose <u>vis a vis</u> the national economy:

            Accountable to almost no civilians,
            the NRC did not particularly see
            fit to guage the political conse-
            quences of its austerity measures
            with the same degree of sensitivity
            as might a civilian government.
            Juxon-Smith stressed this view in
            a 'State of the Nation' address in
            February 1968. "Never again", said

the NRC Chairman, "must the timely
implementation of national economic
policies be delayed or even prevented
because the government in power is more
interested in party politics than in the
well being and prosperity of the nation
as a whole".27

The junta removed those members of the Board who had
been closely identified with the previous regime. The
failure, however, of the NRC to resolve the political
crisis, its high-handed treatment of senior politicians
of both parties, its institution of austerity measures,
the pomp and circumstance of grotesque proportions
clearly enjoyed by the Chairman and other leading
members of the junta, evidently led to their removal
from office by the junior ranks of the army in April
1968.

     The financial crisis of the mid-sixties involving
most importantly a shortage of foreign exchange,
clearly affected the economic performance of the
Authority. Operating surpluses fell below the levels
of the old Port Management Department. During the
first two years of operations, a deficit of Le29,748
was incurred for the year ending 31st December 1965, 28
and Le184,136 for the year ending 31st December 1966.
29 In a statement, prepared for the Board, the
Authority's financial manager outlined the reasons for
the deficits. Some of these were associated with the
increased overheads of an autonomous public corporation
or beyond the control of the Authority. Other reasons
for the deficit, however, had their origins in trends
in the parastatal sector in the post-colonial state.
The junior staff of the Authority had succeeded through
their union in reversing the old policy under which
they were employed as daily-paid workers with no fringe
benefits. While the casual labour system for workers
involved in shore cargo-handling was maintained,
clerks, artisans, and other skilled or semi-skilled
labour were now entitled to paid holidays and pensions
on retirement:

          Leave gratuity not previously paid to
          all members of staff is now being paid
          and this is around Le16,000 per annum.30

Moreover, overtime payment amounted to over a third of
the total wages and salary bill and the permanent staff
of the Authority had increased by seventeen times

between 1962 and 1967 (see Table 4.1). The Authority
had also undertaken to provide accommodation for its
senior management at a subsidised rent.

The main action taken by the Board with regard to
the economic performance of the Authority was to secure
cuts in overtime payments by introducing the shift-work
system. Efforts were made to recover large outstanding
debts from port users. The Board further decided that
senior officials could apply for mortgages (financed by
the Authority) under certain conditions rather than
provide them with subsidised housing. By the middle of
1967, the shift system had been fully implemented, and
the cost control strategy applied throughout the
Authority. The Accounts Department prepared a statement showing that the Authority was out of the red by
the first quarter of 1968. The statement also asserted:

> Prior to September 1967, much control
> had not been exercised on soaring
> departmental costs. There has been
> great improvement in this control
> aspect since the first quarter of
> 1968 as departmental heads were
> often requested to explain adverse
> variances, i.e., when actual costs
> exceeded budgeted figures.[31]

Complementing the IMF stabilisation programme
which led to an upturn in the national economy by 1968,
was a reasonably successful attempt at maintaining the
port organisation as a viable 'quasi-commercial'
enterprise.

The Port Authority 1970-76: Erosion of Accountability and Financial Collapse

With the restoration of civilian rule, the return
of party politics, and the withdrawal of the IMF,
the politics of patronage were reestablished. In
1970, the Chairman of the Board of the Port Authority
appointed by the junta was replaced by a veteran civil
servant and businessman and a known sympathiser of
the APC during its years in opposition. The choice
of other Directors seems to have been influenced by
their loyalty to the regime. These included three
party stalwarts and among them the organiser of the
women's wing. As before, some civil servants with
kinship and other connections in the hierarchy of

87

TABLE 4.1

Port Work Force 1954-1967

CATEGORY	1954	1962	1967
Permanent	40(1)	76(3)	1303(5)*
Daily Wage	320(1)	629(3)	103(5)
Casual	1628(2)	6052(4)	5678(6)
Total Lower Paid	1948	6681	6783

*Includes managerial staff which was 106 in 1967.

SOURCES:
1. Port Authority Archives, Governor's Annual Address, 8 October 1954 (notes prepared by the Port Manager on the activities of the port for the governor's annual review of the work of the administration at the Legislative Council).

2. Annual Report of the Labour Department 1954 (this figure excludes stevedores registered at the port labour pool).

3. Port Authority Archives, Work Force, March 1962.

4. Annual Report of the Labour Department 1962 (this figure is the total number of dock labourers and stevedores registered at the port labour pool).

5. Port Authority Archives, General Manager to Secretary, Sierra Leone Employers' Federation, 18 July 1967.

6. Annual Report of the Labour Department 1967 (figure includes casual stevedore labourers).

the ruling party were appointed. The major port users
and the shipping companies were represented through the
Chamber of Commerce. The incumbent Secretary of the
Dock Workers' Union was also appointed. The report of
the commission of inquiry appointed after the financial
collapse of the Authority in 1976 was particularly
scathing as to the composition of the Board. This is
worth quoting at length as it gives an indication of the
source from which the rot began to spread within the
Corporation:

> The Board of the Authority is in the
> opinion of the commission not only
> too large but also ill composed.
> It was evident from the history of
> its activities culled from its
> minutes, that it was lacking in
> commercial expertise and overweighted
> needlessly by Government appointed
> members. True enough, the Authority
> is wholly owned by Government, but
> if it is to be of economic viability,
> it must be run on economic lines,
> implying a prerequisite of commer-
> cial expertise...The Board seemed
> incapable of making a firm decision
> and holding on to it...It clearly
> maintained a double standard as is
> evidenced by its treatment of
> members of staff deserving of
> punishment for malpractices or
> grave misconduct...The Board
> displayed much weakness in failing
> to formulate any guiding policy,
> and worse, by not insisting on any
> laid down policy being carried out.32

With the reassertion of the influence of patron-
clientelist relationships in appointments to key
positions in the public sector under the APC, it is
evident that a gradual breakdown in effective accountability at the level of the port bureaucracy occurred.
The Ministry of Transport and Communications which had
nominal responsibility for the Authority never did
impose formal procedures for the accountability of the
corporation. In parliament, the official Opposition,
gradually undermined by APC authoritarianism, raised
few questions about the government's management of the
public sector. It was the Forster Commission which

discovered that the accounts had been repeatedly falsified during the seventies:

> The Commission was appalled at what it found...Management's Profit and Loss Accounts and the Balance Sheets thereon have not reflected the true financial operations of the Authority. Most of the adjustments necessary for this are seldom put through the records even though these adjustments are normally submitted to the Accounts section and discussed with them after each audit... The deteriorating financial position of the Authority which became apparent in the past few years had been so much earlier...In 1972/3 for example, Management Accounts showed a record net profit of Le620,193. When the same account was audited by the external auditors, the net profit was reduced to Le309,384, a net difference of Le310,809. 33

Given the laxity with which the Ministry and the Board approached the affairs of the port, the professional management fully exploited the resulting situation. The commission discovered several instances of serious financial malpractices. First, foreign currency to the value of Le2,266 was held in the office of the Chief Cashier for the use of certain members of senior management named by the commission.34 Second, cheques were exchanged for cash by the cashier, and the commission discovered that cheques to the value of Le196 had not been forwarded to the banks of the individuals concerned for payment.35 Third, 'I owe you' chits were also exchanged for cash:

> The Commission was able to confirm that recovery was either delayed, slow, or abandoned as some chits dated back to 1974. Lack of recovery and control over their issue has resulted in an outstanding balance of over Le9,000 as at 30th April 1976. Furthermore, between 1975 and March 1976, a total of over Le10,369 was approved by management as advances-- personal, domestic, which in the Commission's view was meant to replace the chit system, but the latter was

continued without any reason being
given therefore.36

And fourth, the commission discovered that the procedures governing loans for mortgages, cars, and refrige-
rators were repeatedly flouted:

> The Commission was satisfied that there
> was a lack of adequate supervision and
> control in the administration of salary
> advances to staff and this has resulted
> in a huge outstanding balance of
> Le178,000. 37

Of this amount, housing loans accounted for Le105,841,
and car loans for Le62,150. The commission also
discovered serious irregularities in the purchase and
administration of the Authority's stores and supplies,
as a result of which several hundred thousands of
leones were lost to the Authority.

These malpractices appear to have spread all the
way down the line. For the lower placed employees, the
system of overtime payments was the most obvious
opportunity for graft. Hence the system which had been
brought under control in 1968 was again being abused by
the early 70s:

> With the introduction of the shift sys-
> tem, the Authority hoped to have helped
> relieve unemployment among dock workers
> and that working extra hours would have
> been kept at a minimum. On the contrary,
> it was the rule rather than the exception.
> A wide spectrum of the staff and workers
> earned overtime...and though it gave the
> Commission cause for concern, yet it
> seemed it had the blessing of management
> itself, notwithstanding the various
> circulars issued ad hoc, since provision
> for overtime in the budget was inva-
> riably about 50 percent of the amount
> provided for salaries/wages...The
> annual budget was usually overspent
> by as much as 70 percent.38

With the work force already artificially inflated (the
permanent work force had increased from 1,303 in 1967
to 2,064 in 1976, "...in the opinion of the Commission
much in excess of that required for the economic

productivity of the Authority"),39 the abuse of the
overtime system also took its toll on the finances of
the Authority.

Given the erosion of accountability within the
port bureaucracy, and given the large scale diversion
of resources, the economic viability of the Authority
was soon in doubt. By the middle of 1975, it was clear
that the Authority had great difficulties in meeting
its financial commitments and that it was on the brink
of financial collapse. One of the earliest indications
of the plight of the Authority was its inability to
finance the removal of siltation from the seabed of the
berths--an operation routine enough and which would
normally be provided for in budget estimates. The
Acting General Manager solicited a loan from the Oil
Refinery for the purpose and suggested that it would be
repaid by waiving future claims against the Refinery for
port dues.40 Ten days later, the acting General
Manager wrote to the Electricity Corporation requesting
permission to pay outstanding bills in monthly install-
ments of Le5,000. 41 By the end of the year, the Crown
Agents made it clear that the Authority's orders would
not be processed until all outstanding debts to the
tune of Le300,000 had been settled.42 Early in 1976,
the Authority had difficulties in meeting its own wages
and salary bills. A series of sensational articles
soon appeared in We Yone, the newspaper of the ruling
APC exposing 'corruption' at the port. These served
notice that the system of patronage could not be
expected to protect the Directors and senior officials
of the Authority. A few months later, in August, the
Forster Commission was appointed.

The management for its part argued at the commission that there were other reasons which equally
contributed to the financial collapse. First, it was
pointed out that the government had entered into an
agreement with the mining companies exempting them from
harbour dues. Between 1968 and 1972, it was contended
that revenue to the tune of Le875,297 was lost as a
result of the agreement. Indeed, the commission
accepted that "...the Authority has been deprived of
much revenue because of government's agreement with the
mining companies concerned, and some way should be
found to make payments to the Authority for the services
rendered to these companies, or the Authority would
found to be subsidising the mining companies".43
Second, the management argued that of the Le918,497 owed
to the Authority at the time of its financial collapse,

Le217,001 was owed by government departments and other parastatal corporations.44 Third, the management contended that although the Port Act had stipulated that stevedoring should be one of the functions of the Authority so that a fully integrated system of porterage would be provided, the shipping companies had, in 1964 successfully lobbied to retain this function. In 1971, stevedoring was nationalised and the newly formed National Shipping Company was given monopoly rights to provide the service. It was pointed out that stevedoring is an extremely profitable business (the overheads are very low) especially where casual labour is used. The commission accepted that "...this is a very sore point with the Authority and justifiably so...Incredible as it may seem the Authority is wholly owned by government and cutting the nose to spite the face never did anyone any good".45

The conclusion reached by the commission was that the bureaucratic organisation of the port (including the chain of responsibility to the Ministry of Transport and Communications and ultimately to parliament) was adequate to maintain effective accountability:

> The Commission is firmly of the opinion
> that the infrastructure of the Authority
> is substantially sound and, but for the
> pronounced human failings due to greed
> and selfishness of many senior officials,
> the Authority would not have been as
> financially crippled and demoralised as
> it was immediately preceding 4th July
> 1976. 46

Following the logic of this conclusion, the commission recommended the dismissal of several senior officials and the reconstitution of the whole Board. In 1977 the management of the port was sub-contracted to a foreign company.47

The Dynamics of Post-colonial Parastatal Politics: Some Conclusions:

While Forster may have been right in laying blame for the financial collapse on the Board and the manage-ment of the Authority (after all a public inquiry is usually appointed in order that a government may be seen to be doing something about an important or embarrassing problem), corruption in Sierra Leone does not originate

from the personal characteristics of individuals. On
the contrary, it originates from within a political
culture in which a low premium is placed on the accountability of public servants, notwithstanding the moral
indignation expressed from time to time in budget
speeches and on other occasions of the statement of
government policy. It cannot be overemphasised that in
Sierra Leone, political competition is quite literally
a struggle for access to the resources of the state.
Once such access has been obtained, prominent and
influential members of the elite are coopted into the
ruling establishment by the offer of rewards for their
cooperation and support. Those so rewarded are then
expected to use their influence among their communal
groups to build up loyalty to the ruling party. In
this way, a pervasive system of political clientelism
became established. If the adage 'seek ye first the
political kingdom and all things will be added
thereafter' had a figurative meaning for Nkrumah, it
must be taken quite literally here. Perhaps no other
politician has demonstrated so fundamental an understanding of the structure of politics and of the
political culture as has President Siaka Stevens.
Acutely aware of the potentialities of the patronage
system from his years in Opposition, and having seen the
army intervene (initially at the behest of the defeated
government) to deny him the victory he had so narrowly
won in the relatively freely contested elections in
1967, Stevens has been better placed than his political
rivals to manipulate the system of patronage. Tinkering
with the Westminister style constitution bequeathed by
the British first to create a Republic, and more
recently a single party state, has provided him with
greater control and more opportunities for patronage.
It is a feature of the patronage system that openings
have to be created for fresh appointments so as to
coopt emerging leaders as clients. The key to understanding the significance of the Forster Commission is
that the actions of those officials of the Authority
who had formerly been coopted as clients had to be
exposed in a way that left them isolated and politically neutralised. The strategy depended on the
continued belief in the society at the formal and overt
level in principles of accountability as being appropriate for a quasi-commercial corporation. Basic
values associated with the port organisation in the
colonial period--and whose practical benefits the
society had experienced--are exploited to undermine the
credibility and political power of former clients in
the Authority. To be successful such a move has to

emasculate the former clients. In this case therefore, the process began with a series of articles in the party's newspaper and the exposure was then fully and authoritatively endorsed by an investigation undertaken by an impartial and credible commission which could settle the terms of debate about behaviour in the Authority using principles of accountability, propriety and so on.

The effects of the strategy were, first, that former clients could be discarded without too damaging consequences for the patron-client system. Secondly, the President avoided the opprobrium that could have resulted from serious failure in the service provided by the Authority. And, thirdly, new patronage opportunities were created. In this instance, such an expartriate firm was brought in to manage the port and the award of contracts provided at least the opportunity for benefits in the patronage system.

With regard to the problem of situating lower-paid workers in a public corporation in the political economy, two propositions are now offered (and these will be taken up again in the chapters which follow). First, as a parastatal in the post-colonial state, the Authority did not operate in the manner or by the criteria of a typical capitalist enterprise (i.e. profit-making via surplus appropriation). With the gradual erosion of accountability within the Authority what emerged was the tendency of its employees (including lower-paid workers) to plunder its resources. As Forster saw it:

> There was clearly prevalent throughout
> the Authority an enervating attitude of
> 'how for do?', as it is nebulously
> expressed in Krio. A yet more delete-
> rious penchant as widespread as the
> foregoing attitude is to be found in
> the satiric Krio proverb of the cow
> eating grass where it is tethered.48

Given the prevalence of such attitudes, the notion of anti-capitalist protest may not be quite relevant. Second, (and this point will be more fully illustrated in the next chapter), dock workers cannot be accurately regarded as an aristocracy of labour. Notwithstanding a system of patronage to which many owe their jobs, life at the bottom of the social heap (in what is really a poor country even by Third World standards) in terms

95

of housing, family access to education and medicare, rules out such considerations. Nor can dock workers be said to be doing work which is not essential to the market economy even if their productivity is low as a result of overmanning. (At the very least, they make a valued-added contribution). Patrons do not in fact 'look after their own' on a continuous basis. Help may be given in finding jobs and at times of acute adversity but there are no regular handouts. That casual dock labourers survive at all is because of the resilience of the informal economy. Indeed, Forster felt moved to recommend some kind of a social security system for this category of docker.

Hence, therefore, the economic and political dynamics (or rules of operation) of a public corporation such as the Port Authority has been affected by the development of a system of political clientelism (and associated corruption) in the post-colonial state in Sierra Leone. These rules of operation are not those of efficiency in profit maximisation such as characterises capitalist enterprises. In view, however, of their pretty low rates of renumeration and the extensive use of the casual labour system (and in spite of their relatively low productivity), the dockers can still be said to be exploited. The latter proposition is examined in greater depth in the third section of this book.

SECTION 3

THE PROBLEM OF SITUATING LOWER-PAID DOCKERS IN THE

POLITICAL ECONOMY OF SIERRA LEONE: AN EXAMINATION

CHAPTER 5

DOCK WORKERS OF THE PORT OF FREETOWN:

A SOCIOLOGICAL PROFILE

An important dimension to the further elaboration
of the problem of situating the dockers in the political economy of Sierra Leone is an appraisal of the
general sociological characteristics they exhibt, the
material conditions in which they find themselves
relative to the other 'classes', their 'world view',
and their relationship to processes of patron-clientelism. The pursuit of these empirical questions by the
researcher in the field may be greatly affected by his
approach to the workers, their acceptance of him, and
his own definition and selection of what is to be
regarded as important. Nonetheless, the research
strategy was formulated with these problems in mind as
will be evident from the discussion of research method
that follows. While the 'objective conditions' are the
first to be considered, the appraisal of the social and
cultural relations of the dockers cannot be ignored.
Class consciousness (without which classes can hardly
be said to exist as political entities) is expressed
in, and conditioned by, prevailing social and cultural
formations.1 Before examining the empirical evidence,
however, it is necessary to outline the method employed
and to visit the theoretical ground.

Research Method

Four separate strategies were adopted in the
attempt to reconstruct the world of the docker from his
own standpoint. Formal interviews were held with
certain key individuals including union officials, shop
stewards, union activists, and a cross section of the
rank and file on issues relating to the history of
their union, leadership crises, and union struggles.
Most of these informants had been participants in these
events or reliable observers of the growth and evolution
of the union. Similar interviews were held with past
and present officials of national labour centres.
Second, informal conversations were held with many
dockers covering a wide range of issues from the
trivial to the more serious consideration of the
society of which they are a part. These conversations

99

took place over a five-month period from January to July 1980 at road-side bars in the Kanike and Cline Town areas near the port, usually during the mid-day work break or in the evenings at the end of the day's work, and also during the second period of field work, in February 1982, mostly in the evenings. Third, a questionnaire survey of a 1 in 96 sample of casual dockers and a 1 in 12 sample of non-casual dockers was undertaken. The questions asked had been designed to tease out some of the various strands in the ideological beliefs held by dockers with particular regard to what may be termed their 'class consciousness'; to assess their knowledge of, and participation in the Dock Workers' Union and to elicit information on their attitudes to trade unionism, trade union leadership, and strike action; and, finally, to obtain some basic sociological data on the dockers and their material environment (see annexe). Permission had been granted by the port management to undertake research at the port and the Secretary of the Dock Workers' Union had asked all shop stewards to cooperate and inform workers of the research. The questionnaire was administered during the second half of May 1980 with the help of an assistant engaged only for this purpose. He was Alfred Josiah, a literacy instructor in the employ of the Port Authority. Josiah was chosen because of his totally unassuming character, his sense of humour, and, because--as a literacy instructor--he was held in high esteem by many dockers, some of whom had attended his classes. It was impressed upon him, as it had been impressed upon all others, that the author was wholly independent, and that the purpose of the research was academic and specifically for a University of London thesis which may eventually be published. The internal organisational politics of the Port Authority, the Labour Department, the Ministry of Transport and Communications, or the government, it was repeatedly emphasised had nothing to do with the research. The workers had been selected randomly from each of the categories of docker (clerical, skilled manual, unskilled manual, and casual) after a total enumeration of dockers in each category. The venue chosen for the administration of the questionnaire was a classroom in the training department of the Port Authority. The workers participating in the survey were invited during working hours, two at a time to the classroom where Josiah and the author interviewed each in Krio, translating from the questionnaire and simultaneously writing down the replies in English. Clerks and other literate dockers were encouraged to fill in the questionnaire themselves with Josiah and the author being available to clarify queries.

The fourth strategy was pursued during June 1980. The research had until that stage been largely concerned with dockers at work and related issues. In order to broaden the perspective by a small degree, it was decided to observe some dockers in their home environment. This was a rather difficult task as dock workers do not live in any particular area of Freetown, although a significant proportion have residences scattered over the eastern part of Greater Freetown--an area covering some fifteen square miles. Twelve dockers were selected from amongst those who had become particularly friendly with the author and evening visits to their homes were arranged. These dockers belonged in equal proportions to the clerical, skilled, unskilled and casual groups. The conversation during such visits was trivial and informal; the opportunity was used to observe living conditions and to assess their standard of living.

Throughout the fieldwork the author endeavoured to present himself in a manner that was intended to convey to the dockers that he fully identified with them and was broadly sympathetic to their hopes and aspirations. Complete informality was maintained in all encounters with dockers. Krio was the main medium of communication but words of greeting in Mende and Temne were expressed when appropriate in a conscious attempt to convey that the author had no ethnocentric illusions. Dock workers participated willingly in the project; the author was fully accepted.

Visitation to the Theoretical Ground: The Relevance of Data on Social Stratification

The relevance (and importance) of Kitching's work on class in Kenya to the debate on class formation in contemporary African societies lies in his contention that the 'exploiting' and the 'exploited' classes are not at all neatly and simply identifiable in terms of their position in the mode of production. This is essentially because 'socially necessary labour' and 'surplus labour' (or surplus value) cannot be unambiguously identified and also because it is generally the case that the same person occupies differing positions ('exploiter' and 'exploited') in different modes of production at one and the same time (e.g. the urban wage earner who also employs hired labour on his farm). On the other hand however,

101

> ...if there was not surplus labour
> time being worked in Kenya it would
> not be possible for money to be
> accumulated and to become capital.
> We must look for exploitation then
> not in the direct relation of surplus
> labour appropriator to surplus labour
> source but in the capacity of various
> strata to accumulate money in the form
> of capital...those who can accumulate
> money and capital on any scale at all
> must be in control of part of the pro-
> duct of Kenya's surplus labour. The more
> and faster they accumulate, the greater
> must be their share of surplus labour.[2]

Kitching goes on to identify the most likely groups in control of this surplus:

> merchant capitalists proper...both
> foreign-owned import/export firms,
> and on a smaller scale African and
> Asian merchant capitalists operating
> in the domestic market, and (in a
> few cases) in the international
> market too; the best-paid public
> sector employees, and especially
> officials in the state and parastatal
> sectors...and to a small extent,
> domestic retailers and wholesalers...[3]

Now, although Kitching does not admit as much, this amounts to a sophisticated Marxist rationale for treating income levels or levels of capital accumulation (normally dismissed by Marxists as the criteria of 'bourgeois stratification theory') as the clearest possible indicator of class position to which one can aspire in African conditions.[4] Hence, in the context of African societies and economies where the capitalist mode of production is only incipiently developed, and where the same individual might be both wage-earner (in urban centres) and employer (on his relatives' farm), the most reliable guide to the question of "who is appropriating the surplus value?" lies in answer to the question of "who is making how much money out of this system of relations?" The endemic corruption (which Kitching does not take sufficiently into account as a means of capital accumulation) associated with political clientelism in the post-colonial state is, of course, also relevant.

The pattern of income distribution in Sierra Leone closely resembles that depicted by Kitching for Kenya. Table 5.1 shows the distribution of national incomes amongst rural and non-rural groups in 1968/69 and 1975/76, and in particular, draws attention to a trend for rural (farmers') money income to rise faster than that of urban incomes. Although this shows the cash incomes of urbanities to have been much higher, in general, than that of rural dwellers, it must be doubted whether the difference in total incomes, taking subsistence and accommodation expenses into account, is very great, certainly as far as urban manual workers are concerned.

TABLE 5.1

Rural and Non-rural Per Capita Incomes in Sierra Leone, 1968/69 and 1975/76 (figures in Leones)

	1968/69	1975/76
Rural per capita*	56	115
Urban per capita	238	354
Non-rural per capita (includes mining areas)	249	376
Average Income	108	186
Non-rural: Rural Ratio	4:1	3:1

*Excludes imputed income from subsistence farm production.

SOURCE: The JASPA Report, p.34.

103

Table 5.2 shows the distribution of national income amongst aggregated groups in 1975/76 and confirms this view. In aggregate, farmers are better off than manual workers. This does not mean, however, that farmers have been given a fair deal or that they have been treated generously enough to stem the flow of rural-urban migration. Farmers' incomes depend on the type of crop cultivated. Farmers producing export crops such as coffee, cocoa, or ginger, would have received higher incomes relative to farmers producing food crops such as rice. This is because of the deliberate policy of successive post-colonial governments to intervene in the market (under pressure from urban dwellers) to keep the price of food artificially low. Thus Table 5.3, in giving a breakdown of the distribution of income amongst disaggregated groups, provides a more detailed over-view. It is clear from this table that not all farmers are better off than urban manual workers. In reading the table, however, the categories which should be isolated for comparison with the others are unskilled (per capita income, Le425 per annum), skilled (per capita income, Le895 per annum), and clerical (per capita income, Le2,333 per annum). The vast majority of dockers belong to the unskilled category; but, that aside, minimum wages obtaining at the port in 1976 (for dockers eligible to join the union or who did not fall within grades A-B of the Port Authority's pay scale) stood at Le585 per annum (this assumes 300 working days a year for casual dockers) and maximum wages stood at Le1,780. 5 Moreover, these wages amounted in real terms to about half their value in 1965. While nearly all groups must have suffered an erosion in the real value of their incomes as a result of the inflationary tendencies in the economy, particularly after 1973, this would appear to have been especially acute in the case of lower-paid workers. Although the total incomes of such workers, certainly the dockers', were supple-mented by (often dishonest) claims for overtime payment and, as we shall see, by their involvement in secondary employment in the informal sector, this supplement was not at all comparable in (even relative) magnitude to the windfalls obtained by better placed individuals (members of the elite) from political and bureaucratic corruption. While the availability of such monies to well placed individuals among the elite arguably accounts for the major proportions of their real incomes, this is certainly not the case for lower-paid parastatal employees. The latter are therefore far from being the most direct or favoured beneficiaries of the system of patron-clientelism and corruption; and,

TABLE 5.2

Functional Distribution of Income,

Aggregated Groups 1975/76

GROUP	AVERAGE* INCOME	PERCENTAGE		CUMULATIVE PERCENTAGE	
		NOS.	INCOME	NOS.	INCOME
Unskilled	425	6.1	3.2	6.1	3.2
Informal Sector	425	18.3	9.5	24.4	12.7
Non-agri-cultural	522	13.7	8.8	38.1	21.5
Semi-skilled	630	4.1	3.2	42.2	24.7
Farmers	640	48.8	38.4	91.0	63.1
Skilled	895	2.9	3.2	93.9	66.3
Clerical	1,870	2.3	5.2	96.2	71.5
Profess-ional	6,500	0.9	7.2	97.1	78.7
Entre-preneurs	9,800	2.9	21.2	100.0	100.0

=656,000   =Le536M

*In Leones per annum; NOS. = Numbers; M = Million
SOURCE: The JASPA Report, p.279.

105

TABLE 5.3

Distribution of Income (Disaggregated Groups) 1975/76

GROUP	NUMBER (1000)	INCOME (M.LE)	PER CAPITA	PERCENTAGE	
				NOS.	INCOME
Farmers I	48	8	171	7.3	1.5
Hawkers	45	10	300	6.9	1.9
Farmers II	93	37	399	14.2	6.9
Unskilled	40	17	425	6.1	3.2
Non-agri-cultural	90	47	522	13.7	8.8
Vendors	40	21	530	6.1	3.9
Artisans	35	20	566	5.3	3.7
Farmers III	70	43	619	10.7	8.1
Semi-skilled	27	17	630	4.1	3.2
Farmers IV	45	39	869	6.9	7.3
Skilled	19	17	895	2.9	3.2
Farmers V	51	58	1,131	7.8	10.8
Farmers VI	13	21	1,585	2.0	3.8
Clerical	15	35	2,333	2.3	5.2
Retailers	14	58	4,143	2.1	12.2
Professional	6	39	6,500	0.9	7.2
Entrepreneurs	5	49	9,800	0.8	9.1

M. = Million; NOS. = Numbers
SOURCE: The JASPA Report, p.282.

106

in several respects, may be seen to suffer from it. The embezzlement of government or parastatal monies by these members of the elite, for example, clearly has an adverse effect on government's ability to finance wage increases for lower-paid workers (at least without resort to simply printing money).6

Furthermore, while there are immediate differences between low income rural groups and low income urban groups over such issues as the official level of food prices7 and, in particular, the importing and subsidising of rice, it is clear that these are really subsidiary to the major conflict between the political and administrative elite together with some capitalist business on the one hand, and the low income rural and urban work force on the other.

That there is considerable inequality of incomes (and in the rate of accumulation) between the various socio-economic groups should be evident. Less than 4 percent of the population receive almost a third of national income. The highest income group receive almost sixty times as much as the lowest income group.

These indices do not by themselves provide a full picture. For instance, it is preferable to use the household of the dockers as the unit of income assessment since wives and other inmates contribute to family income typically via participation in the thriving informal economy. Some dockers themselves undertake secondary employment in this sector. The questionnaire survey was designed to probe these (and other aspects of their social and cultural as well as economic lives) more deeply.

The Material Environment of the Dockers and Aspects of Their Social Lives

One consequence of the low incomes of the dockers and the resulting pressure to make ends meet is that some resort to secondary employment. There is clearly a demand for various types of service outside the formal sector of the economy where capital intensive methods are prevalent or formal contracts mandatory. Cheaper labour intensive methods create a thriving market in the informal sector. Of the dockers sampled, 8 percent of the clerks, 20 percent of the skilled manuals, 21 percent the unskilled manuals, and 15 percent of the casuals reported having some form of secondary employment.

Amongst the jobs listed were tailoring and secretarial
work (including writing letters for a fee) by clerks;
mechanical repairs, carpentry, and other building
repairs mentioned by skilled manuals; night watching
and woroko woroko (or load carrying) mentioned by casual
and unskilled dockers (see Table 5.4(a)).

TABLE 5.4(a)

Incidence of Secondary Employment Among the Dockers

CATEGORY	% IN SECONDARY EMPLOYMENT	SAMPLE SIZE (n)	SAMPLE POPULATION (N)
Clerks	8	36	432
Skilled Manuals	20	60	720
Unskilled Manuals	21	29	348
Casuals	15	68	6,528
TOTAL		193	8,028

(Figures are given in percentages and have been
rounded). Sample size (n) and sample 'population' (N)
are also shown.

The average annual household income of the dockers
(including estimated earnings from secondary employment)
is provided in Table 5.4(b). It will be evident that
these averages are considerably higher than the minimum
and maximum wages obtaining at the port in 1976. The
range of incomes within each category of dockers,
however, more clearly illustrates the importance of the
contribution of secondary employment and of household

TABLE 5.4(b)

Household Annual Incomes Among the Dockers

CATEGORY	MEAN	RANGE
Clerks	1422	1080 - 3360
Skilled Manuals	1910	744 - 3660
Unskilled Manuals	1022	660 - 1824
Casuals	633	45 - 1560

(Figures are given in Leones)

members to family income. Household members were
invariably petty traders, accounting for 66 percent of
the occupations of inmates of casual dockers' homes; 69
percent of unskilled manual dockers'; 67 percent of
skilled manuals'; and 53 percent of clerical dockers'
homes (see Table 5.4(c)). The predominance of petty
traders in the informal economy of Freetown has been
noted by David Fowler in his 1976 survey8 and by
Katherine Mosley9 in her 1979 study of Safroko Limba
migrants in Freetown. Both report high proportions of
women petty traders, typically hawking foodstuffs
ranging from cookery or home-produced meals to fruits
and vegtables as well as gara or tied-dyed cloth.
Fowler notes that this trend is a consequence of the
"...stagnation in opportunities for wage employment
expansion of the urban economy; most job seekers face a
choice of self-employment or indefinite unemployment."10
The low-capital input, flexible working hours, and
relative simplicity of petty trading, which can be con-
veniently combined with other domestic chores such as
looking after young children, make this form of employment particularly attractive to women. Accordingly, an
inescapable spectacle on the streets of Freetown is of
women and their fannah markits (or tray or wares). The
1966-69 series of household surveys by the Central

TABLE 5.4(c)

Occupations of Household Members (by percentage)

OCCUPATION	CLERKS	SKILLED MANUALS	UNSKILLED MANUALS	CASUAL
Trader	53	67	69	66
Unskilled (Labourer, Domestic)	3	17	7	7
Skilled (Clerical, Artisan, etc.)	8	3	-	-
Unemployed	6	-	17	20
Students	30	13	7	7
TOTAL	100	100	100	100

Statistics Office11 significantly listed 'sales work' as among "...predominant occupations in Freetown and other urban places".12 More specificially, a full quarter of the Freetown labour force at the end of 1967 was involved in petty trading.13

Apart from undertaking secondary employment, or having household members who are employed therein, most dockers' households make purchases of their basic necessities in this sector. Ninety percent of casual dockers reported that their households purchased more than half the items listed in the questionnaire in small quantities (e.g. sugar by the spoonful) and con-sequently from this sector. All unskilled manual dockers, 58 percent of skilled manual dockers, and

53 percent of clerical dockers also reported making purchases of more than half of the items listed in the questionnaire outside the formal economy (Table 5.4(d) has the details).

TABLE 5.4(d)

Percentages of Occupational Categories

Purchasing More than Half of Selected Items

From the Informal Sector

CATEGORY	%
Clerks	53
Skilled Manuals	58
Unskilled Manuals	100
Casuals	99

In view of the widespread belief that the African extended family system has built into it some form of social security mechanism--with automatic redistribution from more affluent relatives to poorer ones--which cushions off lower-paid workers from some of the hardships of urban life, the sample was specifically asked whether they had ever resorted to borrowing money at the end of the month (pay day) as a result of not being able to meet all commitments. No less than 64 percent of each of the four categories of dockers reported that they sometimes borrowed money at the end of the month (Table 5.5(a)). Of those replying that they sometimes borrowed, however, less than 20 percent of each of the four categories reported that they borrowed from well-off kinsmen and relatives (see Table 5.5(b) for the details). Most rather borrowed from friends or neighbours or, in the case of unskilled workers especially,

TABLE 5.5(a)

Percentage of Sample Reporting Making Loans

CATEGORY	%
Clerks	64
Skilled Manuals	80
Unskilled Manuals	90
Casuals	78

TABLE 5.5(b)

Sources of Loans (by percentage)

CATEGORY	FRIENDS/ NEIGHBOURS	OSUSU	RELATIVES/ KINSMEN	MONEY LENDER
Clerks	92	-	8	-
Skilled Manuals	63	12	10	15
Unskilled Manuals	46	-	19	35
Casuals	76	-	11	13

from professional money-lenders. The sample was then
asked whether they were assisting any relative other
than immediate family, financially or materially. No
less that 56 percent of each of the categories replied
that they were helping relatives (Table 5.5(c)). This
confirmed the impression which had been formed during
informal conversations with the dockers. Assistance may
be given by more affluent relatives or kinsmen in
finding jobs or at times of acute adversity, but there
are no regular cash handouts. Moreover, the principle
of reciprocity--an important cultural phenomenon in
Sierra Leone as in other parts of Africa--precludes
many lower-paid workers from seeking assistance from
affluent relatives.

TABLE 5.5(c)

Percentage of Sample Reporting Helping

Relatives Other than Immediate Family

CATEGORY	RELATIVES	FRIENDS	NIL
Clerks	56	3	41
Skilled Manuals	62	12	26
Unskilled Manuals	66	3	31
Casual	62	6	32

The proletarianisation of lower-paid dockers can
be further illustrated by some indices of their
standard of living. None of the unskilled manuals, 6
percent of the casuals, 18 percent of the skilled
manuals, and 19 percent of the clerks were owner-occup-
iers of their homes (Table 5.6(a)). A very liberal
index of six persons to one room en parlah (or one
bedroom and parlour/living-room) was used to define
overcrowding in the households of the dockers.

113

TABLE 5.6(a)

Percentage of Sample Reporting Home Ownership

CATEGORY	%
Clerks	19
Skilled Manuals	18
Unskilled Manuals	-
Casuals	6

By this definition, 41 percent of unskilled manuals, 38 percent of casuals, 18 percent of skilled manuals and 14 percent of clerks lived in conditions of overcrowding (Table 5.6(b)). 14

TABLE 5.6(b))

Overcrowding in the Households of Dockers (by percentage)

CATEGORY	%
Clerks	14
Skilled Manuals	18
Unskilled Manuals	41
Casuals	38

The type of material out of which the home is constructed is also evidence of status and position in the class
structure. More than two-thirds of the clerks and over
half of the skilled manuals lived in cement houses. By
contrast only 21 percent and 26 percent of the unskilled
manuals and the casuals respectively lived in such
houses, with a greater proportion living in pan body
homes (i.e. houses constructed out of shanty-type sheet
metal; see Table 5.6(c)).

TABLE 5.6(c)

Type of House Lived in by Dockers (by percentage)

CATEGORY	PAN BODY	BOARD	CEMENT	MUD
Clerks	11	6	83	-
Skilled	28	17	55	-
Unskilled	55	21	21	3
Casuals	60	11	26	3

Over 80 percent of the clerks had both electricity
and running water in their homes. About half of the
skilled manuals had electricity but only a third had
running water. On the other hand, less than 10 percent
of the unskilled and casuals had either electricity or
running water in their homes (see Table 5.6(d)). The
sample was asked which of these five luxury items they
owned: 'fridge, radio or tape, TV, car, motorbike or
bicycle. None had all five items. Six percent of the
clerks owned four of the items. A further 8 percent of
this category and 3 percent of the skilled manuals owned three of the items (see Table 5.6(e)), but the large
majority of unskilled and casual workers owned none.

Various aspect of the social lives of the dockers
were examined. Ninety-eight percent of the sample

TABLE 5.6(d)

Public Utilities Enjoyed by Dockers' Households (by percentage)

CATEGORY	RUNNING WATER	ELECTRICITY
Clerks	81	83
Skilled	33	52
Unskilled	10	7
Casuals	9	7

TABLE 5.6(e)

Luxury Items Owned by Dockers (by percentage)

CATEGORY	0	1	2	3	4	5
Clerks	28	30	28	8	6	-
Skilled	32	50	15	3	-	-
Unskilled	62	38	-	-	-	-
Casuals	75	24	1	-	-	-

attended a church or mosque. In Freetown (as well as in other parts of Sierra Leone), churches and mosques tend to cater for particular ethnic groups. Thus, for example, Christian Mende dockers tend to worship in a Mende church while Temne Muslim dockers tend to worship in a Temne mosque or to belong to a Temne jamaat (or Muslim burial society).15 Sixty-three percent of dockers not born in Freetown were members of a descendants' association such as the Tonkolili District Descendants' Association (TODDA) or the Moyamba District Descendants' Association (MADDA). Since the APC came to power in 1968, and particularly since the mid-seventies, these descendants' associations have proliferated. They typically serve as the power base of important national politicians, have undercut the influence of the chiefs in national politics, and have clearly become channels for the dispensation of patronage and the mobilisation of support. The tribal headman system in Freetown, which has always been closely related to religious communities,16 is by now all but fully integrated into descendants' associations. Fifty-eight percent of the sample also reported belonging to secret societies such as the Gbangbani, the Ojeh, the Porroh, or the Hunting Society. Membership is usually related to ethnicity. Thus, for example, the Krios are found in the Hunting Societies while the Mendes and Temnes are found in the Porroh.17

Outside the world of work, in their social and cultural activities, dock workers may therefore be said generally to belong to organisations which provide a certain degree of communal cohesion. This point will be taken up again below when political clientelism vis a vis recommendation for employment in the public sector is discussed.

Dock Workers: Some Basic Sociological Characteristics

It is perhaps not surprising that all dockers undertaking manual tasks are male. It was estimated from the total enumeration of all dockers that some 28 percent of the clerical group (N = 433) were female. The sample of the clerical group yieled eight women or 22 percent (n = 36).

The dockers are drawn from most of the ethnic groups in Sierra Leone and from all the main linguistic groups (Table 5.7(a), (b), (c), (d)). Among casual dockers (made up of stevedore and shore cargo-handling labourers) it had been observed impressionistically that Kroo men were in the minority. This suggested

TABLE 5.7(a)

Ethnic Groups Among Clerks

ETHNIC GROUP	PERCENTAGE
Krio	41
Temne	19
Mende	19
Fulah	6
Loko	6
Limba	6
Sherbo	3
TOTAL	100

TABLE 5.7(b)

Ethnic Groups Among Skilled Manuals

ETHNIC GROUP	PERCENTAGE
Temne	25
Krio	25
Limba	18
Mende	15
Sherbro	5
Mandingo	3
Loko	3
Koranko	2
Susu	2
Fulah	2
TOTAL	100

TABLE 5.7(c)

Ethnic Groups Among Unskilled Manuals

ETHNIC GROUP	PERCENTAGE
Temne	38
Limba	24
Loko	11
Susu	11
Mende	7
Fulah	3
Mandingo	3
West African National	3
TOTAL	100

TABLE 5.7(d)

Ethnic Groups Among Casual Dokers

ETHNIC GROUP	PERCENTAGE
Temne	39
Mende	30
Loko	9
Limba	8
Sherbro	3
Kroo	3
Fulah	2
Krio	2
Susu	2
Mandingo	2
TOTAL	100

119

(and was indeed confirmed during informal conversations)
that the traditional dominance of this occupational
category by the Kroos has over the years been eroded.
The sample yielded only 3 percent Kroos. Krio dockers,
having been long exposed to formal education, dominate
the clerical grades, while Temne dockers dominate the
manual grades as a result of their relative proximity
to Freetown.18

    In his sociological study of Freetown, Banton
suggests that a multiplicity of factors influenced
rural-urban migration.19 These include the imbalance
of opportunities as between the provinces and Freetown,
the desire to 'break out' of the restrictions (particularly for women) in rural society, and the pull of
the 'bright lights'. Some attempt was made by the
present author to assess the extent to which dockers
are migrants. Just over two-thirds of the sample were
born outside Freetown (see Table 5.8(a)), though less
than half of the clerks--suggesting a correlation
between birth in Freetown, good schooling, and clerical
employment. Of those not born in Freetown, 19 percent
of the clerks said that they came to seek wage employment. Thirty-seven percent said they came for educational purposes, but a greater proportion, 44 percent
said they came for personal reasons such as to seek
medical care or to live in the household of a relative.
Among skilled manuals, a third came for personal
reasons with the remaining two-thirds coming for employment and education. A greater proportion of the casual
and unskilled labourers, 62 percent and 74 percent
respectively, reported coming solely for employment.
None came for education (Table 5.8(b) has the details).

    These dockers were also asked about their previous
occupations before coming to live in Freetown. A clear
pattern emerged. A small proportion of the clerks and
the skilled manuals had been farmers, fishermen, or
traders. On the other hand most of the unskilled
manuals and the casuals, 72 percent and 73 percent respectively, had been farmers (see Table 5.8(c)). Table
5.8(d) provides data relating to the number of years
dockers not born in Freetown had lived there and Table
5.8(e) gives a distribution of the ages of the dockers.

    The educational attainment of dockers obviously
varies with their occupational roles, as will be
evident from Table 5.9(a). Their social background--
using fathers' occupation as the index--also appears to

TABLE 5.8(a)

Percentage of Dock Workers Not Born in Freetown

CATEGORY	%
Clerks(16)	44
Skilled Manuals(33)	55
Unskilled Manuals(26)	90
Casual Labourers(53)	78
TOTAL 128(a)	66(b)

Numbers in parentheses are the actual numbers within each category of the sample. (a) Refers to the total number of dockers in sample not born in Freetown; (b) refers to the total number of dockers not born in Freetown as a percentage of the whole sample.

TABLE 5.8(b)

Main Reasons for Coming to Live in the Capital

(by percentage)

REASON	CLERKS	SKILLED MANUALS	UNSKILLED MANUALS	CASUALS
Employment	19	46	62	74
Personal	44	33	38	26
Education	37	21	–	–
TOTAL	100	100	100	100

121

TABLE 5.8(c)

Previous Occupation of Dockers Not Born in Freetown

(by percentage)

OCCUPATION	CLERKS	SKILLED MANUALS	UNSKILLED MANUALS	CASUALS
Student	88	58	4	4
Farmer	12	21	72	73
Fisherman	-	3	-	2
Same	-	9	12	15
Unemployed	-	3	-	2
Trader	-	6	12	4
TOTAL	100	100	100	100

be related to occupational roles. About half the clerks in the sample had fathers who had been profess-ional, managerial, clerical, or skilled manual workers in occupation. Just under a third of the skilled manuals had such fathers. Ninety-four percent and 81 percent of unskilled manual and the casual groups by contrast had fathers who had been peasant farmers (Table 5.9(b)). Such data of course suggests differ-ences in the possibilities for intergenerational mobility among lower-paid workers (which must be even more pronounced between the latter and the more elite groups). These inequalities are, moreover, not at all attenuated by a declining economy, the consequent con-traction in employment opportunities, or by an official agricultural polity which discourages the small farmer

TABLE 5.8(d)

Years of Residence of Dockers Not Born in Freetown

(by percentage)

YEARS	CLERKS	SKILLED MANUALS	UNSKILLED MANUALS	CASUALS
1 - 5	-	9	12	2
6 - 10	12	13	-	4
11 - 15	12	3	8	4
16 - 20	12	21	23	17
21 - 25	19	21	15	7
26 - 30	19	9	11	13
31 - 35	-	3	4	13
36 - 50	-	3	8	23
41 - 45	26	18	19	17
TOTAL	100	100	100	100

and thereby encourages migration to the towns.

The survey also shows that the work force at the port is fairly stable with a low incidence of job turnover. (This stability is in part a consequence of the lack of alternative and attractive opportunities either

TABLE 5.8(e)

Ages of Dockers (by percentage)

YEARS	CLERKS	SKILLED MANUALS	UNSKILLED MANUALS	CASUALS
Under 20	-	2	-	-
20 - 29	25	30	-	12
30 - 39	55	33	21	26
40 - 49	11	13	14	12
50 - 59	6	7	21	22
Over 60	3	3	14	15
D. K.	-	12	30	13
TOTAL	100	100	100	100

D. K. = Don't know.

of or to urban employment). Seventy-five percent of the clerks in the sample had been working at the port for more than five years. The corresponding figures for the other groups were 64 percent of skilled manuals, 87 percent of the unskilled manuals, and 75 percent of the casuals (see Table 5.10(a)). This stability may also be related to marital status and parenthood. Less than a fifth of each category of dockers reported that they had no children. More than two-thirds of each category were married (see Table 5.10(b)).

TABLE 5.9(a)

Educational Attainment Among Categories of Dockers

(by percentage)

CATEGORY	PRIMARY	FORM 1-2	FORM 3-5	COLLEGE	NIL	TOTAL
Clerk	6	6	58	22	8	100
Skilled Manual	13	12	53	5	17	100
Unskilled Manual	3	-	3	-	94	100
Casual	10	5	8	-	77	100

The sample was asked how they had obtained jobs at the port. Sixty-nine percent of the clerks reported that they got their jobs by direct application to the Authority or through placement by the Freetown Labour Exchange. Sixty-seven percent of the skilled manuals, 21 percent of the unskilled manuals, and 40 percent of the casuals reported using these channels. The remaining proportions (see Table 5.11), gave replies which can best be summarised as by 'recommendation', a slightly euphemistic term for the working of the system of patron-clientelism in the public sector.

What has emerged so far is as follows: dockers are predominantly male with a small proportion of women in the clerical group only. They come from all over the country but the two largest ethnic groups, Temne and Mende, are over-represented relative to their national percentages among all categories of dockers. Krios are also over-represented among clerical and skilled dockers. It had been observed impressionistically that there was little sign of ethnic tension among dockers. This observation was borne

TABLE 5.9(b)

TABLE 5.9(b)

Fathers' Occupation Among Categories of Dockers

(by percentage)

SKILLED MANUALS	%	CLERKS	%
Labourer & Domestic	6	Labourer	3
Trader	17	Skilled Manual .	19
Farmer	45	Trader	17
Clerk	2	Professional & Managerial . . .	25
Skilled Manual . .	15	Farmer	30
Professional & Managerial	12	Clerical	6
Don't know	3		
TOTAL	100	TOTAL	100

UNSKILLED MANUALS	%	CASUALS	%
Farmer	94	Farmer	81
Fisherman	3	Trader	4
Trader	3	Skilled Manual .	13
		Clerical	2
TOTAL	100	TOTAL	100

out in the survey. Dockers were asked with which group
of workers they particularly liked to 'mix'; the

TABLE 5.10(a)

Labour Turnover Among Categories of Dockers

(by percentage)

NO. OF YEARS AT THE PORT	CLERKS	SKILLED MANUALS	UNSKILLED MANUALS	CASUALS
Less than 1 Year	6	17	-	3
1 - 2 years	-	2	3	9
3 - 5 years	19	17	10	10
6 - 8 years	22	15	31	12
9 - 10 years	22	15	7	9
11 - 14 years	12	17	21	7
15 - 20 years	19	10	21	18
More than 20 years	-	7	7	29
Don't know	-	-	-	3
TOTAL	100	100	100	100

alternative responses were deliberately standardised to include 'workers from your ethnic group or region' (see annexe, question 2.8).

TABLE 5.10(b)

Percentage of Married Dockers

CATEGORY	%
Clerks	64
Skilled Manuals	82
Unskilled Manuals	83
Casuals	96

TABLE 5.11

Means of Obtaining Employment Among Categories of Dockers by (percentage)

CATEGORY	BY RECOMMENDATION	BY APPLICATION
Clerks	31	69
Skilled Manuals	33	67
Unskilled Manuals	79	21
Casuals	60	40

128

Without exception, the replies cut across the alterna-
tives which had been isolated. It was perhaps significant here that one of the slogans of the Dock Workers'
Union was "One union, one (cooking) pot". The heavy
sybolism in this slogan must not be overlooked.

About two-thirds of the sample were not born in
Freetown. In most cases it appears that the various
facilities available and the possibilities of realising
a higher standard of living in the capital have been
the main attractions and have contributed to the
decision ot continue living there. There is little
evidence of inter-generational mobility. In relative
terms, the social backgrounds of individual dockers are
related to their educational attainment and, hence,
occupational status. While clerks and other skilled
workers are in this (and other) respects relatively
privileged, their economic and social distance from the
truly elite groups is quite vast. This was clearly
evident from observation of their standard of living
during visits to their homes. It is also evident in
their cultural and recreational activities.

The frequently repeated assertion (and the basis,
very largely of the Fanonist position) that most urban
workers are very much better off than most rural farmers
does not appear to be clearly supported by the evidence
for Sierra Leone. It is clearly not the case that,
according to official income figures at least, the
majority of manual workers (who in turn constitute the
majority of urban workers) are very much better off.
(Tables 5.2 and 5.3 on pp. 105-106 illustrate this
point neatly). Further evidence is provided by their
low standard of living as expressed through over-crowd-
ing in their homes, the fact that they live in
shanty-type sheet metal housing largely without running
water or electricity, their inability to afford items
such as bicycles and radios and their dependence on the
informal economy. Manual workers are very clearly not
better off than the poorer sections of the peasantry
even if, in recent years, the latter have been identified as the most disadvantaged group in Sierra Leone
and have become beneficiaries of the ubiquitous integrated rural development projects (IRDPs) financed by
World Bank and EEC multilateral aid. The objective of
IRDPs is to provide primary health care, basic education, sanitation and improved housing while encouraging
increased agricultural productivity via improved
techniques. On the basis of the evidence presented
here, the urban poor in Freetown qualify for similar

assistance in community and evironmental development. This does not mean that the rural farmers have been fairly treated; it is not to deny that they are exploited in order to finance the provision of public sector jobs which, collectively speaking, are somewhat parasitic. The degree of parasitism, however, is highly unevenly distributed within this collective (class) situation as between not only individuals but also different categories of urban wage-employees. It is, to say the least, somewhat over-simple and misleading, therefore, to view the majority of lower-paid workers as parasitic on the rural peasantry.

It would seem that the rural-urban migrants are attracted not by any real improvement in the living standards of the majority of urban wage-employees but by the need to supplement a family rural income with a male member's urban cash income (or by the greater opportunities for social mobility in the urban areas). Such opportunities are, the evidence would suggest, decidedly and increasingly limited. In so far as they exist, however, they would seem to hinge on two possible avenues of advancement: (1) via combination of employment in the formal sector with entrepreneurial success in the informal sector; (2) via cultivation of political patrons and of the opportunities presented by government or by parastatal employment for increased income through corruption. The second of these avenues is largely closed to lower-paid manual workers and the reason why, once they have secured a job at the port, the great majority of the dockers stick to it, is rather to be found in the increasingly high incidence of unemployment and severe underemployment.

Trade Unionism and the World of Work

The Port Authority is virtually a closed shop. All persons in the sample were members of the Dock Workers' Union with the exception of the stevedore casual labourers who accounted for 20 percent of the sample.20

Lower-paid workers at the Port Authority are subjected to very close supervision during the work process. It was also observed that the fringe benefits of employment at the Authority were distributed highly disproportionately among the work force; while members of the senior staff and their families, for instance, were

entitled to free medicare at the well-equipped port
health clinic, which was attended by two full-time
doctors, a team of nurses and other para-medical staff,
the families of lower-paid dockers were prohibited from
using the clinic.21 Moreover, casual dockers could
only use the clinic if they happened to fall ill on the
day that they had actually been working. A particularly sore point among the dockers therefore was the
spectacle of medical teams being rushed to attend
foreign crews and their families on board visiting
ships. A canteen was also maintained at the port for
the use of the work force. It was observed that the
canteen was divided into two lounges for the senior and
junior staff. The former was by far the more comfort-
ably furnished.

Another issue frequently mentioned by dockers when
asked about the problems they experienced at work, was
the infrequency of promotions. Because the port is so
heavily overmanned, individual competitiveness and an
achievement ethic are conspicuous by their absence.
Accordingly, the management does not seem to have found
it necessary to institute programmes of manpower development as distinct from literacy classes and some
basic training among the junior members of the work
force.

The psychological ramifications of these aspects
of the organisation of work at the port are conducive
to adversarial industrial relations. When asked
whether their work made them feel within their hearts
that they were doing something worthwhile, more than
two-thirds of each of the four categories gave an
affirmative response. This may, however, be related to
the lack of alternative employment opportunities in
Freetown. When asked what they generally thought of
trade unions, the dockers' most common reply was that
"unions protect workers from being taken advantage of
by management". An accounts clerk wrote on his
questionnaire that "the only effective way workers can
be powerful enough is through the union. It is the
vehicle through which workers can be heard". A welder
(of the skilled manual group) wrote that "unions are
there to seek the interest of the workers and must also
educate them". Such manifestations of a developed
trade union consciousness were rare in the sample as a
whole, more especially amongst the unskilled workers.
This suggests, however, that skilled workers (relatively well-off as they might be), far from being
complacent about their position in the emerging class

131

structure, are more likely to develop radical attitudes vis a vis their relative deprivation, in consequence of their possession of skills and generally higher level of educational attainment. The latter, also, no doubt, helps them to see through the facade of government claims to be pursuing the general interest in an impartial manner.

These differences within the sample as regards attitudes to trade unionism were also evident as regards attitudes to strike action. When asked what they thought of strikes, just over half the sample were ambivalent, a typical reply being, "it is good to join trade unions but I do not favour strikes except when absolutely necessary" (a cleaner of the unskilled manual group). The more educated workers in the sample gave replies which might be regarded as militant: "Strikes are necessary when workers are dissatisfied with either the conditions of service or some other reason" (an electrician of the skilled manual group).

It was noticeable and impressive that each docker in the sample knew the name of the shop steward representing his/her section and the name of the union secretary or a senior official. When asked what they considered to be the qualities of a good trade union leader, 69 percent of the whole sample listed 'honesty' among their replies. Other frequent replies were that a union leader must be well informed (53 percent), approachable (42 percent), and articulate 'like a lawyer' (38 percent). Forty-three percent of the whole sample had had some experience of strike action.

Ideology and Consciousness

The ambivalence in the attitudes of the dockers to the inequalities in the society around them, and more especially towards elite corruption, had been noted during informal conversations. Some questions were deliberately written in the questionnaire to bring out these contradictions. The dockers were told that, in Sierra Leone, there are Big Men or 'gentry people', there are those who are 'managing' and there those who are poor. Dockers were then asked to which of the these groups they thought they belonged. Ninety-seven percent of the clerks, 62 percent of the skilled manuals, 76 percent unskilled manuals and 80 percent of the casuals replied that they were 'managing' (Table 5.12(a)). They typically reasoned that, since they

TABLE 5.12(a)

Self-assessment of Socio-ecnomic Position

(in Percentages)

CATETORY	POOR	'MANAGING'	GENTRY
Clerks	3	97	-
Skilled Manuals	33	62	5
Unskilled Manuals	17	76	7
Casuals	20	80	-

were in good health, had a job, and every reason to be
hopeful, to say that they were poor was being ungrate-
ful to God or Allah. Dockers were than asked how and
why they thought inequalities occurred in Sierra Leone
society. Eighty-nine percent of the clerks, 61 percent
of the skilled manuals, 90 percent of the unskilled
manuals and 88 percent of the casuals gave some variant
of the reply that people were unequal because it was
the will of God. (In making this point during informal
conversations, a docker would typically spread out all
the fingers and say with impeccable logic that they were
not all of the same size because God didn't want them
that way). However, 42 percent of the clerks, 47
percent of the skilled manuals, 31 percent of the
unskilled manuals, and 34 percent of the casuals also
gave replies suggesting that the personal situation of
the individual (education, inheritance, etc.) could
contribute to his position in society. Seventeen
percent of the clerks, 48 percent of the skilled
manuals, 31 percent of the unskilled manuals, and 29
percent of the casuals also listed political power,
influence, and corruption as factors that could
contribute to inequalities in society. (The details
are provided in Table 5.12(b)).22

TABLE 5.12(b)

Main Views on the Origins of Inequality

(by Percentage*)

CATEGORY	DIVINE DESIGN	EDUCATION, INHERITANCE	DON'T KNOW	POWER, INFLU-ENCE
Clerks	89	42	3	17
Skilled	61	47	–	48
Unskilled	90	31	7	31
Casuals	88	34	7	29

*The sample was allowed to give up to four replies.

     The ambivalence in such replies contrasted sharply with the replies given when dockers were asked, 'Compared with other people, do you think you and your family are getting a fair share or benefit for the job you do?' Fifty-three percent of the clerks, 68 percent of the skilled manuals, 86 percent of the unskilled manuals, and 82 percent of the casuals replied in the negative. When asked to explain, they typically drew attention to their low standard of living, and frequently mentioned that prices were rising faster than wages. Similarly, when asked what their future intentions and aspirations were, the dockers were clear about their priorities. Fifty-eight percent of the clerks, 47 percent of the skilled manuals, 14 percent of the unskilled manuals, and 23 percent of the casuals wanted to further their education or to learn a skill. Seventeen percent of the clerks, 42 percent of the skilled manuals, 28 percent of the unskilled manuals, and 24 percent of the casuals wanted to become involved in business or commerce. (More than a third of the unskilled manuals mentioned commercial farming).

Twenty-one percent of the casuals intended investing in their children's education.

The sample was then asked to assess the country's politicians and top civil servants and, more specifically, to gauge whether politicians and public servants were setting an example by making a sacrifice or whether they were capable of improving the country's economic situation. Over two-thirds of each category in the sample gave a negative response to either one or the other of the two propositions (Table 5.12(c)).

TABLE 5.12(c)

Assessment of Politicians and Public Servants

(by percentage)

CATEGORY	NEGATIVE	POSITIVE	DON'T KNOW
Clerks	67	30	3
Skilled	62	38	-
Unskilled	76	17	7
Casuals	82	16	2

The sample was also amenable to the idea that the government's priority ought to be rural development. (The survey was carried out some six weeks before Sierra Leone lavishly hosted an OAU summit conference-- and at a time when the preparations in the capital were intense--at a reputed cost of Le200 million). Table 5.12(d) has the details.

Political Clientelism and the World of the Docker

As already stated, a third of the skilled dockers,

TABLE 5.12(d)

Rural Development as a National Priority

(by percentage)

CATEGORY	POSITIVE	NEGATIVE	DON'T KNOW
Clerks	81	3	16
Skilled	90	2	8
Unskilled	76	17	7
Casuals	98	-	2

and a much higher proportion of the unskilled report using informal channels to obtain employment. As we have seen in Chapter 4 (when documentary evidence from the port archives and the report of the Forster Commission was cited), influential persons can exert pressure on the port management to place political supporters and kinsmen on the payroll. A senior official of the Port Authority claimed that the port bureaucracy as a whole was overmanned by at least a third.23

It has also been shown that, at the work place, the ethnic identity of the docker is submerged and their union, the Dock Workers' Union is properly a vehicle for the advancement of their interests. Work mates from different ethnic groups 'mix' freely with each other quite easily. In their social and cultural lives outside the work place, however, some degree of ethnic cohesion is maintained through their religious activities and through their membership of descendants' associations. In their social and cultural activities therefore, dockers have the opportunity to 'mix' with influential Big Men or Mammies. Favours such as assistance in finding a job may be requested and granted. Dockers were specifically asked in the survey whether there were 'any groups who are helping you so that you

136

can go before' (or improve your situation in life).
Just under a third of the whole sample replied in the
affirmative that influential people could give assistance in finding jobs and on family occasions such as
births, marriages and deaths. There were no suggestions, however, of regular cash hand-outs. Most
dockers do recognise that they live in a political and
economic world where patron-clientelism is the main
answer to advancement--and many are prepared to use it.
This keen sense of political realism helps to explain
their somewhat ambivalent attitudes. In one word then,
ambivalence, provides the answer to the question of what
influence is exerted on their political perceptions (or
ideology) and behaviour by the role of patron-clientelism. This is not to suggest that the absence of an
'authentic' working-class ideology leads the dockers to
a readiness to accept patron-clientelist relations (or,
alternatively, that their acceptance of patron-clientelist relations leads to a 'watered-down' working-class
ideology). It is rather to suggest that the dockers
recognise the realities of the world in which they live
and, accordingly, are prepared to make compromises with
it. This is the essence of Marx's aphorism in The
Eighteenth Brumaire of Louis Bonaparte:

> Men make their own history, but they
> do not make it just as they please;
> they do not make it under circum-
> stances chosen by themselves, but
> under circumstances directly encoun-
> tered, given, and transmitted from
> the past.

It is the essence, too, of Gramsci's struggle to
develop an appropriate 'revolutionary praxis' and of
the heart-searching attempts of the leaders of socialist movements in contemporary Western Europe to remain
relevant to the interest they claim to champion. If
further comparisons may be drawn, the populism (not
socialism) exhibited in the behaviour of the railwaymen
of Sekondi-Takoradi and their willingness to 'take on'
Ghanaian regimes in 1961 and in 1971 (as described by
Jeffries24) or, for that matter, the 1919, 1926, 1955
and 1981 strikes (discussed in this book) are special
cases of African working-class radicalism.

Hence, therefore, it must not be assumed that 'Big
Men' can rely on the loyalty of dockers to whom they
have been patrons. However poorly they express their
consciousness of the inequalities in the society around

them, dockers do resent some of the activities of this
political and bureaucratic kleptocracy. When specifically asked to assess the politicians and top civil
servants (Table 5.12(c)), the dockers were overwhelmingly negative in their assessment. The chapter which
follows continues this evaluation of the dockers'
response to their economic situation by examining the
most notable features of their trade union organisation
and behaviour.

CHAPTER 6

A SHOP STEWARDS' MOVEMENT: THE INTERNAL DYNAMICS

OF THE DOCK WORKERS' UNION 1963-79

        Following the formation of the Dock Workers' Union
in May 1963, a powerful shop stewards' movement--which
has since become the 'keeper of the conscience' of the
union--gradually emerged. Not originally provided for
in the union constitution, and thereby having only an
informal status, shop-floor representation on the union
executive via elected stewards descended directly from
the system of workers' representation on the discredited
Works Committee (see Chapter 3). Being the driving
force behind the formation of the union, these representatives continued to act in an informal capacity as
the recruitment agents of the union in the sections
they had represented at the committee. Within a few
years another function evolved: Shop stewards became
the main channel of contact between the ordinary
members and the full-time leadership. Grievances for
transmission to the Union Secretary or his assistant
were reported to stewards; the interpretation of agreements reached with management, the union constitution,
and other documents and notices were undertaken by
stewards. Two important considerations appear to have
influenced this development in the role and status of
shop-floor representation within the union. First,
most stewards were literate, articulate, or had the
experience of the procedures of bargaining in a committee of workers and management. These 'qualifications'
were recognised and respected by their work mates.
Second, the institution of an automatic check-off
system shortly after the registration of the union
meant that the leadership were in receipt of monies
subscribed by the workers. The stewards made it their
business to know how this money was being spent. In
their attachment of much importance to this issue,
informal means of accountability became established
within the union. The term 'shop steward' appears not
to have been in use at the port before 1967 when the
union constitution was revised, the role formalised,
and provisions made for annual elections. The year
before, shop-floor representatives had provoked a
crisis over a proposal of the management to replace the
overtime system with shift work as part of the re-organisation of the public sector urged by the IMF. The

Union Secretary, a member of the Board of the Port
Authority, had acquiesced in the implementation of the
proposals. Urged on by floor representatives, dock
workers resisted the introduction of shift work until
it had been properly negotiated with the union. The
dispute necessitated the setting up of a public inquiry
which published a report giving valuable insight into
the union organisation during its early years.1 The
report recommended the dismissal of the Secretary who
was by then thoroughly discredited. Four years after
this dispute, in 1971, stewards forced the second
Secretary out of office on allegations of fraud and
dishonesty. Throughout the seventies, this tradition of
union 'watch dog' was maintained. In 1979, stewards
again precipitated the dismissal of the third Union
Secretary for misuse of union funds and instituted
legal proceedings. In between leadership crises, floor
representatives fully participated in the mapping of
strategies to be adopted in bargaining with management,
in securing the support of influential politicians on
these occasions, and in the strategic use of such
support. This chapter examines the most notable
features and internal dynamics of the Dock Workers'
Union by studying the structure of accountability
within the union and the responses of the dockers to
their employment by a parastatal organisation.

The Structure of Accountability Within the Dock Workers' Union

     The formation of the Dock Workers' Union was a
somewhat acrimonious affair as two of the older unions
operating at the port, the Maritime and Waterfront
Workers' Union and the Railway Workers' Union were
determined to strangle the new organisation at birth.
The organisers were equally determined to resist these
attempts. At the Labour Department, where all trade
unions were required to be registered, they argued
forcefully that to prevent dock workers from forming
their own organisation would be an infringement of
international labour codes of freedom of association.
Attention was further drawn to the practice in other
countries where dockers are organised separately.2 It
was strongly believed by the organisers that "our
interest will not be properly protected in a bigger
union. Apart form that, the railway union and the
stevedore union were not progressive unions"3. Due to
the success of the former representatives on the Works
Committee in persuading their work mates to join the

union, the Port Management Department became a virtual closed shop. Subscriptions were set at 6d. a month.4 The Works Committee itself became redundant. For the first year of its existence, the elected officials of the union--drawn mainly from the clerical and artisan grades--were part-time; but in 1964 two clerks, J. I. Sandy and M. I. Mansaray, became the full-time Secretary and Assistant Secretary respectively. Both resigned their appointments whith the Port Management Department.5 Other members of the union executive in 1964 were M. M. Fatoma, Union President, J. C. Solomon, Vice-President, M. A. Jalloh, Treasurer, A. J. Johnson, and F. J. Seibure, Internal Auditors, H. B. Macauley, and F. J. O. Johnson, Trustees.6 These were part-time appointments. The decision to appoint two full-time officials was a product of the realisation among the membership of the practical difficulties facing the main individuals who were employees in the port organisation but also involved in routine negotiations with the management on behalf of the union.7 Since the union had accumulated some funds from membership subscriptions,8 it was felt that these ought to be used to employ two full-time officials at rates comparable to those obtaining for clerks at the port organisation. The union also leased office space at Fourah Bay Road in the vicinity of the port and employed office staff, a typist and a messenger. In order that these overheads would be met, monthly subscriptions were increased to 15 cents in 1964 9, to 30 cents in 1965 and to 40 cents in 1966. 10

During these early years, however, a problem which was to become perennial in the administration of the union emerged. This was the use and control of union finances. It can be shown that about half (at the maximum) of the union's monthly revenue between 1964 and 1967 was used to meet overheads, leaving a healthy balance in reserve (see Tables 6.1(a) and 6.1(b)). It is clear, however, from conversations with dockers, and indeed from the evidence heard by the Panda Commission in 1966/67, that a clique within the union executive converted monies from these balances for their personal use and the use of their friend. Here, it is worth quoting Panda at some length:

> The finances of this union, if
> properly handled, would be a handy
> asset to the union itself...Evidence
> was adduced that union funds were
> utilised in advancing loans to
> members and non-members of the

141

union...There are several amounts
outstanding to the union and steps
should be taken to recover these
immediately. I find the executive...
were in default in granting loans to
members of the union under the guise
of benefits. For trade union
purposes, benefits may include relief
in sickness, accident, and unemployment from victimisation in the
furtherance of a trade dispute.11

These allegations firmly placed the issue of
accountability within the union on the agenda for
debate amongst the entire membership. This directly
resulted in the re-organisation of the union structure
in ways more radical than even Panda had envisaged.
The Panda report recommended that the Labour Department,
and specifically, the Registrar of Trade Unions, should
periodically examine the audited reports of the union.
12. At the docks, however, where the laxity of public
service bureaucratic control was fully understood, a
consensus emerged that elected floor representatives
from each section of the port organisation should be
made members of the executive. "We felt that we don't
have to wait for the Ministry to come and tell us that
our money has been stolen. It is our money which we
pay for the union to be organised to protect us. So it
is we who should decide how to use the money and to
know if it is being stolen."13 At the union's annual
conference of March 1967 (in effect a mass meeting of
the entire membership), the union constitution was
amended to accommodate floor representatives, designated shop stewards, on the executive. Another amendment created the position of Financial Secretary whose
function it was to maintain the financial records of
the union and to approve all transactions carried out
by the Treasurer.14 Elections to all executive positions were held, and in all cases, none of the former
members of the old executive were returned. Jack Sandy,
the founding Union Secretary, having been thoroughly
discredited, did not contest. The former Assistant
Secretary, M. I. Mansaray, was elected Secretary.
These two positions continued to be full-time.15

It is clear that M. I. Mansaray was instrumental
in bringing about these changes. At the end of 1964,
Mansaray, then Assistant Secretary, was awarded a six
months' scholarship to study aspects of trade union
organisation in the USSR. Sandy, as Union Secretary,

TABLE 6.1(a)

Estimate of Union Revenue 1963/64 - 1966/67

YEAR	MONTHLY SUBCRIPTION	MONTHLY UNION REVENUE
1963/64	6d.(5c)	£55.1.6d (Le 110.30c)
1964/65	15c	Le 396.35c
1965/66	30c	Le 794.70c
1966/67	40c	Le1,059.60c

Basis of estimate: Union membership in 1963 was 2,649 (see Labour Department, Annual Report 1963). It is assumed that membership remained at this level (though it in fact increased over the period). The bias is, however, in the right direction as it is not known whether each member paid the subscription.

having cultivated a personal relationship with the leaders of the ruling SLPP, had himself attended a short course in industrial relations in Europe in 1964, and had secured the scholarship for Mansaray.[16] On Mansaray's return to Freetown in July 1965, he discovered the financial irregularities that were later investigated by the Panda inquiry. "I was angered, because this was a young union, and within a year all these things were happening."[17] Furthermore, Sandy had been appointed a member of the Board of Directors of the Port Authority in January 1965, and Mansaray on his return recognised that the former's position as Union Secretary had, as a consequence, been hopelessly compromised. He decided to undermine Sandy's position among the membership and, in particular, the former representatives on the Works Committee.[18] The Panda inquiry also heard evidence to this effect:

TABLE 6.1(b)

Estimate of Average Union Monthly Expenditure

1963/64 - 1966/67

ITEM	EXPENDITURE
Union Secretary's salary	Le 80
Union Assistant Secretary's salary	Le 60
Typist's salary	Le 30
Messenger's salary	Le 20
Other overheads (e.g. office lease, stationery, bills, etc.)	Le 150
TOTAL	Le 340

N.B.:   First full year of union expenditure on these items is 1964/65.

SOURCE: These estimates are based on figures provided by Aziz Kassim who was elected Union Financial Secretary in 1967 (interview with Aziz Kassim, 6th March 1982). Actual figures on union expenditure are available from 1971. These show that average monthly union expenditure was in the region of Le650 (Dock Workers' Union, Minutes of Executive Meeting, 17th February 1972). Assuming a gradual increase in union expenditure over the years, the 1963/64 - 1966/67 estimates are realistic.

...allegations were preferred against
Mr. Mansaray to the effect that he had
been engaged in moves aimed at bringing
the good name of the union to disrepute;
that Mr. Mansaray had been heard on
several occasions telling groups of
members of the Dock Workers' Union that
they were being exploited by Government
because the union was very weak and was
always taking sides with the employers.19

A power struggle then ensued between Sandy and
Mansaray, the former drawing his support from the union
executive, and the latter from the union rank and file.
In August 1965, the executive expelled Mansaray from
the union in circumstances which Panda found "to be not
in accordance with the provisions of the constitution
of the union".20 Mansaray, ignoring the expulsion
order, continued his campaign to remove Sandy from the
leadership of the union. The Panda Report noted that
"from the time Mr. Mansaray was expelled...there
existed a complete rumpus within the union".21 Sandy
completely misjudged the mood of the membership. He
compounded this error with other tactless actions. The
1965 annual union conference was held behind closed
doors at the V.I.P. lounge of the Port Authority, Sandy
being a Director on the Board. The delegates to the
conference were carefully hand-picked by Sandy, who was
consequently able to secure a vote of confidence and a
further term of office. Mansaray retaliated by organis-
ing an 'alternative' mass union conference at which it
was resolved that the following letter of protest be
sent to the Labour Department:

Dear Sir,

        Resolution of fully paid-up members of the
Sierra Leone Dock Workers' Union at a meeting
assembled at Cline Town on Tuesday, 5th October,
1965, at 6.30 a.m. attended by approximately
1,600 fully paid-up members of the Sierra Leone
Dock Workers' Union, the following matters
regarding the mal-administration of the union
were discussed and decided upon:-

1.   Illegally convening of a so-called Annual
      Conference for the election of officers
      at which only thirty members including
      the present officers attended at a Very
      Important Personalities lounge of the

Sierra Leone Ports Authority, instead of at the union's registered office.

2. Unsatisfactory and illegal use of union's fund.

3. Summary dismissal of fully paid-up members without a charge being prepared against them.

4. Contravening Rule 22 of the union's rule regarding elections.

In view of the above we the undersigned fully paid-up members unanimously resolve as follows... That the authorities concerned appoint an independent enquiry to probe into the matters complained of.

We remain to be Sir

(signed) Members
(Dock Workers' Union)22

No immediate action was taken in response to the letter. Sandy, however, attempted to consolidate his position by issuing a press statement in which he declared the support of the union for the single-party state mooted by the ruling SLPP which was being debated in parliament. This was regarded by Mansaray and others as a very skillful move, as Sandy had succeeded in giving the dispute a political dimension and could therefore count on the support of his patrons in the SLPP.23 The Labour Department was eventually forced to intervene as the rank and file was resolute in their determination to make Sandy accountable:

> The Commissioner of Labour in his evidence said that his Ministry had done everything to educate the leaders of the union. He had personally insisted that the union should be run in accordance with its constitution. When he made efforts to reconcile the relationship between the General Secretary...and Mr. Mansaray...he received no cooperation from the former. It was after this that he was compelled to relax his efforts because the latter group had taken the matter

to court to seek an injunction to
restrain the executive from function-
ing.24

The injunction was not granted because of a legal
technicality.25 The Mansaray faction, however,
appealed to a higher court. While the case was being
heard, the rank and file of the union took action over
the introduction of a shift system which had been
approved by Sandy at Board level, but which had not
been negotiated with the union. It was in response to
the continuing dispute within the union that the Labour
Department advised the government to appoint a commission to examine these issues and the relations between
the union and the Port Authority.26 Mansaray and
others immediately dropped their action.27

The commission found the convening of the 1965
annual conference of the union in the V.I.P. lounge of
the Port Authority to be profoundly improper as this
was meant to exclude the participation of workers'
representatives in the deliberations and in the election of union officers. Moreover, since membership of
the Port Authority Board had compromised the position
of Sandy as union leader, the commission felt that some
person, other than the Secretary, ought to be appointed
as the workers' representative on the Board:

> The General Secretary of a trade
> union is the chief executive of
> that union. He runs the day to day
> business of the union under the
> guidance of the executive council.
> A Union Secretary may find himself
> in a very untenable position as a
> member of the corporation. There
> is no doubt that the present Secre-
> tary, Mr. Sandy found himself in
> the position described, having
> acquiesced at a Board meeting
> held in June, 1965, in a decision
> to introduce the shift system at the
> port. In order to give the workers
> effective representation and at the
> same time to avoid putting the Union
> Secretary in an embarrassing posi-
> tion, the Minister responsible for
> the appointment of members of the
> Board may consider appointing someone
> else outside the industry; for

147

example a retired trade unionist of
wide experience and knowledge of
industrial relations in this country.28

This recommendation has never been heeded in spite
of its inherent logic. As governments attempt to extend
their influence in the trade union movement, a paid
Directorship on the Board of the Port Authority has
always been offered as a carrot to the Secretary of the
union.29

The crisis within the union, however, exposed the
whole of the membership to a learning process which
resulted in a widespread realisation of the importance
of maintaining and fostering means of accountability
within the union. The measures taken at the union conference of March 1967, and in particular the amendment
of the constitution to provide for floor representation
on the executive, were a natural consequence of this
learning process. Moreover, in becoming a part of the
union folklore (as extended conversations with dockers
has revealed), these lessons are being constantly rein-
forced. Mansaray's own eventual dismissal during the
second leadership crisis of 1971, and indeed the third
leadership crisis of 1979, can be related to the
lessons which had been learnt.

One of Mansaray's priorities as Union Secretary
was to increase the membership of the union, particularly among casual dockers. "I realised that casuals
are very difficult to organise but they needed union
protection badly".30 Of a total lower-paid work force
of 6,978 at the port in 1967, 5,678 dockers were
casuals.31 (Almost the whole of the non-casual dockers
were members of the union and it was in this sense a
virtual closed shop). During his Secretaryship,
Mansaray succeeded in increasing membership from "just
below 3,000 when I took over to about 4,200 when I
left".32 This was achieved by extending membership of
the union also to labourers employed by the Produce
Marketing Board engaged in the packing of produce for
export in the Cline Town area close to the port. "In a
sense these labourers are cargo-handlers. They pack
produce for export which is sent to the port, where our
own boys take over. I realised that these labourers
needed union protection".33 Accordingly, Mansaray wrote
to the General Manager of the Produce Marketing Board
to inform him that over 200 labourers employed in his
establishment had joined the Dock Workers' Union. The
letter presented the issue as a _fait_ _accompli_:

148

> I should inform you...that your
> workmen have expressly decided
> voluntarily, and have accordingly
> joined the Sierra Leone Dock
> Workers' Union with effect from
> November ending 1967. 34

The management of the Produce Marketing Board was initially reluctant to accept this development, but,
following several meetings and exchanges of letters, the
issue was eventually resolved.35 Two shop stewards
were elected by the workers from among their numbers to
represent them on the union executive.36

   As Union Secretary, Mansaray supported the APC
which came to power in 1968 and benefited from its
patronage. (Since the formation of the union, it had
been affiliated to the APC-leaning national centre, the
Council of Labour--see Chapter 7). In 1968, contrary
to the recommendations of the Panda Report, Mansaray
was appointed to the Board of the Port Authority. The
following year, O. B. Conteh, Mansaray's deputy, was
sent to Britain to pursue a course in industrial
relations.37 Mansaray's appointment to the Board was
viewed with some dismay by many of the shop stewards
and the union rank and file.38 He argued that his
appointment would improve the union's intelligence
network and that he would never enter into any agreement without the mandate of the executive.39 "He kept
to his promise and we never suspected him of selling
out".40 Mansaray himself has said he never "betrayed"
the union and has insisted that he is very proud of his
record as union leader.41 As a part-time Director on
the Board, he received Le1,080 a year in Director's fee
and was entitled to other perquisites.

   During the absence of the Assistant Secretary in
1969-70 however, some irregularities in the use of
monies voted for the administration of the union were
discovered by the executive. The executive decided to
bring this matter to a head at the 1970 annual conference of the union. Mansaray attempted to pre-empt this
by drawing up a programme for a one-day conference--even
though it had become the established practice for conferences to be spread over three days--at which the
elections of members of the executive was the main item.
(Except for minor changes, the 1967 executive had been
re-elected each year). C. T. Patnelli, a shop steward
in the Accounts Section, wrote to Mansaray to insist
upon a detailed programme spread over three days:

> A day for annual conference is in my
> view too short for us...Three days
> at least could be utilised for putting
> things straight. You yourself as
> secretary-general of the union have
> been privileged to see the union run
> on democratic principles...The agenda
> as I see it calls for some re-arrange-
> ment and additional items. 42

This agenda, supported by other members of the executive, was adopted. At the conference, Mansaray drew
attention to his successes in negotiations with
management at the Produce Marketing Board and at the
Port Authority. When the audit reports were discussed,
it was clear that he had fraudulently converted monies
voted for the administration of the union to his use.
"The mood of the conference was that he had done a good
job, so we warned him, and decided to increase our own
vigilance."43

It is clear from union records that the vigilance
of the stewards was indeed increased after the conference. At an executive council meeting in June, a
steward, J. T. Mahoi (representing Traffic and Claims
Section) was selected for the award of a scholarship to
undertake a course in trade union studies in Israel.
It was proposed that he should be given some spending
money, a 'purse', to meet some of his expenses. An
interesting discussion ensued:

> On the union's recommendation of
> Comrade J. T. Mahoi for a four months'
> study fellowship of Israel...it was
> decided that the purse should be voted
> for, but should not be made payable to
> the comrade until notification for his
> departure to Israel is received.44

Another instance of vigilance of the executive is
evident from discussions on salary increases for the
Union Secretary and his staff at the union office:

> Comrade Patnelli (representing Accounts
> Section) expressed some reservations
> about the salary increase to the
> Secretary-General but supported all
> the other recommendations...He pointed
> out that the Secretary-General was
> receiving a renumeration of Le90

150

monthly as a member of the Sierra
Leone Port Authority Board which put
together with his salary of Le110
from the union should be quite sufficient for him. He did not therefore
consider a salary increase to the
Secretary-General justifiable...
Comrade Amadu Wilson (representing
Marine Slipway Section) reflected
on the working conditions of members
whose 40 cent dues is being so spent,
and ended by warning that careful
thought should be exercised over the
way spending is approved by the
council.45

In the event, however, the meeting voted for a monthly
increase of Le10 in the salary of the Secretary.46
Aziz Kassim has explained that "each time the union
gives the Secretary more money, we have to consider
that he is trying to get us more money; so we should do
the same for him. Scratch my back and I will scratch
your own."47 The records of the union show that, over
the months, the executive continued to exercise its
role as the 'conscience' of the union. When it was
discovered the following year that monies voted for the
administration of the union had been misappropriated, a
stormy meeting took place:

>...Comrade Santigie Sesay (represent-
ing casual tally clerks) wanted the
Secretary-General relieved of his
duties...He concluded by saying that
he was tired to see the Secretary
always falling short of expectations
and precious time should have been
otherwise spent discussing urgent
issues wasted in repudiating the
Secretary-General.48

It was eventually decided that Mansaray should be
relieved of his position.49 A mass meeting of all
union members was convened to convey and ratify the
decision of the executive:

>The meeting was called to order by
Comrade N. R. Sesay (representing
Lighterage). He said that as the
executive was the government of the
union, we the members of the executive

151

have sacked the Secretary-General
Comrade M. I. Mansaray...Contribu-
ting to the issue, Comrade Salfu
Turay (representing Harbour Master's
Section) praised the workers and
said that it is not a crime to be
illiterate. But that though some of
them were illiterate, it was the
workers who put Comrade Mansaray
in the position he found himself...In
contributing, Comrade J. D. Saidu
(representing coopers) said that we
have all been disappointed at the
action of the Secretary-General
because all of us fought hard for
him to become Secretary-General
of this union...At this juncture,
Comrade O. B. Conteh (the Assistant
Secretary) was asked to say something.
In his speech, he said that he wanted
to reserve his position...He swore to
the almighty God that he was not a
partner in the accusation against
Comrade M. I. Mansaray. He said that
if he wanted to fight Comrade
Mansaray for his position as was
rumoured, he will fight him consti-
tutionally...He asked members to listen
to the words of the executive who were
prepared to set everything right...
One of the workers was asked to say
something. In his speech he asked for
a short prayer; the Alfatia. He then
addressed the executive. He said that
he has many things to say which if he
wanted to say all, will talk endlessly.
He said there have been a number of
thieves and crooks in this union. It
began from Sandy's time...He said that
as Comrade Mansaray had been suspended,
let no man touch the union's money...
He said that he was looking to the
executive for appropriate action.50

The meeting also resolved that the General Manager of
the Port Authority, the press, the Commissioner of
Labour, the Minister of Labour, and other important
politicians should be informed of the decision to ter-
minate the services of M. I. Mansaray as union
leader.51 O. B. Conteh was voted in as Secretary

and J. T. Mahoi, a clerk and shop steward representing the Traffic and Claims Section, became the Assistant Secretary.

Conteh having inherited Mansaray's seat on the Board, it was decided at the beginning of the former's term that his Director's fees should be paid into the union's bank account "...in view of the general feeling of workers always against the Secretary-General being paid such fees by the Port Authority thereby weakening his position on the Board..."52 But it was also decided to increase the Secretary's salary by a "full Le90 (a month) bringing his fixed salary to Le210 with effect from the month ending January 1972 which view was unanimously accepted and passed by the council".53 Thus the principle that Director's fees should be paid to the union was established and the Secretary's salary increased by the same amount he would have received from the Port Authority.

The balances from expenditure on the administration of the union, affiliation fees to local trade union centres and the International Transport Workers' Federation having accumulated over the years, it is evident that the union's financial position was extremely buoyant. The main financial assistance the union offered its members was a death benefit of Le20 paid to the relatives of a deceased docker. Salary advances for the purchase of consumer durables were offered to the union's small staff from time to time and 'purses' were voted for union members attending courses or conferences abroad. In April 1972, the executive voted Le7,000 to be held in a fixed deposit bank account.54 In 1974, Le1,000 worth of shares were purchased as a contribution to a consumer, cooperative venture sponsored by the Labour Congress.55 Two years later, the union purchased Le3,000 worth of shares at Standard Bank (Sierra Leone) Limited.56 By August 1978, the union's total bank balances was Le18,015.58 cents.57

Throughout Conteh's leadership of the union, the records show that the executive continued to monitor the unions' expenditure carefully. Several instances of attempts to reinforce a system of accountability within the union can be cited. In February 1972, for example, a few weeks after some new office equipment was bought, a steward suggested that an inventory of the union's assets should be made:

"Comrade D. E. Kamara suggested that

153

it is necessary that an inventory of
equipment at the Secretariat with
particular reference to those recently
bought...be drawn up and displayed for
the perusal of any interested member
of the union...After this, Comrade
Salifu Turay appealed to members to
try to forget past occurrences perpetrated by the previous and past administrations headed by Jack Sandy and
M. I. Mansaray which he felt were
perpetuating these tendencies of
mistrust among executive members.58

It is evident, however, that these tendencies of
mistrust continued to manifest themselves among executive members and could be related to an apparent division of the executive into 'hawks' and 'doves' over the
question of union expenditure. The leading hawks were
Alfred Jackson, Kadrie Kamara, and J. T. King. The
doves included E. P. K. Ceisay, F. M. Abu, and the
Secretary himself. Some sharp exchanges between these
protagonists took place regularly at executive meetings.
In March 1972, for example, it was suggested that a
'purse' of Le600 be given to the Secretary who was
about to leave for a conference in Geneva. A majority
of the members voted for this suggestion:

After this, Comrade J. T. King sounded
a note of warning that members should
always try to appreciate that the
union's money was not just the asset
of a few members as some members felt,
but owned generally by all the members;
and that the Secretary-General was
just going to be away for a few weeks.
Next was Comrade R. M. Abu who reminded
him and asked members to just take a
quick mental stock of what the union
has achieved just the past few months
under the Secretary-General's leadership; and that the members should be
certain that when he is back from
this very worthwhile course more will
be achieved.59

Another bitter exchange took place later that year over
a suggestion by R. M. Abu and E. P. K. Ceisay that the
union should host a dance in honour of some visiting
Port Managers from other West African countries:

154

Expressing his own view, Comrade
Alfred Jackson said that it was
rather preposterous for the union
to spend the poor labourer's money
on a dance just to please the Sierra
Leone Port Authority and their guests.
The Vice-President supported this view
and added that the money will not only
provide ugly rumours but will also
bring confusion in the union. Making
his own contribution, Comrade Kadrie
Kamara said that the union should not
take the entertainment of the Authority's guests on its head.60

In the event, the suggestion was not accepted. In the
absence of clearly defined objectives to which the
union's accumulating balances were to be put, problems
relating to the use of union funds obviously emerged.
It has been established that the funds were not being
held to provide assistance to members during any protracted strike action.

We never thought of that...because
we always reached agreement by
negotiation. But this is possible
now...Yes, benefits to members
were virtually non-existent, but
two years ago, the union started
to give (school) scholarships to
the children of members...We have
also made some good investments.61

One of the individuals best placed to exploit this
vacuum relating to the use of union funds was the
Secretary, O. B. Conteh. In December 1972, he
presented the union executive with an application for a
Le2,500 loan for the purchase of a vehicle which was to
be paid back over a two-year period. Although a
majority of the members of the executive at the meeting
voted for the application to be approved, it was clear
that several other members resented this development.
"Comrade Aziz Kassim expressing his views maintained
that all seniors officers of the Sierra Leone Port
Authority who took loans are paying interest...and
insisted on interest at five percent".62

The Secretary did not in fact purchase a vehicle.
He bought a house and came back to the executive for a
further loan of Le2,000 to complete the transaction.

155

This application was also approved but the Secretary was required to write and inform the executive that the original purpose of the loan had been changed. His discomfiture is evident in the letter which was not, however, lacking in boldness:

> ...I have no alternative but to honestly submit the fact that I cannot...discharge the understanding of buying means of transport...I am constrained, and for the discreet consideration and understanding of you all, to withdraw the understanding of my original application to buy means of transport in place of which I wish to offer my house and landed property bought at four thousand two hundred leones, situated at No. 26 Will Street as a safe guarantee towards the repayment of salary advance of Le4,500 which I have already started repaying at 5 percent interest.63

Those members of the executive who resented these developments were not prepared to be 'discreet' or 'understanding' over this issue. The hawks quickly spread the word among the union rank and file that the executive had approved a loan of such magnitude to the Secretary. At an executive meeting in May, they were warned that discord would be created within the union as a result of this 'gossiping':

> Comrade E. P. K. Ceisay intimated members...to stop the way some of them have started to spoil the smooth running of this organisation by means of gossiping. He referred members to a resolution taken some time ago...that all decisions taken by the executive should be confidential, but yet still some members are fond of telling other people what the executive decides on each executive meeting.64

The warning was directed particularly at J. T. King, Kadrie Kamara, and Alfred Jackson. Ignoring the warnings, they convened a series of meetings among

156

dockers in the various sections of the Port Authority
in order to undermine confidence in the Secretary and
the executive. O. B. Conteh himself interrupted one of
these meetings after having been informed that papers
relating to the loan had been removed from the union
office:

> ...the Secretary General first of
> all reported about how he was
> called down the Marine Slipway,
> Cline Town, in the early afternoon
> of the date of the meeting (August
> 22) where he was handed a copy of
> the letter of his application
> regarding his salary advance loan
> with a copy of the draft agreement
> said to have been seized from
> Mr. J. T. King who he met concluding
> his address to workers against the
> Executive's decision granting the
> loan they had made to him. The
> papers in question he said were
> kept inside one of the drawers of
> his office desk and could not
> imagine that these papers could
> ever have found their way out...
> this state of affairs the Secretary
> concluded was one which the executive
> must view with all seriousness
> especially when it was now clear that
> the question of papers related to
> matters of a confidential nature were
> a security risk; and finally urged the
> executive to consider appropriate
> measures to preserve confidentiality
> in the Secretariat.65

The Secretary also presented a resolution to the
meeting purporting to be a popular endorsement of the
decision to grant him the loan:

> We the members of the constituent
> sections comprising the general
> membership of the Sierra Leone
> Dock Workers' Union having today
> been addressed at this meeting
> concerning unscrupulous allegations
> documented by three members of the
> executive, and also having heard a
> detailed factual account offered by

> our union Secretary-General supported
> by inspected authentic documents in
> relation to the Executive decision of
> having made a Le4,500 salary advance
> loan to the Secretary-General, do by
> this unanimous resolution endorse that
> decision of the executive council which
> we take to be very consistent with
> conducive conditions of employment.66

In retrospect, it is clear that confidence in
Conteh's leadership was badly shaken, and the events
which were to eventually remove him from the leadership in 1977 may be said to have their origins in the
divisions created within the union over this affair.
Three sections of the union, Civil Maintenance, Marine
Slipway, and Mechanical Plant Yard, made up primarily
of artisans, and represented on the executive by King,
Jackson, and Kamara respectively, were determined to
bring about a change in union leadership.67 Being a
sensitive political animal, Conteh himself attempted to
consolidate his position by creating a clientele among
unskilled workers, particularly the casual labourers,
numerically the largest group within the union:

> He successfully created a personal
> following among the casuals...The
> strategy I would say was to remind
> them that he was doing his best to
> improve things for them and that
> they should ignore the artisans,
> who as skilled workers did not
> have any problems and were secure
> in their jobs. It should also be
> remembered that what was at issue
> was not his suitability for being
> Secretary-General, for he was a
> shrewd negotiator who could deliver
> the goods, but his honesty and his
> tendency to behave like a dictator.68

It is a tribute to his skills that, having failed in an
attempt to expel King, Jackson, and Kamara from the
union, he was successful in having them voted off the
executive.69 Conteh also attempted to consolidate his
position further by seeking office in the Labour
Congress. At the end of 1974, he was elected First
Deputy Secretary of Congress.70 It was from this
position of influence that he presented the executive
with a request for a 25 percent salary increase in

March 1975. This time, however, he was careful in
securing the approval of his 'constituency' among the
casual labourers before bringing the matter to the executive. For this he was warned by the Union President
to refrain from 'going over their heads' to the membership:

> The President, Comrade Amadu Wilson
> warned the Secretary-General that
> whenever he needs anything from the
> union, he should first of all inform
> the executive instead of the masses.71

Again, he was awarded the increase, and by the time he
left office in 1979, Conteh had succeeded in increasing
his salary by over 50 percent, from Le210 to Le333.33
cents.72 The artisan wing of the union had quietly
been securing changes in the membership of the executive. At the 1975 union conference, two of O. B.
Conteh's strongest supporters, E. P. K. Ceisay and
R. M. Abu, were voted off the executive.73 The
following year, the artisans made their biggest gain
when the Assistant Secretary, J. T. Mahoi, was voted
off and replaced by Alfred Conteh (no relation of the
Secretary). The position of O. B. himself remained
impregnable due to his strong popularity among the
unskilled workers, but it is evident that he resented
these developments, and in particular, the appointment
of an Assistant Secretary with an independent power
base in the union:

> The Secretary-General reported that he
> intended having a mass meeting of all
> members on the matter of an Assistant
> Secretary as no one will impose someone
> on him, otherwise he would leave the job.74

Conteh did in fact make an attempt to leave the job.
In October 1977, he triumphantly informed the executive
that he intended to present himself as a candidate for
the Secretaryship of the Labour Congress.75 In the
event Conteh did contest the elections, only to withdraw his candidature at the very last minute when it
was clear that J. B. Kabia of the Mine Workers' Union
commanded the support of a majority of the delegates at
the conference (see Chapter 7). "It was a humiliation
from which he did not recover. Since we wanted to get
rid of him, we gave him support. But it was not fana-
tical support".76

Although it is clear that a majority of the members of the union executive were, by the end of 1977, resolved that Conteh must be relieved of the Secretaryship, it has been established from conversations with dockers that his negotiating skills and his ability to create a network of contacts with important politicians continued to be widely admired by the union rank and file. Conteh appears to have been fully aware of the sources of his strengths and was apparently determined to resist attemps to remove him from the leadership. He must also have been aware that his position as Union Secretary was secure (for a year at the very least) as periodic Trade Group Council negotiations for the review of wages and benefits in public utility establishments (as was required under the 1971 Industrial Relations Act) were due in 1978. The executive was also aware of this and indeed granted a 25 percent salary increase to Conteh while the negotiations were in progress in September 1978.   In November, the Secretary reported to the executive that negotiations had been concluded:

> ...The Secretary-General then
> informed the meeting that after
> some hard bargaining the Trade
> Group Negotiating Council has
> awarded Le96 per annum, and an
> increase to all junior employees
> earning up to Le1,780 per annum,
> and an increase of 30 cents
> per diem to all casual workers.
> Other conditions like free
> Saturdays and proper medical
> care will now be enjoyed by all
> workers immediately the agreement
> is signed.77

Once these negotiations were over, Conteh's position again became vulnerable. The resentment, particularly of the skilled workers, that the Secretary was using his position to exploit the union again surfaced. The old power struggle continued. At the union annual conference in March 1979, where Conteh triumphantly reported his successes in the previous year's negotiations, the executive successfully secured an amendment to the union's constitution which had been carefully designed to strengthen their position vis a vis the Secretary. This was that "...the general membership which is the supreme authority of the union shall call for elections after every three years".78

160

The significance of this amendment was that executive members (but not the Secretary or the Assistant Secretary) were no longer to be subject to annual election. Since a majority on the executive were critical of Conteh's leadership, this meant that the Secretary would be unable to undermine them for the ensuing three years at the very least.

In April, the Internal Auditors on the executive discovered that two separate incidences of fraud had been perpetrated on the union by the secretary and reported the matter to a meeting of the executive council.79 The total amount involved was Le13,200; Le1,200 having been voted for the Secretary to attend a meeting in Ghana, which he did not attend, and Le12,000, having been voted for the purchase of land at Newton, near Freetown, as an investment, for which there was no receipt. Since the secretary could not offer a convincing explanation to the meeting, it was decided to withdraw one of the allowances he had been receiving from the union until he did so.80 The meeting also decided to report the matter to the Minister of Labour, one of Conteh's many patrons in the APC. Conteh, meanwhile, presented the issue to the union membership as being that "...his enemies among the skilled workers wanted to remove him as Secretary-General. He refused to work with the executive and secured a court injunction to seal up the office of the union until the matter was resolved".81 In May the executive voted to remove him from the leadership. The deliberations of the meeting are worth quoting at some length:

> Comrade Luseni (representing clerks of the Operations Section)...moved a motion that the Secretary-General be suspended from office indefinitely...Full Text of the Motion:...Mr. Chairman and members, considering certain predominant factors which tend to disrupt the smooth running of this important and essential organisation, I am left with no alternative but to move a motion that the present Secretary-General be suspended from office and an interim committee be formed to manage the affairs of the union... Finally, I ask you Mr. Chairman and members to invoke the provision of Rule 7.5 prescribed in the constitution of the Sierra Leone Dock Workers' Union for the suspension of Mr. O. B. Conteh for gross

inefficiency and insubordination in
the execution of his official
duties...82

After the meeting voted in favour of the motion:

Brother Khalil Kamara (representing
floating staff, Harbour Master's
Section) moved that the Secretary-
General's suspension should be made
known immediately to the following:

(a)   His Execellency the President,
      (President Stevens)

(b)   The Secretary-General, APC

(c)   The Honourable Minister
      of Labour

(d)   The Honourable Minister
      of Transport and Communi-
      cations

(e)   The General Manager, Sierra
      Leone Ports Authority

(f)   The Commissioner of Labour

(g)   The Registrar of Trade Unions

(h)   The Secretary-General Sierra
      Leone Labour Congress

(i)   The Consultant, Sierra Leone
      Port Authority, etc.83

The meeting also decided that "...court action be taken
against the Secretary-General on the points raised in
the motion of suspension".84

Conteh fought back. He organised a deputation of
his supporters among the unskilled workers to present
the Minister of Labour, who was also his kinsman,85 with
a resolution expressing confidence in his leadership of
the union. The Minister subsequently intervened in the
dispute to persuade the executive to drop the court
action against Conteh in view of the service he had
given to the union since 1971, or else to convene a
union conference to ratify the decisions they

had taken.86 Meanwhile a new Secretary, Francis Brimah, formerly a Branch Secretary of the Mine Workers' Union, was appointed after the executive had interviewed other nominees suggested by the Labour Congress. Congress, however, also required the executive to have its decisions ratified by a union conference:

> Comrade Alfred Sesay expressed the opinion that it was rather unfortunate that the Labour Congress had supported the Minister's proposal but that if even it was to be, the executive will surely win the conference. After a lengthy exchange on the matter, the President (D. F. Kanu) advised that the date of the conference should be announced after the meeting. Brother Mark Luseni expressed the opinion that every shop representative now had an important role to play (in ensuring that the executive wins) but suggested that before ever the conference will be held, the Minister of Labour should agree and sign the following proposals by the executive for the safeguard:
>
> (a) That the conference was only to show the popularity of Mr. Brimah
>
> (b) That if Mr. Brimah wins, he will become substantive holder of the post
>
> (c) That whether Mr. Brimah wins or not the executive will remain in office until their term expires
>
> The president suggested that the proposals of the executive should be given to Lawyer Campbell (the union solicitor) who will then write and forward them to the Minister for his approval before ever the conference will be held. This was unanimously agreed by all members present.87

In the event, the executive did win the conference, albeit by a narrow majority.88 All the decisions of the

163

executive were ratified including the court action
against the former Secretary.89

Having examined some of the more important aspects
of the structure of accountability within the union
during the sixteen years after its formation in 1963,
the focus now shifts--before discussing the theoretical
conclusions towards which this account points--to an
appraisal of the strategies of bargaining adopted by
the union over the same period.

The Responses of Dock Workers to Their Employment by A Parastatal Organisation: The Dynamics of Bargaining

The main priority of the union at the time of its
formation was to secure the reversal of the illiberal
employment policies of the port organisation. Where
the colonial authorities had employed a host of
measures to keep the costs incurred in the employment
of lower-paid workers fairly low, the Albert Margai
regime was favourably disposed to an improvement in
working conditions and benefits in the public sector
in general. Indeed, at the first Board meeting of the
Port Authority (at which Jack Sandy as Secretary of the
Dock Workers' Union was present), the Minister of Transport and Communications, Kandeh Bureh, in his address
to the Directors as guest speaker, emphasised that it
was government policy to ensure that acceptable terms
of employment were maintained in the public sector.90
The nomination of the Union Secretary as a Director by
the Minister was not only a concrete manifestation of
the policy, but was arguably a calculated attempt to
increase the influence of the ruling party in the
labour movement which generally supported the APC Opposition. In its attempts to reverse the illiberal
employment policies at the port, the union was impress-
ively successful. By 1967, a large proportion of daily-
wage workers had been absorbed into the permanent work
force (see Table 4.1) Reliable figures as to wage
rates of dock workers are not available on a time-series
basis for the 1960s. To the extent, however, that the
wage indices for unskilled and skilled dockers were
126.3 and 95.2 respectively between 1965 and 1971, it
would appear that the union was largely successful in
maintaining the real value of wages during this period
at least (see Table 6.2).

Successive leaders of the union have long recognised that much could be achieved for the union member-

TABLE 6.2

Movement of Daily Wage Rates,

1965 – 1979, Dock Workers

YEAR	(a) UNSKILLED WAGE RATES	(b) SKILLED WAGE RATES	CPI* 1961=100	UN-SKILLED REAL WAGE INDEX	SKILL-ED REAL WAGE INDEX
1965	1.06	4.83	116.5 (100)	100	100
1971/72	1.46	5.03	127.3 (109.3)	126.3	95.2
1974/75	1.73	5.33	171.1 (147)	111	75.1
1976/77	1.95	5.93	238.7 (205)	89.8	60
1978/79	2.26	6.25	295.8 (254)	84	51

(a) Unskilled dockers' wage rates (bottom end of the scale; (b) Skilled dockers' wage rates (top end of the scale), both expressed in Leones and Cents.

* The official Consumer Price Index has 1961 as its base year. In this table, 1965 has been taken as the base year and the figures in parentheses have been adjusted accordingly. (See also Table 7.3).

SOURCES: 1. The Forster Report, Appendix 3 for 1965 – 1976/77 figures on wage rates.

2. Dock Workers' Union, Minutes of Executive Council Meeting, 30th November 1978, for 1978/79 figures on wage rates.

3. Bank of Sierra Leone, Annual Report 1969; Annual Report 1979, for figures on the Consumer Price Index.

ship through the personal intervention of influential
politicians. Given, as we have seen, the flexibility
in the rules governing the management of public corporations, and the considerable scope for the exercise of
power and influence, leaders of the union have naturally
turned to politicians not only for support in bargaining with with management, but also, as in O. B. Conteh's
case, for assistance in preventing his dismissal by the
union executive. This is the background against which
the responses of dock workers to their employment by a
parastatal organisation and the dynamics of bargaining
should be examined.

After the formation of the union, Sandy carefully
cultivated the friendship of certain politicians, including the Prime Minister himself, Albert Margai. As
union leader, Sandy was consulted over the plans to
establish the Port Authority as an autonomous public
corporation. He used the opportunity to secure the
absorption of daily-paid workers and a good number of
casual workers into the permanent work force, and to
negotiate new wage rates which came into effect in
1965. 91 Sandy appears to have been able to 'pull off'
these successes for three reasons. First, he flirted
with the SLPP at a time when most trade union leaders
supported the APC Opposition. Second, as a southerner,
he could claim affinity with the leaders of the SLPP
most of whom were southerners. Third, the government
itself was favourably disposed to an expansion of wage
employment in the public sector and an improvement in
its benefits. Sandy was therefore in a position to
enjoy the patronage of the government. He was nominated
by the Labour Department for a short course in
industrial relations in Europe in September/October
1964, and at the end of the year, M. I. Mansaray, then
Assistant Secretary, was nominated for a Soviet Union
scholarship.

As a Director on the Board, Sandy could take the
demands of the union to the highest policy-making body
of the Port Authority. In March 1965, he persuaded the
Board to meet a part of the medicare expenses of
dockers and, subject to certain conditions, to give
salary and wage advances for the purchase of consumer
durables. The management was also required to provide
protective clothing for dock workers exposed to dirt
and grease.92 Prior to the dispute within the union
over misuse of funds and the introduction of shift
work, it is clear that the union leadership had the
upper hand over the management as a result of Sandy's

influential contacts. The Panda inquiry heard evidence
to this effect:

> ...it emerged from evidence that
> management allowed the union to have
> an unusual say in its affairs which
> to all intents and purposes made the
> union a very powerful weapon against
> management...93

As a result of the IMF stabilisation programme
which came into effect in mid-1966, public corporations
were, as we have seen, required to make substantial cuts
in expenditure. Since redundancies would have been
politically unacceptable, the overtime system, which
was known to have been widely abused, was selected as
the area to be subjected to economy at the Port
Authority. The Panda Report noted that "...there were
employees in the port industry who earned over 200
percent of their salary as overtime".94 The Board
decided to begin the introduction of shift work with
the crane drivers as "...there were already sufficient
men employed to permit the introduction of shift
working without further recruitment or training of new
staff".95 The workers involved refused to cooperate
with the management:

> It is clear from the evidence that the
> question of the shift system for portal
> crane drivers was never discussed either
> by the executive of the union or with
> the workers concerned. It was only
> after management had given the green
> light to enforce the shift system, that
> Mr. Sandy discussed the question with
> the portal crane drivers and the leading
> hands. As it was to be expected, they
> were violently opposed to the proposal
> ...Mr. Sandy realised that with the
> introduction of the shift system the
> total emoluments of employees in the
> industry would be reduced...It is not
> understood, however, why Mr. Sandy
> should have acquiesced earlier in the
> decision of the Board to introduce
> the shift system.96

Recognising the unpopularity of shift work, over which
the rank and file had begun to take unofficial action
in the form of a work to rule, Sandy decided to make the

action official and accordingly issued the management
with a formal notice.97 However, the action of the
rank and file was also a protest against the Union
Secretary's leadership and, in particular, his initial
agreement to the introduction of shift work without
demanding any concessions as a quid pro quo. Management responded by 'spreading the word' throughout the
port that it had been prepared to negotiate but Sandy
had not pressed for negotiations.98 Sandy, who was by
then thoroughly discredited, informed the Minister of
Transport and Communications that the management, had
presented the issue of the introduction of shift work
as not negotiable, and that accordingly he was calling
a strike. The rank and file, however, were satisfied
with the assurances given by the management that shift
work would be negotiated. As it was the Union Secretary
who had failed to enter into proper negotiations in the
first instance, they were not prepared to go on strike
merely to 'save his face':

> ...some members of the union advised...
> (the executive)...to withdraw the
> notice of work to rule and enter into
> negotiations with management. This
> request fell on deaf ears and it was
> at this juncture that a splinter group
> of the union emerged which later became
> vocal throughout the crisis. By that
> time, the workers had resumed normal
> working time and with the work to rule
> being clearly flouted, the executive
> council proceeded to give a 21-day
> notice to go on strike. The serving
> of the notice was rejected by a
> majority of the workers...There was
> now a complete rift in the union and
> the workers had become frantic over
> the manner in which the executive...
> had controlled the affairs of the
> union and the unnecessary hazards to
> which they had been subjected.99

By this time, Sandy had become an embarrassment to the
government, which appointed an inquiry to examine the
dispute within the union as well as between the union
and the management.

     Sandy's Secretaryship is still remembered,
however, for its early achievements. It was noted
during conversations with dock workers that his method

of cultivating the friendship of politicians, whose
influence was used to alter the balance of power between
management and the union, was regarded with approval.
Dockers also spoke with regret of the fact that the
Secretaries who succeeded Sandy had not been able to
attain the same degree of influence.

As Union Secretary, M. I. Mansaray negotiated the
shift system with the Port Authority Mananagement.
Agreement was reached that a special shift allowance
would be paid. It was further agreed that meetings
between the management and the union to review differences would be held regularly.100 Over the years,
these meetings became the main forum for aggressive
bargaining between the union and the management.
Issues discussed ranged from the provision of small
increases in the wages of "workers who have passed a
trade test in their field of work..."101, to the provision of leave gratuity or holiday bonus to workers
entitled to paid holidays.102 It was a testimony to the
confidence of the union that, in December 1968, it put
forward a proposal that the Internal Audit Department
of the Port Authority should be made completely independent of management.103 The idea behind this
proposal was to facilitate the access of the union
leadership to documents which showed the correct financial position of the Port Authority, and which could be
used in bargaining. Some of the union demands were
accompained with strike threats as a tactical means of
manoeuvre during the negotiations. Strike notices were
issued in May 1968 and in January 1969, 104 but subsequently withdrawn. At the port JIC negotiations in
September 1969, Mansaray was able to secure a per diem
increase of 10 cents for all categories of workers.
Working hours were reduced from 48 to 45 hours a week
and a food allowance of 24 cents per shift (subject to
a minimum of four hours being worked in each shift was
introduced for casual cargo-handlers.105 Many dockers
readily admit that Mansaray was effective in bargaining
and could therefore deliver the goods. He was also
fortunate that his period in office coincided with a
period of buoyant revenue receipts at the port and the
regime of a competent managerial team. In 1971, the
year he was voted out of office, the Authority recorded
a profit of over Le1 million. It was after this period
that the diversion of funds by senior port officials
became an increasingly worrying--and, from the point of
view of lower-paid workers--damaging trend.

After the military interregnum and the return to

civilian rule Mansaray, like Sandy before him, cultivated the friendship of APC politicians and, in particular, D. F. Shears, the Minister of Transport and Communications (with responsibility to nominate Directors
of the Port Authority), and C. A. Kamara-Taylor,
Secretary-General of the APC, who as Minister of Lands,
Mines and Labour was in charge of the Labour Department.
In November 1968, Mansaray was nominated Director of
the Port Authority. In a lengthy interview interview,
Mansaray was forthright in elucidating his reasons for
cultivating the politicians:

> Even though the appointment of the
> Secretary-General as Director was
> not popular with our members, I was
> convinced that to be effective, I
> should be on the Board. Also it
> had happened before (i.e. Sandy
> had created the precedent). If I
> was not a Director, it will look
> as if I don't have prestige and
> contacts. Management like to snob
> we union people and carry on as if
> they are the only people in this
> world with education. But as
> Director, I sit on the Board
> whether they (management) like it
> or not and become an important
> personality as far as Port Authority
> is concerned.106

It is in the nature of clientelist politics that
prominent national politicians should seek to renew and
extend their network of clients. This was recognised
by union leaders like Mansaray who were prepared to
adopt tactics of aggressive bargaining to increase
wages, improve conditions, and defend gains at the work
place or at the industry level, but were also willing
to enter into clientelist relations in the political
arena as another channel (and an effective channel) to
reach the same objectives. Clientelist relationships
are also attractive for the material rewards that are
offered, such as the Directorship in Mansaray's case,
or the scholarship awarded to his assistant, O. B.
Conteh, in 1969. This strategy, however, was not
without risks. At the very least, it compromised the
independence of union leaders to criticise (and to
encourage union members to criticise) the performance
and the policies of the regime publicly. This failure
was (as we shall see in the next chapter) shared with

other union leaders in the labour movement.

These strategies of bargaining continued to be
adopted during O. B. Conteh's Secretaryship. In the
face of an attempt in 1972 by the management of the
Port Authority to introduce comprehensive terms of
conditions of service for all workers in its employ,
for instance, Conteh skillfully employed his
clientelist relations to force the maximum number of
concessions from the management. Given the absence of
comprehensive terms of employment, the management had
grown to believe that the union had exploited the
resulting state of affairs by forcing concessions--via
patron-clientelism as well as with threats of strike
action--vis a vis working conditions. By setting out
the conditions of service as part of the contract of
employment of each worker, the management hoped that
the union would become limited to bargaining at the
trade group council periodic wage reviews. It was
recognised by the union executive that comprehensive
terms of employment would greatly circumscribe the
leverage which the union had hitherto exercised. In
October 1972, when Conteh was abroad with another union
official, the management issued the service booklets to
workers, who were requested to sign them. The
Assistant Secretary, J.T. Mahoi, acting as Secretary,
wrote to the General Manager of the Authority to
protest:

> ...the whole executive council of the
> union at its emergency meeting held
> yesterday, has authorised me to again
> convey the union's stand on the issue
> of these conditions of service. Accord-
> ingly, all union members in the Authority
> have been asked NOT to complete the forms
> accompanying the booklet containing the
> conditions of service until further
> notice. A copy of the circular is
> attached. In the name of industrial
> peace and goodwill, the union is asking
> management to suspend the issuing of
> these booklets to employees until the
> President and Secretary-General return
> from an overseas tour...We believe that
> by doing so an explosive situation
> could be avoided.107

As it had always been the strategy of the union to
acquaint influential politicians with the details of

171

difficulties with the management, this letter was copied to the Minister of Transport and Communications and to the Minister of Labour. The Management for its part was insistent that:

> ...there had never been any compre-
> hensive conditions of service for
> employees of this Authority which
> is the bed-rock of contract whereby
> workers become acquainted with the
> terms and conditions governing their
> employment and safe-guarding their
> interests. It is therefore overdue
> for positive action to be taken in
> this direction as the present
> conditions of service provide these
> vital ingredients which are nece-
> ssary in any industrial set up.108

This letter was also copied to the Ministers. On Conteh's return from abroad, the matter was again taken up with management which insisted that the conditions could not be negotiated. The management only relented when the Minister of Transport and Communications inter- vened.109 Conteh laid down no less than twenty-six amendments.110 Most of these were eventually accepted and included as a supplement to the conditions. It is clear that shop stewards on the union executive fully supported the strategy of involving the two ministers in the dispute.111

Conteh's personal stature and influence within the labour movement had grown considerably since assuming office as Union Secretary. He represented the union on the executive of the Labour Congress and in October 1973, he was asked to act as Secretary of Congress during the absence of the substantive Secretary, George Palmer, from the 20th November to the 10th December.112 A year later, in December 1974, Conteh was voted First Deputy Secretary of Congress.113

Another preoccupation of the union around this was with the changing technology in cargo-handling. During the seventies, shipping companies increasingly adopted the containerised method of cargo movement. Its many advantages include the reduction of the time a ship spends at port since containers enable great quantities of cargo to be handled at the same time. Containerisa- tion, however, reduces the demand for cargo handling la- bour since special equipment is used to move containers.

172

Throughout the seventies, Conteh expended considerable
energy in persuading management to introduce a 'supple-
mentation of earnings' scheme for casual labourers (his
'constituency' in the internal politics of the union)
threatened with loss of earnings as a result of contain-
erisation. This campaign did not meet with much
success. The present management of the Port Authority
holds the view that "...since Sierra Leone is at the
receiving end of the container revolution, there is not
much that can be done to save jobs in the longer
term".114 It has, however, been the strategy of management to generate more business at the port by making
Freetown an important centre for the transhipment of
cargo. At the first meeting between union representatives and the team of consultants (to whom the management of the port was subcontracted following the financial collapse of the Authority, the publication of the
Forster Commission Report and the dissolution of the
Board of Directors), Conteh was quick to make his
anxieties over the new technology known:

> Mr. Osman Conteh, Secretary-General
> of the union introduced individually
> the entire body of representatives to
> management...He pledged the coopera-
> tion of the executive to the new man-
> agement from whom in return he expec-
> ted the continued realisation of the
> basic conditions of service which
> workers should enjoy...and for workers
> who become unemployed through the
> application of advanced technology,
> the introduction of a supplementation of
> earnings scheme...He asked that these
> processes be not unduly delayed.115

Although Conteh failed in his attempt to become
Secretary of Congress at the end of 1977, he had become
an important figure in the labour movement in his own
right. Dock workers have pointed out, however, that
his kinsman relationship with Formeh Kamara, Minister
of Transport and Communications from July 1975 to June
1978 when he became Minister of Labour, considerably
'helped along' his career in the labour movement. Be
that as it may, it is clear that Conteh was never
impeded by any lack of self-confidence in his bargaining with management. The Forster Commission was
evidently impressed with his resolute determination to
defend the interest of dockers in bargaining with
management.116 During the dispute between Conteh and

the union executive however, the Minister did intervene,
initially to prevent his dismissal, and later to insist
that the union membership must ratify the decisions of
the executive.

The Internal Dynamics of the Dock Workers' Union: Some
Conclusions

        Two main conclusions may be drawn from this account
of the responses of dockers to their employment by a
parastatal organisation, and the structure of accountability within the union. First, dockers, through
their union leadership are prepared to use the usual
channels of management--union contact in bargaining,
or in the frequent review of the multitude of problems
inherent in any organisation with relatively
large-scale employment, as well as the channels
afforded by patron-clientelist accommodation of the
union leadership by prominent national politicians.
Individually or through their union leadership, and via
patron-clientelist accommodation, dock workers have also
been prepared to maintain and defend the many irregular-
ities--tolerated in a public enterprise--being practiced, such as dishonest claims for overtime payment,
overmanning, low productivity, the use of material and
equipment belonging to the Port Authority in private
contracts in the informal sector, etc., as documented by
the Forster Commission. These strategies and their
substantive consequences circumscribed the extent to
which the Port Authority operated as a typical capitalist enterprise.

        Second, it is clear that the main conflicts within
the union have centred on the effectiveness of its
leadership in bargaining with management, defending
gains, or on their 'honesty'. After extended conversations with dock workers, there should be no doubt that
they resented and increasingly became paranoiac over
the appointment of successive Union Secretaries as
Directors on the Board of the Port Authority, even going
to the extent, in 1972, of insisting that Directors'
fees must in principle be paid into the union account,
and reimbursing the Secretary with the same amount.
But union leaders, generally having an inferior level
of education than management, correctly perceived that
a Directorship (or an appointment at the national
labour centre) can enhance their status, and hence
their effectiveness in bargaining with management.
In insisting, however, that the funds from the

174

accumulating balances of the union must not be 'stolen',
skilled workers, especially, have placed a high premium
on the honesty of the leadership. To the extent that
this became a problem, it reflects the absence of any
commitment to radical political objectives of the rank
and file and the leadership alike. Throughout the
history of the union, it was never envisaged that the
union's substantial balances could be used to sustain
workers in a protracted strike action, or to further
clearly defined political objectives. Trade unions in
post-colonial Sierra Leone have (as we shall see in the
next chapter) shown little evidence of political radicalism and appear to be oriented towards aggressive
bargaining at the work place, displaying a concern with
more parochial issues, and an 'economism' so much
derided by Lenin. It is clear that no union leader,
Wallace-Johnson included, has been able to sustain the
interest of workers in mobilising for the furtherance
of radical political objectives. It is significant
that the two major strikes in the country's history
(February 1955 and August/September 1981) occurred
during periods when there had been an erosion in the
value of real incomes and a shortage of rice, the
nation's staple food. During negotiations to facilitate the representation by the Dock Workers' Union of
workers engaged in the handling of produce at the
Produce Marketing Board, M. I. Mansaray clearly spelt
out the orientation of the union, and his ideology on
trade union organisation:

> Mr. Mansaray then addressed the
> meeting...he said that the union
> had the same aims as the employers:
> these call for the maintenance of
> good discipline, promotion of
> better understanding between
> employers and employees leading
> to the maximisation of profits,
> and ultimately resulting in general
> prosperity, increased earnings and
> better conditions for all concerned.117

The 'accommodation' of lower-paid workers in parastatal organisations and their involvement in the various
irregularities--politically acceptable in public enter-
prises--does not necessarily imply that they are unpro-
ductive and unexploited. At the Port Authority, the
productivity of dock workers is quite low (as a result
of overmanning and the widespread use of casual labour),
but, as argued earlier, at the very least, dock workers

make a value-added contribution in the handling of cargo
and related activities. In spite of the dockers' involvement in graft, the requirement that the Authority must
be commercially viable has resulted in the conceptuali-
sation of wages as a 'cost of production', and subjected accordingly to measures of economy. Morever, in
the day-to-day administration of the enterprise, the
professional management employ a variety of labour
control systems designed to minimise their perception
of the adequacy of the worker in the performance of his
tasks, and in so doing, reduce the autonomy of the
worker. The rise of professional management in work
organisations, the choice of technology, the adoption
of labour control strategies, have resulted in what
Braverman has called the 'degredation of work'.118

Furthermore, in the pursuit of daily work activities at the port organisation, dockers encounter a
managerial power structure which seeks to minimise the
uncertainties arising out of the work process, and in
so doing, subjects them to intense supervision as well
as finding new ways to increase the rationalisation of
work tasks. Moreover, the rules which govern behaviour
at the enterprise (such as the amount of time to be
allowed for breaks) reflects the prevailing balance of
power between management and lower-paid workers.
Dockers particularly resented the policy of the Port
Authority which allowed supervisors and senior management and their families to use the medicare facilities
at the port, but which denied them the same privilege.
The power structure within the port organisation, as
perceived by the docker, makes it clear to him that, in
addition to his involvement in clientelist political
relationships, he needs a trade union to protect his
interests at the work place. When asked the purpose of
joining the union, dockers frequently remarked that the
union is 'like a lawyer'. During periodic wage reviews,
or during the making of the rules of the work place, the
union presents the workers' case. Indeed, this was the
reasoning of the artisans and clerks who master-minded
the formation of the Dock Workers' Union in 1963.

The absence of radical political pursuits in the
actions and ideological orientations of the rank and
file as well as the leadership of the union, does not
necessarily suggest that dock workers constitute a
'labour aristocracy'. The poverty and squalor of their
city life alone (as was shown in Chapter 5) ruled out
the entertainment of such notions. Moreover, lower-paid
workers in Sierra Leone are not even the most direct

beneficiaries of the appropriation of the resources of the state by the political kleptocracy. Indeed, there is evidence of an attitude of antipathy towards corrupt politicians and officials (and even towards their own union leadership) amongst lower-paid workers, thus confirming the observation of Melson and Wolpe that clientelist relationships inherent in communalism are essentially opportunistic.119 At the same time, however, it is clear that traditionally-held beliefs mediate the responses of such workers to their situation of relative poverty. For instance, when asked to explain the origins of inequality in Sierra Leone, dock workers often expressed a fatalism, couched in religious terminology, and best captured perhaps by the Temne expression, <u>sababun</u>, meaning, one's lot in life.

CHAPTER 7

THE RESPONSES OF ORGANISED LABOUR TO POLITICS

IN THE POST-COLONIAL STATE

The union leadership of the dock workers has inevitably been constrained in its strategy and deci- sions by the policy and orientation of the trade union movement in Sierra Leone as a whole. Having located this study in its proper historical perspective, having argued and documented the thesis that the extent to which a public corporation in the post-colonial state operates as a typical capitalist enterprise is circum- scribed by the system of political patronage, corruption and graft, and having assessed the responses of the dockers and the more general sociological characteris- tics they exhibit, this final chapter situates their trade union behaviour in the context of the nature and orientation of the labour movement in post-colonial Sierra Leone. The discussion which follows therefore focuses on the political posture of the labour movement (and assesses the extent to which it has confronted successive governments over major policy issues) and on its own internal dynamics during the two decades of independence.

Main Trends in Labour Politics in the First Decade of Independence

With the SLPP as the party of government, Sierra Leone became an independent state within the British Commonwealth on 27th April 1961. In the period between the constitutional talks in London and the first elections held on the basis of universal suffrage in Sierra Leone, i.e., between August 1960 and May 1962, new political realignments became apparent. These resulted in divisions (over questions of political strategy) within the labour movement. The realignments began with the formation of the All People's Congress (APC) by Siaka Stevens, who had broken ranks with the United National Front (UNF), the coalition of all parties formed under the leadership of the SLPP to nego- tiate the administrative arrangements for the transfer of power from the British. Having lost his seat as an MP following the 1957 elections, and having unsuccess- fully advocated 'elections before independence', Stevens

left the UNF apparently over concessions made to the
British for the continued use of Freetown as a naval
base and other defence purposes. Refusing to sign the
constitutional and independence instruments, Stevens
flew back to Freetown and floated the idea of a populist political party in opposition to the SLPP-dominated
UNF. A former political associate of Stevens who was
also at the conference has written:

> Stevens found the courage to assume
> this posture because he was fully
> aware that he stood little chance
> of personally deriving much advan-
> tage from the arrangements of the
> UNF. The plum of a cabinet
> portfolio as he might have seen
> it was beyond his grasp...whatever
> his real motives, Siaka Stevens...
> announced in September 1960...the
> creation of a new political party
> under his leadership, the APC.1

In floating the idea of the formation of a new party
with radical pretensions, Stevens was fully alive to the
possibilities of deriving a solid base of support from
various groups disenchanted with nine years of SLPP
rule. The constituency to which they hoped to appeal
included liberal intellectuals (and especially faculty
members of Fourah Bay College) who deplored the elitist
nature of the transfer of power and, more especially,
the reliance of the SLPP on a clientele of Big Men and
chiefs throughout the country for its power base; at
the local level lower-paid workers who, during the
early sixties registered their discontent in a series of
strikes, mainly over issues of work place industrial
relations; peasant farmers of the North, ever resentful
of their chiefs who, as APC organisers were quick to
point out, had allowed themselves to be incorporated
into the southern-dominated SLPP; and the people of Kono
amongst whom a communally-based anti-elitist political
organisation had flourished for many years. This was
essentially the same constituency as that to which the
UPP had appealed in 1957 with some degree of success.
By the end of 1961, however, only five MPs considered
themselves as part of the opposition in parliament:
two Kono MPs representing the KPM; two UPP MPs; and
Wallace-Johnson who had left the UPP to become the sole
voice of the APC in parliament. He was detained along
with Stevens and other APC organisers during the independence celebrations.

As was expected, several trade unionists supported
the APC, the most influential being H. N. Georgestone.
He had been most impressed with the stated objectives
of APC organisers and had grown to believe--given the
communal support of the new party in the North and in
Kono--that its prospects of success and of becoming a
radical force in Sierra Leone politics was promising.2
Marcus Grant, who was preparing his candidature as an
'independent' in the general elections of May 1962, did
not express support for Stevens and the APC. Recalling
Stevens' earlier career as a member of the Margai
ministry of 1951-57 and, in particular, their confrontation during the 1955 strike, he has argued:

> I cannot accept that the APC was the
> party of the working-class. Its
> leader came to prominence through the
> trade union movement; it is not
> necessarily working-class. And my
> views are shown to be correct by
> recent history.3

Stevens himself now regards the formation of the APC as
having been motivated by nationalist aspirations, by
the need to assert control over the mining companies,
and as an attempt to "open up the country and provide
the leadership for the aspirations of the masses".4
Wallace-Johnson shared this analysis and was until his
death in 1965 a fully paid-up member and activist of the
APC.

In the run-up to the elections of 1962, many union
leaders openly campaigned for the APC and encouraged
their members and families to vote for the party. The
Mine Workers' Union, whose founding Secretary was the
APC leader, played a prominent role, campaigning for the
APC in the mining centres of Lunsar-Pepel in the North,
Moyamba in the South, and Kenema and Kono in the
South-east. In Freetown itself, where most of the
unions were concentrated, trade union officials address-
ed APC rallies. Prominent among them were H. N.
Georgestone (the part-time Secretary of the national
centre, the Council of Labour) and A. O. Walker of the
Transport and General Workers' Union, Basco George and
George Palmer of the Clerical, Mercantile and General
Workers' Union, A. W. Hassan of the Motor Drivers'
Union, A. Bai Conteh of the Artisans and Allied Workers'
Union, P. S. Mammah of the Railway Workers' Union, and
Amos Sawyerr of the Articled Seamen's Union.5 It is
significant that each of these union officials origi-

nated either from Freetown or from the North.

The results of the 1962 elections clearly revealed not only that the SLPP was faced with a formidable opposition for the first time, but also that the old Freetown-upcountry cleavage had been replaced by a new ethnic and regional cleavage between the Mende south and south-east and the Temne north. The APC concentrated its campaign in the North and in the Greater Freetown area. It won 12 of the 19 northern seats and 4 of 12 seats in Freetown and its evirons. It failed to win any seats in the South and South-east. The SLPP on the other hand won most of these seats, five of the northern seats, and five seats in the Greater Freetown area. The Kono-based KPM (an ally of the APC) won all four Kono seats.6 Reflecting on these results, Cartwright observes that the APC combined an anti-chief appeal with a clear sectional base in the North:

> (Stevens apart)...The APC leaders and members of parliament constituted a 'new class' entering the political elite for the first time. Relative to the SLPP oligarchy, the APC members came from lower status occupations, had more limited formal education, were younger, and had fewer links with traditional ruling families. They did not articulate any coherent set of beliefs that could be called a radical ideology, but they did have rather strong feelings about the existing social structure, and in particular about the abuses they felt the chiefs were able to perpetrate against their people...this...served to some extent to innoculate them against the ever present temptation to move en masse to the government side...7

The SLPP, however, failed to win an overall majority, the balance of power being held by independent MPs. These MPs, including Marcus Grant who won a seat in the Freetown suburb of Waterloo, were induced to join the SLPP. Approaches were also made to APC MPs, two of whom 'crossed the floor' to the SLPP side a few months after the elections. Three of the four Kono MPs declared themselves members of the SLPP in July 1963.

Marcus Grant's 'defection' to the ranks of the
SLPP, as it was regarded by his colleagues in the
labour movement, precipitated a crisis. A large
section of the rank and file of his union, the Artisans
and Allied Workers' Union, proceeded to remove him from
the leadership:

> Bai Conteh (the Assistant Secretary),
> the shop stewards and myself (Regional
> Secretary at Bo, southern province),
> could never understand why Pa Marcus
> did that. He knew that the rank and
> file were solidly for the APC. He
> could have even remained independent.
> It was a stab in the back, so it was
> decided that he should go. Some of
> the things which we had overlooked in
> his leadership were exposed.8

At the national centre, the Council of Labour,
Georgestone as Secretary, demanded his explusion.9
Anticipating that this would be carried out, Grant and
two union Secretaries who supported his decision to
join the SLPP resigned their affiliation to the Council
and formed a rival centre, the Federation of Labour.10
Grant himself has explained that it was his electoral
constituency which recommended that he supported the
SLPP in parliament. His constituency supporters presumably calculated that they would receive favourable
consideration of applications for development grants
and other benefits that normally went with support for
the ruling regime. The Artisans' Union, however,
demanded his resignation. As an MP of the ruling
party, he was supported by influential Cabinet Ministers
and a sympathetic Labour Department.11 In 1965,
however, following a long campaign against him by union
officials and the rank and file, Grant resigned:

> Allegations were made against me,
> even though I had been with them for
> 26 years as founder and organiser of
> that union.12

In 1963, four new unions, including the Dock
Workers' Union, had joined the Council of Labour,
bringing the total number of affiliated members to
19,441 as compared with 14,191 in the Federation of
Labour. (See Table 7.1). Encouraged by the Minister
with responsibility for the department, Labour officials attempted to bring the two sides back together.

TABLE 7.1

Registered Trade Unions and Affiliations December 1963

COUNCIL OF LABOUR		FEDERATION OF LABOUR	
UNION	NO. OF MEMBERS	UNION	NO. OF MEMBERS
Railway Workers' Union	1,785	Artisans and Allied Workers' Union*	7,612
Mine Workers' Union	5,500	Maritime and Waterfront Workers' Union	5,600
Clerical, Mercantile, and General Workers' Union	3,259	Sherbro Amalgamated Workers' Union	979
Transport and General Workers' Union	1,606		
General Union of Construction Workers	800		
Articled Seamen's Union	960		
Motor Drivers' Union	1,500		
Dock Workers' Union	2,649		
TOTAL	19,441		14,191

* The Artisans' Union rejoined the Council of Labour after Marcus Grant was ousted from the leadership.
SOURCE: Labour Department, Annual Report 1963.

184

This was for the obvious reason that SLPP leaders
concerned with the growing momentum of the APC, realised
that it was politically inept for a large section of the
labour movement to be on the side of the Opposition.13
Following Albert Margai's assumption of the Premiership
in 1964, he personally intervened to persuade Grant as
Secretary of the Federation and Georgestone as Secretary
of the Council to form one national centre which,
presumably, could be more controlled by the government.

The Brussels-based International Confederation of
Free Trade Unions (ICFTU) was also concerned to bring
about a settlement to the dispute. From the point of
view of ICFTU officials, the numerical strength of the
unions in Sierra Leone being relatively small, the
logical strategy for local trade unionists would be to
remain united in one national centre in order to consolidate their resources and foster the development of
trade unionism.14 Such reasoning, of course, did not
take account of local political realities. The ICFTU
also found it expedient to concentrate its financial
(and other) assistance on one union centre, rather than
duplicate such hand-outs between small rival centres.
After much persuasion by ICFTU officials, the two
factions finally came together in 1966. As E. T. Kamara
has pointed out, however, this was only made possible
by the fact that Marcus Grant had been ousted from the
leadership of the Artisans' Union. Although he had
taken over the Secretaryship of the Maritime and Waterfront Workers' Union (following the death of its Secretary, George Thomas), this union, with a membership of
casual stevedore workers, was far less influential than
the former union. The new national centre was named the
Sierra Leone Labour Congress. Marcus Grant and
Georgestone agreed to work under E. T. Kamara, who
became the part-time Secretary of Congress.15

Regarding the tendency for the fragmentation of the
labour movement and the setting up of rival national
centres, a Labour Department official has perceptively
commented:

> Splits (within the labour movement)
> always take the same pattern. One
> faction overtly supports the govern-
> ment; another wants to hold back.
> They split...(but) they all come
> back to government to beg favours...
> To set up a national union centre
> was too easy in this country.

> 1. You print your letter heads.
> 2. You stick a sign on your office
> door. 3. You obtain a cable
> address. 4. You inform fraternal
> organisations the world over that
> you represent so many thousands (of
> workers). That's all. You don't
> need to worry about salaries,
> organisation, and so on, because
> you are all part-time officials
> in the centre, and full-time in
> your union.16

The four-year rift in the labour movement was as much
as consequence of disagreements over political strategy
as of personality differences. Georgestone and Grant
both belonged to that generation of union leaders who
spent their formative years in the Youth League. They
had both been the standard bearers of the League during
the period of decolonisation. While Grant appears to
have reached an understanding of the realities of patronage and political influence in the post-colonial
state, however, Georgestone appears to have preferred
to remain 'uncontaminated'. Grant could not bring
himself to believe, quite rightly as it turned out, that
the APC could possibly become a radical political force.
From this point of view, union leaders would be wise to
seek some kind of accommodation with the party in power.
Several union leaders in fact adopted this strategy
while remaining affiliated to the Council of Labour.
Jack Sandy, the Secretary of the Dock Workers' Union,
for instance, carefully cultivated the friendship of
leading SLPP politicians and, as we have seen, was
'rewarded' with a Directorship of the Port Authority in
January 1965 (see Chapter 5). It has been established
that even the Mine Workers' Union exploited the patronage of the SLPP during disputes with the management of
the mining companies and during wage negotiations.17

   The attempt to introduce a one-party state stemmed
from the realisation of SLPP leaders of the potential
threat posed by the APC. Ironically, when the Bill
approving the principle of a one-party state was voted
on in parliament, Stevens and his group of APC MPs
abstained. Cartwright comments:

> The most striking feature of the
> debate was the lack of criticism
> by the All People's Congress of
> the principle of a one-party

system...This failure of the APC
leaders to argue for the desirability
of an organised Opposition was no
momentary aberration. Nowhere in the
columns of We Yone (the party newspaper)
up to this time had there been a
rejection on principle of the one-party
state; all its arguments had been
concentrated on the unrepresentativeness
of Sir Albert and the SLPP. Stevens
himself some months earlier had said
that it was only the SLPP's weakness
that disqualified it from seeking a
one-party system.18

Georgestone, in his capacity as Secretary of the Transport and General Workers' Union, joined other APC
supporters in making a successful application for a
supreme court injunction to prevent the meeting of a
committee set up to work out the details of a constitution for the one party state.19 Georgestone therefore continued to uphold what he saw as the anti-autho-
ritarian traditions of the Youth League. Younger labour
leaders, on the other hand, displayed remarkably agile
footwork in mobilising support for the APC, in
exploiting the patronage of the SLPP, and at the same
time in articulating the demands of their members,
especially after 1966 when the stabilisation programme
of the IMF imposed some hardship on lower-paid workers.

Union leaders played an important role in the 1967
election campaign, addressing APC rallies and ensuring
that workers and their families turned up to vote on
election day.20 The Mine Workers' Union was
particularly influential in mining constituencies where
its officials campaigned for the APC. In the mining
constituencies of the South and South-east where the
party failed to win seats, its vote was still appre-
ciably high.21 The APC narrowly won an election which
revealed the importance of the growing regional cleavage
as the basis of the division between the two parties.
The SLPP won only three seats outside its southern and
south-eastern strongholds: one in the North, and two
in Kono. The APC won all the remaining northern and
Kono seats, and all seats in the western area of
Freetown and its environs. It is evident that a coalition of northern ethnic groups, supporters of the Kono
movement, the Krios, urban workers and the liberal
intellectuals of Freetown, swept the APC to electoral
victory. The intervention of the army prevented

the party from taking office for a year.22

This account of the history and dynamics of union-government relations should not obscure the fact that considerations of political strategy were not the only concerns of the union leadership. Serious and genuine attempts were also being made to consolidate and develop trade unionism in the country. Once the two factions of the labour movement had been brought together, the ICFTU concentrated its assistance on the new Labour Congress. The priority area was to be trade union education: the training of shop stewards and union officials in bargaining procedures and trade union practices. E. T. Kamara was asked to assess training needs in Sierra Leone:

> Trade union sponsored education
> programme for workers in Sierra
> Leone is comparatively recently
> gaining root. No educational
> programme was embarked upon either
> by the Council of Labour or the
> Federation of Labour until they
> were replaced by the Labour
> Congress...From this dry-as-dust
> background, the Congress is
> building up an educational
> programme in coordination with
> individual trade union programmes
> and the Sierra Leone Workers'
> Educational Association...(which)
> ...was formed in 1963 with the
> help of an International Labour
> Organisation expert.23

In cooperation with the ICFTU and other interested parties, the Labour Congress ran a series of courses in labour education from 1967 in the main areas of large-scale employment throughout the country. Individual unions also embarked on campaigns to increase member-ship; in the case of the Dock Workers' Union, labourers at the Produce Marketing Board were organised for the first time.

The relationship between labour leaders and the military junta of 1967-68 was fundamentally different from the relationship with civilian politicians. Within a few days of taking office, Andrew Juxon-Smith, the Chairman of the National Reformation Council, made it clear that his mission was to rescue the country from

political and moral decay. Political patronage as
practiced by civilian politicians and 'corruption' in
official circles were no longer to be tolerated. This
meant that neither the union leaders nor the employers
could seek the assistance of members of the government
and other important officials to influence the outcome
of bargaining as before. All leading trade unionists
were invited to meet the Chairman, who urged them to
show restraint in wage demands. Marcus Grant, who lost
his seat as an SLPP candidate in the elections, was a
member of the delegation, but Georgestone, who personally never recognised the junta, declined the invita-
tion.24 As part of its economic strategy, the junta
encouraged the newly created Employers' Federation and
the Labour Congress to sign a special 'code of conduct'
designed to reduce the likelihood of strike action.
In spite of the code, strike statistics for 1967 and
1968 show significant increases in man days lost and
number of workers involved. The issues were mainly
concerned with working conditions and work place
industrial relations.25

    The relationship between labour leaders and the
junta was evidently strained by the IMF austerity
measures which the NRC implemented with much enthusiasm.
In his 1967 budget statement, Colonel Juxon-Smith went
out of his way to dispel notions, especially current
among labour leaders, that the IMF was running the
country or that it was a tool of the imperialist powers:

> I should like to record our sincere
> debt of gratitude to the IMF for
> coming to our rescue in time...I
> wish to reassure my countrymen
> that Fund visitation is neither a
> sign of national failure nor an
> abrogation of national sovereignty.
> Rather, it is a sign of our deter-
> mination to seek and implement
> sound economic policies. It is
> an indication to interested
> observers that we recognise our
> difficulties and with international
> support we are resolved to overcome
> them.26

The deflationary impact of the budget resulted in
redundancies both in the public and private sectors of
the economy. The government wages bill was reduced by
a significant proportion:

The total for personal emoluments for
1967/68 is Le9,919,000 compared with
Le10,555,500 in 1966/67, a decrease of
6.03 percent.27

E. T. Kamara has described the reaction of labour
leaders to the NRC's economic policies:

> We challenged the NRC on these points.
> They said that the outgoing SLPP
> government had ruined the economy and
> therefore there was no alternative
> but to reduce employment in the public
> sector. Employers (in the private
> sector) were also given a free hand to
> make redundancies. When a government
> practices redundancies as its policy,
> workers lose their rights. Trade
> unions become weak...The NRC men were
> hypocrites. They made the rest of us
> suffer, but they were enjoying.28

As the Labour Congress was represented on the largely
civilian NRC Advisory Committee, it was decided that a
detailed memorandum, stating the dissatisfaction of the
labour movement with the regime's economic policies, be
forwarded to the committee. According to the memorandum:

> Unemployment is the present day
> problem...and the future does not
> look very bright due to probable
> redundancies in some corporations...
> No one is against these measures
> (the economic strategy) but those
> concerned, i.e., Employers' Federa-
> tion, Labour Congress, and the
> Department of Labour should of
> necessity be consulted when it
> is proposed to take decisions on
> this matter of unemployment of
> such magnitude.29

The statement also drew attention to government figures
on employment, 7,294 in 1967, which were "unreliable in
view of the fact that most of the unemployed...are unre-
gistered".30

One suspects that the suggestion for meetings of
employers, labour leaders, and Labour Department

190

officials, was an attempt to return to the status quo ante military intervention when trade unionists and employers could use informal means to influence the outcome of bargaining or government policy. Moreover, the NRC member with responsibility for the Labour Department, Mr. Alpha Kamara, a senior police officer, was known to be more flexible with regard to the economic strategy than some of the military members of the junta. The Chairman of the NRC, who was in charge of financial and economic matters, stuck to his guns. The budget proposals were implemented.

The basis of the NRC's power was its military might. It largely ignored the sullen resentment of the coalition which had provided the APC with electoral victory, though the various commissions of inquiry which were set up to investigate the activities of the Margai regime were popular among this group. The economic policies to which the Chairman (with what must have been a sense of messianism) committed the junta, the documentation of the corrupt practices of the previous regime, was partly an attempt to justify the intervention of the NRC. In so far as the junta was to conduct this 'house cleaning' exercise for a limited period, it commanded the support of the rank and file of the security forces, and secured the grudging (or resigned) acceptance of the civilian population. However, when the NRC (and especially the Chairman) wavered over the question of the return to civilian rule, its support among the lower ranks of the military crumbled. In April 1968, junior officers of the army ejected the junta from power and installed Siaka Stevens and the APC in government.

It was with some relief that the leaders of organised labour welcomed the new APC regime. Four days after Siaka Stevens' appointment as Prime Minister, the Congress executive presented a congratulatory message to him in which it was made clear that they anticipated a special realtionship with the government:

> In his address, Mr. Caramba-Coker (President of Congress) commented on Dr. Stevens' trade union links and former career as a trade unionist. "We, as workers' representatives...feel happy and proud beyond measure that we have our own man at the helm of affairs in this

country with whom we can confer and
consult.31

The appointment by Stevens of C. A. Kamara-Taylor as
Minister of Land, Mines, and Labour was welcomed by
Congress. As a former employee in the clerical grades
of the UAC, Kamara-Taylor had worked alongside George
Palmer of the Clerical Union with whom he had maintained
a close friendship. It is further evident that labour
leaders greeted the assumption of office by the APC with
much euphoria and great expectations. On the 24th May
1968, "thousands of workers and trade unionist from all
over the country defied torrential rain to rally in
honour of Prime Minister Stevens...(who) told them that
govenment would consider ways to provide more low-cost
housing for low-income workers and that measures to
control the price of rice would be announced shortly...
E. T. Kamara, Secretary General...of...Congress assured
the Prime Minister and Government of their cooperation
in the tasks that lay ahead".32 On the 7th of July,
Stevens was crowned 'chief motor driver' by the Motor
Drivers' Union. At the ceremony, the Secretary of the
Union asserted that they hoped to be government's
"comrade-in-arms against want, disease, oppression, and
inequality".33

While the APC was formally committed to the reform
of the institution of chieftaincy and to effect a redistribution of income through reformist social and
economic policies, the logic of its political stragegy
once in office--to reduce the numerical strength of the
Opposition in parliament, to create, maintain, and
extend its own network of clientele via political
patronage, and to reward loyalty to the regime and in
particular its leader--conflicted in several respects
with the higher ideals which had surrounded the formation of the party and which had sustained it during the
difficult years in Opposition. Indeed, the APC leadership had served notice of this political strategy by
its refusal to criticise the principle of a one-party
state. Labour leaders, and the leaders of the coalition of interest groups which supported the APC in
Opposition, failed to sustain an interest in, or to
enter into a debate on, how the principles of reform on
which they had campaigned for the APC could be translated into successful policies. Leaders of these
groups readily accepted the ambassadorships and other
appointments offered by the APC. Individual trade union
leaders also reached their own 'accommodation' with the
new regime. At the Port Authority, M. I. Mansaray, the

Secretary of the Dock Workers' Union, was able to
persuade the Minister of Transport and Communications to
make him a Director on the Board, contrary to the recommendations of The Panda Report. In April 1969, E. T.
Kamara, the Secretary of the Mine Workers' Union and
part-time Secretary of the Labour Congress, resigned
from the labour movement to pursue a course in management studies in Britain, and was later to become head of
administration at the APC national headquarters.

In their concern with the more economistic and
parochial issues relating to the practice of trade
unionism (to effect marginal increases in wages and to
secure marginal improvements in working conditions),
labour leaders also failed to address the more important
questions relating to the sources of inequality, or the
nature of power and authority in the post-colonial
state. It was not until an unprecedented bout of infla-
ion had by the mid-1970s considerably eroded the real
value of wages (and after the hopes raised by the coming
to power of the APC had been dashed), that union
leaders began to address themselves to these crucial
issues. On the other hand, in view of the historical
development of the practice of trade unionism in Sierra
Leone, and in view of the political conditions associated with neo-patrimonal leadership, it is perhaps under-
standable (if not justifiable) that union leaders should
have been concerned to reach an 'accommodation' with the
regime and to exploit the patronage of the politicians
for personal advancement. It could also perhaps be
argued that it was only through such an accommodation
that it was possible to secure and defend gains at the
work place. Apart from the adoption of these tactics
of bargaining, some labour leaders did also demonstrate
a genuine commitment to the development and consolidation of trade unionism. The success of these attempts
to create a viable labour movement was invaluable
during the confrontation with the APC regime in the
late seventies. The kind of trade unionism consolidated during the early years of APC rule, however, did
not involve any very strong or consistent assertion of
the right and duty of the labour movement leadership to
criticise government policy and performance publicly.
In a sense, the silence of these leaders was bought.

The main priorities, then, of union leaders at the
beginning of APC rule were to strengthen the viability
of the movement and to secure and defend gains at the
work place. In November 1968, E. T. Kamara proposed
the centralisation of all trade unions into one single

193

national union having a similar organisational structure
to that of the Israeli Histradut.34 The reasoning
behind the proposals was that individual unions had
acquired (via members' subcriptions) the financial
resources to maintain viable organisations with
full-time officials, office accommodation etc., while
the national centre was poorly organised. By coming
together into one national union, the resources of all
unions would be concentrated in the national centre. It
was envisaged that 'departments' within the national
union centre would be in charge of the various areas of
trade union activity, such as the docks, the mines,
clerical workers, artisans, etc. A committee of
Congress was eventually formed to examine the issue. In
its four-point recommendation, the committee ignored
the idea of a Histradut-like national centre, but made
suggestions for the strengthening of Congress:

> That Congress persuade small unions
> of like interest to merge and form
> one strong unit;...that Congress
> endeavours to get the check-off
> system on a national basis...and
> thirty percent of all union dues
> collected at source be paid to
> Congress;...that...a full-time paid
> Secretary be employed with two
> assistants and a clerk-typist;...
> that a campaign be launched for the
> following: The setting up of an
> industrial relations charter...to
> serve as a modus operandi for the
> labour movement...the encouragement
> of trade union education.35

In view of the rejection of the idea of a national
union, one is led to suspect that individual union
leaders wished to preserve their autonomy within a
strong national centre. The suggestions also reflected the more urgent needs of the labour movement as
perceived by the committee. The proposal for a new
industrial relations charter stemmed from a growing
realisation among union leaders, employers, and labour
department officials alike, that the existing institutions of collective bargaining, the Wages Boards and
the JICs, had become outmoded. One of the most notable
features in employment trends during the first decade
of independence was the growth of the manufacturing,
commercial, and services (hotels, restaurants, entertainment, etc.) sectors (see Table 7.2).

194

TABLE 7.2

Changing Pattern of Employment Trends

INDUSTRY	1960 (MONTHLY AVERAGES)	1969 (MONTHLY AVERAGES)
Agriculture, Forestry and Fishing	1,813	3,202
Mining	6,047	9,197
Manufacturing	3,004	6,670
Construction	8,689	7,475
Electricity, Water and Sanitary Services	993	1,857
Commerce	4,355	6,197
Transport, Storage and Communications	8,961	8,444
Services	14,012	20,564
All Industries	47,874	63,542

N.B.   Figures are based on returns from employers of six or more persons.

SOURCES: Labour Department Reports, 1960 and 1969

Newer employers tended to offer more favourable working conditions and fringe benefits than employers in the

traditional sectors.36   While four new JICs had been
created in addition to the Artisan and Transport JICs to
reflect the growing diversification of employment, most
of the benefits offered by employers were negotiated and
awarded outside the framework of JIC or Wages Board
Agreements.   Unlike the Dock Workers' Union, which was
essentially a 'house' union, the Clerical Union, for
instance, operated in several sectors and consequently
there was much heterogeneity in the range of benefits
available to its members.   Indeed the increase in strike
activity in 1968 and 1969 in terms of man-days lost and
numbers of workers involved was directly related to
attempts to reduce anomalies in working conditions and
benefits offered by different employers.

     In May 1969, agreement was reached between repre-
sentatives of Congress, the Employers' Federation and
the Labour Deaprtment that technical assistance should
be sought from the ILO in the formation of the new
charter.   In February 1970, the ILO sent its Regional
Adviser, Charles Spencer-Cooke, to Sierra Leone to
undertake the research relating to the formulation of
the industrial relations charter.37   A month later, the
principles and details were agreed upon.   Its main
provision was the establishment of Trade Group Negotiating Councils to replace the JICs and Wages Boards.38
The economy was divided into fourteen sectors and the
TGNC was to become the forum for negotiations on wages
and other benefits in each sector designated viz:
mining, building and construction, commercial and
insurance, shipping and forwarding, industrial, oil
(marketing and refining), public utilities, banking,
hotels and entertainment, printing, transport, agriculture, municipal and local government, and air transport.
Each TGNC was to be reponsible for setting the minimum
level of wages and benefits in each sector.   As it was
envisaged that these 'agreements' would be given legal
force, the level of wages and benefits reached at negotiations was to become the statutory minimum applicable
in each sector.   Negotiations at TGNCs were to be held
biennially, but "...it being understood that in extraordinary circumstances affecting the national economy it
may within this period be reviewed at the petition of
either party to such aggreement".   Each TGNC was to be
composed of an equal number of representatives drawn
from employers and the unions in the sector concerned.
Disputes were to be referred to the Commissioner of
Labour (the senior industrial relations specialist at
the Labour Department) for arbitration, and if aggreement could not be reached, to an industrial court, the

196

decision of which was to be final. Notices of strikes
and lock outs were to be given at least fourteen days
in advance of the action. A Joint National Negotiating
Baord (JNNB) was also proposed under the agreement. It
was to be responsible for fixing national minimum rates
of pay, maximum hours of work, the rates of pay applicable on public holidays, and terms of employment of
children, young persons, apprentices and the disabled.

This 'formal' model of industrial relations
contained some of the more favoured prescriptions of
the ILO (and in particular the recommendation that an
industrial court should become the final arbiter of
industrial disputes) to take 'politics' out of
industrial relations. Labour Department officials perceived, however, that it was unlikely that the formal
model would work as envisaged in the agreement. Indeed,
in view of the pervasive tendency among union leaders
and employers to use their clientelist relationships
with important politicians to influence the outcome of
bargaining, the model has never worked as envisaged.
Nonetheless, after eighteen months of study by
government legal advisers, a Bill containing some of
these recommendations was submitted to parliament in
September 1971.

During this intervening period, some progress was
made by Congress in the field of trade union education.
An important area of patronage for a ruling party in
Sierra Leone lies in the distribution of government
scholarships. The APC regime had provided Congress with
representation on the national scholarships committee,
and two scholarships were reserved on an annual basis
for the training of trade union officials. In October 1970, the national centre with ICFTU assistance ran
a series of seminars for shop stewards. In accordance
with its official policy of 'non-alignment', Congress
accepted scholarships for the training of workers'
representatives from trade union organisations in
Eastern Europe as well as in the Western countries and
Israel. It is clear, however, that labour leaders in
Sierra Leone have preferred the ideologies underlying
the mildly reformist strategies of American trade
unionists. None of the Sierra Leonean trade unionists
encountered by this author professed a commitment to
socialist or communist ideologies prevalent among
European trade unionists.

The content of educational programmes has been
examined. These have been geared towards promoting

literacy among union members, and towards disseminating
normative information on the purposes and functions of
trade union organisation. Regarding the latter type of
courses, booklets which are used in instruction are
distributed among participants. These contain slogans
which are explained by a simple text and by pictoral
displays. For instance, the Congress Shop Steward
Manual admonishes floor representatives:

> When a worker comes to you with a
> grievance, get the facts, listen
> to the members, look at the job,
> talk to other workers, check
> past grievances...When presenting
> a grievance, find a precedent.
> Cite a similar case that has been
> settled the way you want it...Be
> sure to file the grievance on
> time. A late grievance is a lost
> grievance.39

Shop stewards at the Port Authority have been asked to
assess the usefulness of Congress training programmes.
Without exception, those stewards who had attended
courses maintained that the instruction received was
useful in their role as workers' representatives.
Needless to say, participants have not been introduced
to debates concerned with the political role of trade
unions.

By the end of the first decade of independence, the
trends in national labour politics which had become
established during the years of decolonisation continued
to be manifested. During this period, trade union
leaders also demonstrated a commitment to the strengthening of the organisational base of trade unions in
Sierra Leone, albeit within political parameters that
had been narrowly defined, and within the terms of a
political cosmos which they accepted uncritically and
indeed helped to sustain. Developments during the
second decade of independence initiated a reconsidera-
tion of the assumptions governing the political
behaviour as well as the political values of labour
leaders.

Main Trends in Labour Politics in the Second Decade of Independence

In March 1971, almost three years after coming to

power, the APC was faced with its first major crisis. A corps of senior army officers alleged to be associates of leaders of the United Democratic Party (UDP) attempted to assassinate the Prime Minister, Siaka Stevens, by raking his office and home with gun fire. The leaders of the UDP, Dr. Mohammed Fornah, Dr. John Karefa-Smart, Dr. Sarif Easmon, and the Bash-Taqi brothers (M. O. and Ibrahim) had either been senior Cabinet Ministers or leading supporters of the APC, and had resigned from the party in protest at the harrass-ment of Opposition MPs and at allegations of govern-ment complicity in the Great Diamond Robbery at Hastings Airport near Freetown.40 The formation of the UDP was a serious threat to the ruling party as four of its leaders, Fornah, Karefa-Smart, and the Bash-Taqi brothers were Temnes from the North. Sarif Easmon symolised the growing disenchantment of the Freetown elite with the APC regime. The UDP leadership was also distinguished from senior APC politicians by the fact that they were all highly educated professionals or were relatively affluent in their own right. Three of the senior UDP politicians were successful medical practi-tioners, while Ibrahim Bash-Taqi had been a successful journalist. With the exception of M. O. Bash-Taqi, the others had joined the APC rather late in the day and had been particularly identified with the liberal intellec-tual supporters of the party.41 Thus the banning of the UDP, and the subsequent ascendancy of C. A. Kamara-Taylor and S. I. Koroma in the hierarchy of the party, may be described as the resurgence in political dominance of the original group of APC activists from lower-status occupations as described by Cartwright, who were initially protesting against the elitism of the SLPP and the excesses of the chiefs, but who showed little concern with liberal values and whose own poli-tical survival had replaced the reformist spirit in relevance and in importance. During this second decade of independence, the APC leadership consolidated its position by the adoption in April 1971 of a Republican Constitution giving a wide range of powers to the presidency with Stevens himself assumed, by the coopta-tion of senior army officers, and by the adoption of a single-party regime in June 1978. This the APC had been able to achieve not only by creating an efficient nation-wide organisation which was used to renew and extend its network of clientele, but also by creating a security unit, independent of the army, and loyal to the party leadership. It is against this background that the responses of organised labour to trends in national politics need to be assessed.

Most labour leaders came down firmly on the side
of the APC in relation to the cleavage which had given
rise to the UDP and the assassination attempt on the
Prime Minister. A meeting of Congress was called to
discuss the situation: "...a letter written to the
Prime Minister by the Secretary-General dated 25th
March sympathising with him...was read".42 A statement
was presented to Stevens on 30th March and is recorded
in the official diary of the APC leadership:

> The Sierra Leone Labour Congress,
> representing the entire national
> work force, condemned the actions
> of a small dissident army group
> in their attempts on the life of
> Prime Minister Siaka Stevens and
> pledged their support for the
> government under Dr. Stevens'
> leadership.43

By August, it was clear that this statement of support
was not the unanimous view of leaders of Congress affiliates. Before the events leading to the assassination attempt, H. N. Georgestone who--following Marcus
Grant's loss of credibility and influence after his
unsuccessful foray into national politics--was respect-
fully regarded as the 'father' of trade unionism in
Sierra Leone, had advocated that Congress ought to
re-assess its relationship with the APC.44 George
Palmer the Secretary of Congress, did not share this
view. According to Georgestone, "sometime in 1970" he
had even warned Stevens that the growing authoritarianism of the APC was a betrayal of the ideals of those
who had supported it in Opposition.45

Matters came to a head in June 1971, when the
Labour Department nominated Palmer as the workers'
delegate to the annual ILO meeting in Geneva.
Georgestone interpreted this as an unwarranted exercise
of government patronage and protested that, in principle, an invitation should have been issued to Congress
which should in turn have selected a delegate (usually
the Secretary) as was the established practice. The
Labour Department ruled that there were no procedural
irregularities. Georgestone and three other leaders of
Congress affiliates issued a statement of no confidence
in the elected officers of Congress, eventually resigned
affiliation from the body to establish a rival centre,
the Council of Labour.

Within Congress itself there was no serious attempt to debate the 'activities' of Congress officials or the 'connotations' of the Industrial Relations Bill, to which the statement of no confidence had referred:

> The Secretary-General pointed out
> that it was not proper for an
> organisation to use the name of the
> Sierra Leone Council of Labour as it
> had long been dissolved and replaced
> by the Sierra Leone Congress. For
> this reason, he felt that this
> should be brought to the notice of
> the Minister of Labour and the
> government for appropriate action,
> and that Congress should see to it
> that the govenment makes a press
> release re-affirming its official
> recognition of the Sierra Leone
> Labour Congress...Comrade Hamilton
> (Railway Workers' Union) congratu-
> lated all other speakers who
> strongly criticised the behaviour
> of the two leaders of the seceded
> unions and appealed to all members
> for stronger support and coopera-
> tion in order to work not only
> for the benefit of self but for
> the benefit of the members we
> represent, and concluded that we
> make a statement to the outside
> world for them to know the facts.46

These developments are significant for two reasons. First, the anxiety of the representatives of Congress affiliates that the outside world (including the ICFTU and the AALC, the major donors of aid) should be informed of the 'real' facts (i.e. Congress's position) is obvious. The logic underlying the provision of assistance by these organisations is a genuine desire to help build a united labour movement with a solid organisational base and with an ideological orientation acceptable to Western geo-political interests. Indeed, during the earlier dispute between the Federation of Labour and the Council of Labour under the Margai regime, the ICFTU had helped to bring about a rapproach-ement between the two factions. It is unfortunate that in wanting to create and maintain an influence in Third World labour movements, these international organisa-tions often fail to understand the trends in local

national politics. Throughout the dispute, the AALC
and the ICFTU continued to provide Congress with
various types of assistance. From 1972, the AALC
actually paid the salaries of the full-time officials
of Congress and, indeed, made it possible for these
officials to be able to act on behalf of Congress on a
full-time basis.47

Second, the nature of the issues relating to the
division within Congress posed some key questions cen-
tring on the choice of the future political posture of
the labour movement in Sierra Leone. The statement of
no confidence referred to the 'activities' of Congress
officials and to the 'connotations' of the Industrial
Relations Bill. As already noted, Congress made no
serious attempt to discuss these issues, contributions
to the debate of 23rd September being mere homilies on
the correctness of extending invitations to the 'dissi-
dent' unions to come back to the fold. In view of
trends in national politics under the APC, Georgestone
in particular, with great foresight, wanted Congress to
re-assess its relationship with the ruling party. He
had perceived that certain provisions in the Industrial
Relations Bill were designed to bring the labour movement under the control of the party. The issue, then,
was not whether labour leaders should seek to enter into
clientelist relations with politicians (the effectiveness of these informal channels was fully understood
and not controversial as such), but whether the labour
movement could preserve and maintain its independence
especially to criticise those areas of government policy
that were perceived not to be in the best interests of
lower-paid workers. The failure of Congress to debate
the issue in these terms was tragic. On the other hand,
however, the premium placed on the loyalty to political
patrons by those who enter into clientelist relations
with them is high. Within the terms of such relationships, criticism or oppositional activities which are
directed at the very nature of the political system
(and in consequence, the very survival of the regime)
cannot be accommodated. Having chosen on 23rd
September to (in effect) submerge their own particular
interest beneath those of the ruling party, Congress,
however, lost the tactical advantage to be accrued by
remaining an independent interest group. That is to
say, Congress lost its psychological advantage over the
politicians who would not otherwise have been certain a
priori of the political posture of the labour movement.

By the end of 1971, two conclusions with regard to

APC-Congress relations could be drawn. First, the ruling party had achieved effective control over Congress via clientelist relationships and via industrial relations legislation, just as it had been able to reduce the significance of the SLPP Opposition via inducements to 'cross-the-floor', harassment, and the adoption of the Republican Constitution. During the mid-seventies, university students were to provide the most vocal opposition to the regime. Second, and crucially important to the situation of lower-paid workers, the priorities of the APC were in the area of economic nationalism (reducing the shares of foreign businesses in the mining companies, the setting up of state-owned insurance, commercial bank, trading, and shipping companies--see Chapter 4--all of which increase the scope for the exercise of patronage) and not in the area of reducing inequalities by the adoption of policies of redistribution and of meeting basic needs. These conclusions can be related, respectively, to the Industrial Relations Bill and to a government policy statement on industrial relations.

The provisions of the March 1971 agreement on the Industrial Charter were written into the Bill presented to parliament in September 1971, with some crucial modifications. The government increased the statutory period of strike notice required from fourteen to twenty-one days, and in the public utilities sector, prohibited strikes completely. The Employers' Federation and the Labour Congress were given statutory recognition. Trade Group Negotiating Council disputes were to be mediated by the Minister with responsibility for the Labour Department and not by the Commissioner of Labour before being presented to the Industrial Relations Court if agreement could not be reached. The check-off system was given legal recognition and employers who failed to pay minimum wage rates were to be subjected to stiff penalties.

In making the provision that the Minister of Labour should mediate disputes arising out of industry-wide bargaining, the Bill gave recognition to the existing practice whereby informal political channels are used to influence the outcome of bargaining by the unions and the employers alike.48 The most controversial aspect of the Bill, however, was the provision for the statutory recognition of Congress. This not only implied that such recognition could be withdrawn (and was therefore contingent on the relationship between the party and Congress) but also that unions which wished to operate

out of the framework of Congress might not be able to do
so. These were the 'connotations' (especially in view
of national political trends) about which Georgestone
had expressed reservations. This point was made by
Salia Jusu-Sheriff, the Leader of the SLPP Opposition
during the debate on the Bill in parliament:

> I want to know how those unions
> which are not members of Congress
> are going to go about their bus-
> iness...in view of the fact that
> by ILO convention, no government
> can force them into a secondary
> union.49

The Attorney General, L. A. M. Brewah, replied on behalf
of government:

> The question that the honourable
> member is asking does not arise
> if these people form a union and
> do not want to join Congress to
> enjoy the facilities of Congress,
> whose fault is it?50

At the end of 1971, the government issued an important
policy statement which clearly revealed for the first
time the ideology of the APC on industrial relations
reform:

> When trade unionism started in
> Sierra Leone in the early 1940s, the
> country was a dependent territory...
> Since independence, the position has
> completely changed. Terms and condi-
> tions of service of workers have
> improved much more than they were in
> the early years of trade unionism...
> It is the view of government that
> trade unions should now play a role
> consonant with the overall development
> of Republican Sierra Leone...It should
> constantly be borne in mind that a
> strike in one section of industry inva-
> riably brings out a chain of repercuss-
> ions on various spheres of our gross na-
> tional product. Claims made on both the
> public and the private sectors should be
> realistic...New industries should be
> allowed to grow without unnecessary

industrial strife...Splinter groups
whose aim is merely to publicise the
importance of their leaders and to
peddle patriotic sentiments for personal gain must not expect any support
from government.51

The Council of Labour was allowed to function not only
because it posed no threat either to the regime or to
the Labour Congress, but also because to have banned it
would have been an infringement of ILO codes. The
government, however, never recognised the Council. For
instance, when the Joint National Negotiating Board was
convened in May 1972 to fix minimum wages, Council was
not invited to take part in the deliberations. While
Congress was officially invited to give evidence at the
Barthes-Wilson Commission on Prices in mid-1971, this
recognition was not accorded to Council. Congress also
took pains to present the Council as an "insignificant
minority of disgruntled elements" to the international
organisations to which the former was affiliated.52

   One of Congress's main preoccupations during the
seventies was with the rising trend in prices. It is at
least a tribute to Congress's influence that government
responded by using that familiar instrument of public
administration to show that it was also concerned. A
commission of inquiry under J. Barthes-Wilson, a senior
Cabinet Minister, was appointed to examine the inflationary tendencies in the economy. Congress representatives gave evidence at the commission and, shortly
before the publication of its report, Congress presented
the government with a detailed memorandum on the inflationary situation:

           ...(Congress) notes with grave con-
           cern the persistent increases in the
           cost of food, clothing, drinks rent
           and all necessaries which have no
           bearing on adequate economic factors
           to justify the increase...The cost
           of pharmaceutical products are un-
           necessarily high, and realises the
           predicament of the common man...and
           therefore appeals to government to
           take immediate steps by compelling
           the dealers to drastically reduce
           their profit margin...Government to
           take action to withdraw the monopoly
           of the National Trading Company on

                    (imported) commodities which is
                    chiefly responsible for the present
                    high cost of living.53

When the Commission reported in May 1974, it argued that
the inflationary tendencies in the economy were imported, but recommended the review of the Trading Company's
monopoly and increased vigilance of Price Inspectors of
the Ministry of Trade and Industry.54 The monopoly of
the Trading Company was withdrawn but price control has
been a notorious failure. From 1973, government had
also been subsidising certain essential commodities
including petroleum products,55 but the deterioration in
the relationship between Congress and the regime from
1977 onwards can be related to the considerable erosion
of living standards since the early seventies.

     Towards the end of 1972, the question of the cen-
tralisation of Congress affiliates into one trade union
was again considered. Part of the problem of the loose-
ness of the organisation of the national centre resided
in the fact that individual unions were fairly effective
in achieving their objectives as perceived by their executive councils or union officials. Affiliation to Congress afforded contact with foreign labour organisations
and provided the means of coordinating the activities of
the affiliates as for instance, in the expression of
concern over the inflationary tendencies in the economy.
Congress of itself, however, existed outside the bargaining framework of its affiliates, and was in this
sense remote from the rank and file of unions affiliated
to it.

     In mid-1972, the Transport Workers' Union rejoined
Congress following Georgestone's resignation as Union
Secretary in consequence of continuing internal dissen-
sion. Over the next twelve months, however, the Con-
struction Workers' Union was joined in the Council by
two new unions, the Printing and Allied Workers', and
the Municipal and Local Government Employees'.56
Emerson Davies of the Printers' Union became part-time
Secretary of Council while H. D. Charles of the
Construction Workers' became President. In March 1975,
another new union, the Hotels, Food, Drinks, Tobacco,
Entertainments and Services Union, joined the Council.
Between 1972 and 1975, however, four new unions joined
Congress. These were the Teachers' Union, the Provin-
cial and General Workers' Union, the Public Utilities'
Employees' Union, and the Electricity Corporation
Employees' Union.57 The proliferation of new unions

naturally increased the significance of the Council of Labour vis a vis Congress. There is evidence that the AALC encouraged a rapprochement between Congress and the Council, even suggesting that centralisation of Sierra Leone trade unions would enable Congress to become financially self-sufficient.

It had been decided within Congress that a merger with the Council would be sought as a prelude to centralisation. Approaches made to the Council, however, were rebuffed. It was not until after a new Minister of Labour was appointed following a Cabinet re-shuffle in November 1974 that some progress was made. According to a senior official of Congress:

> Gobio (George Gobio Lamin, the new
> Minister) was a diplomat. He under-
> stood the situation. When we went to
> acquaint him with our difficulties, he
> agreed to use his good offices to bring
> about a solution.58

The Minister assumed office with no major advantage; he had not been involved in the formulation of the Industrial Relations Act or associated with the policy of the Labour Department to 'isolate' the Council. In February 1975, encouraged by the Minister, Congress and the Council agreed in principle to come together to form one national centre. Over the next few months a committee of Congress and Council representatives deliberated the issues related to the merger and towards the end of the year, issued a report for the consideration of the affiliates to the two centres. It recommended that "...a national centre be created and called Sierra Leone Labour Congress...that the constitution of Congress be reviewed and fresh elections of the new body be arranged...that mergers between existing unions be encouraged in the immediate future to make them viable and strong".59 Other recommendations were the adoption of standard rates of union subscription, the creation of a research department of Congress, and with regard to the proliferation of unions, the adoption of "...recognised spheres of influence of existing registered trade unions".

During the early months of 1976, the report was deliberated by affiliates of the two centres and eventually adopted. In September the new centre was formally inaugurated by President Stevens. Elections of officers to serve in the new centre were held prior to

207

the inauguration ceremony and it seems evident that the
outcome had been pre-arranged as all candidates were
unanimously elected. George Palmer retained the full-
time Secretaryship of Congress while H. D. Charles
became part-time President. James Kabia of the Mine
Workers' was elected (part-time) First Deputy Secretary
and O. B. Conteh of the Dock Workers' Union (part-time)
Second Deputy Secretary.

In the months preceding the formal inauguration of
the new centre, the future political posture of Congress
had been vague. The merger committee, for instance,
made no reference to national political trends. During
the early months of 1977, however, it became evident
that Congress had adopted a critical political posture.
This was partly facilitated by the change of personnel
in the hierarchy of Congress.

In January 1977, students of Fourah Bay College,
protesting the deteriorating economic situation,
allegations of official corruption, infringements of
civil liberties, etc., staged demonstrations during a
ceremony of the conferment of degrees by President
Stevens in his role as Chancellor of the University of
Sierra Leone. The vehemence of the demonstration
brought the ceremony to a premature conclusion. The
President and his entourage left the campus of the
University. Hours later, thugs 'invaded' the campus.
Several students were severely beaten and raped. The
leaders of the demonstrations were arrested and
detained.60

The action taken by the students occurred after a
four-year absence of public criticisms of the ruling
party or other oppositional activity. Following widespread incidences of violence and intimidation at the
1973 elections, in which APC candidates were returned
'unopposed' in more than half the parliamentary seats,
the SLPP Opposition withdrew from the contest in protest. Voting actually took place in only five consti-
tuencies.61 Between 1973 and 1977, therefore, Sierra
Leone was de facto a single-party state. This period
coincided with severe economic decline, unprecedented
levels of inflation, and considerable erosion in mass
living standards. In the absence of an Opposition in
parliament, or of a critical press, and in view of the
cooperative posture (or, at least, unwillingness openly
to criticise political trends) of the major pressure
groups such as professional organisations, religious
organisations and the Labour Congress (to which a

majority of the unions were affiliated during this
period), the protest action of the students was an
indication of popular discontent that had for long been
tightly bottled-up. Indeed, the subsequent attack on
the students and the detention of their leaders provoked
demonstrations throughout the capital city which was
brought to a standstill. On the third day of the
students' crisis, a press release signed by James Kabia
as Acting Secretary, (following George Palmer's resignation from the movement in November 1976 to take up an
ILO appointment in East Africa), and H. D. Charles as
President, was issued. This threatened action in support of the students if the harassment and victimisation
of their leaders continued:

> The executive council of...Con-
> gress, meeting at a special emer-
> gency session at Congress' Secre-
> tariat today...reviewed the
> incident at Fourah Bay College...
> the executive regrets the incident
> all the more in that it involved
> the Head of State and Chancellor
> of the University...in the interest
> of national peace, Congress calls
> upon government to secure the
> release of all students detained...
> Congress wishes it to be understood
> that if no immediate action is taken
> to release the students already
> detained, it will sympathise with
> them.62

A few hours later, however, a second statement signed by
Kabia and Charles, as well as senior APC politicians,
withdrawing the earlier statement, was released.63 It
transpired that, after the first statement was issued,
representatives of Congress affiliates were invited to
meet senior APC politicians:

> Appeals were made to us that any
> action taken by us would only lead
> to national chaos. It was agreed
> that the students would be released
> ...that they should apologise to
> His Excellency the President and
> agree to call off the demonstrations.
> We were invited to send our grie-
> vances to government and assured
> that action would be taken.

209

> Government also said that it was
> prepared to call elections within
> three months to seek a fresh mandate.64

The students for their part regarded the action of Congress as a sell-out and have argued that, if Congress had called a general strike, "...a revolution would have taken place".65 Be that as it may, it was evident that the national centre had adopted a critical posture vis a vis the regime. Further evidence is provided by some proposals issued in connection with the pending general elections:

> ...Congress strongly appeals to
> government that the pending general
> elections be conducted in a free
> and fair manner.66

Other proposals contained in the document specifically called for ecomomic reforms:

> as an austerity measure to tide over
> the difficult financial and economic
> period, the Sierra Leone Labour Con-
> gress suggests that government cut
> down on the number of Sierra Leone
> foreign missions...that the number of
> Ministries be reduced to twelve...67

Elections were held in May, a full year before they were due, amid much violence and allegations by the SLPP Opposition of intimidation. APC MPs had been declared unopposed in more than a quarter of the constituencies. The beleaguered SLPP Opposition--which had withdrawn from the 1973 elections in protest at the violence--was determined to fight the elections as there had been much discussion in APC circles of legalising the de facto one party parliment. The SLPP won 15 of the 85 parliamentary seats in the South, South-east, and in Freetown. Its majority in the Freetown Central II constituency, a former APC stronghold, was convincing. A few weeks after the elections, on 30th May, a resolution on the adoption of a one-party system of government was passed at the APC national delegates conference at Mahera, Lungi, in the northern province, and thereby became party policy.68 A year later, in June 1978, one party-government was formally adopted following a referendum which recorded a dubious 97 percent majority in favour of the new system.69

At the delegates conference of Congress held in October 1977, two candidates closely identified with the regime (A. W. Hassan of the Motor Drivers' Union and O. B. Conteh of the Dock Workers' Union) were not re-elected. Most union leaders had grown to believe that, while they should cooperate with the goverment (and continue to use the informal channels of bargaining), they should nonetheless maintain a distinct identity. Indeed, the Teachers' Union had presented a paper to the conference calling attention to (among other things) the "...undue loyalty of union officials to employers and government for renumerative jobs and other rewards".70

Under the single-party constitution, the Secretary of Congress is automatically a member of the Central Committee (the policy-making body) of the recognised party. A senior official of Congress maintains, however, that key policy decisions are taken at Cabinet level.71 The decision to host the 1980 OAU summit and ministerial conference, for instance, widely believed to have cost the government some Le200 million, was taken by senior APC politicians. Although the preparations (construction of a conference centre, a luxurious hotel, villas for the dignitaries, road works, etc.) created about 700 jobs,72 the decision resulted in a further deterioration in Congress-government relations73 culminating in the general strike of August/September 1981.

The profligacy in public expenditure associated with the hosting of the conference and the 'demonstration effect' of the luxurious way in which the delegates were feted (at a period of declining living standards in view of the inflationary trends in the economy) served as a catalyst to the manifestation of anti-pathetic attitudes (which had been latent) toward the political elite amongst lower-paid workers. Graffiti appeared in various parts of the docks (and the capital) prominently displaying slogans such as 'OAU for you, IOU for we' (or we pay the debt for hosting the OAU). While there was much talk among the rank and file of the Dock Workers' Union about misplaced priorities, Congress leaders were resolved, however, to wait for the end of the round of negotiations on wage increases in the various TGNCs which were concluded by December 1980. Dock Workers were awarded 50 cents per diem for the lowest paid, and Le156 per annum (about 52 cents per diem) for those at the higher levels of the wage scale. Even after these awards wages were in real terms about 60 percent below their 1965 levels (see Table 7.3)74. In an interview with West Africa magazine shortly before

TABLE 7.3

Index of Real Wages of Dock Workers in December 1980

YEAR	(a) UNSKILLED WAGE RATES	(b) SKILLED WAGE RATES	CPI* 1961=100	UN- SKILLED REAL WAGE INDEX	SKILL- ED REAL WAGE INDEX
1965	1.06	4.83	116.5 (100)	100	100
1980	2.76	6.77	361.4 (310.2)	39.3	35

(a)   Unskilled dockers' wage rates (bottom end of the scale; (b)   Skilled dockers' wage rates (top end of the scale), both expressed in Leones and Cents.

* The official Consumer Price Index has 1961 as its base year.   In this table, 1965 has been taken as the base year and the figures in parentheses have been adjusted accordingly.   (See also Table 6.2).

SOURCES: 1.   The Forster Report, Appendix 3 for 1965 figures on wage rates.

2.   The Sierra Leone Gazette, 6th June 1980, for 1980 wage awards to the Public Utility TGNC.   (This award has been added on to the 1978/79 wage rates obtaining at the Port Authority).

3.   Bank of Sierra Leone, Annual Report 1969 for 1965 figures on the Consumer Price Index; Economic Review, July – December 1980, for 1980 figures on the Consumer Price Index.

the strike, James Kabia, Secretary of Congress described the strategy which the movement decided to follow with regard to falling living standards:

> Actually there have been two schools
> of thought...the first was to demand
> salary and wage increases to augment
> the rise in the cost of living. The
> second was to submit to government,
> Congress' view on the economic sit-
> uation in the country. This second
> school of thought carried the majo-
> rity. A committee was appointed to
> work out the details.75

The report of the Congress committee was submitted to
government in June in the form of a memorandum. It contained proposals for reducing the number of staff in
Sierra Leone's embassies around the world, reforming tax
collection and foreign exchange control, reforming the
import licensing system, the price control mechanism and
the land tenure system, encouraging small businesses and
farmers producing food as well as setting up state farms
to boost productivity. The memorandum also stated:

> We do not believe that recourse to
> IMF loans is the answer...a look at
> some of the conditionalities that
> follow IMF loans such as devaluation
> of the domestic currency, restrictions
> in public expenditure and removal of
> subsidies on items such as transport
> and food (which hit the poor hardest),
> restriction on bank lending, and encou-
> ragement to foreign investors are all
> positive processes of underdevelop-
> ment.76

Thus, the initial response of Congress to the deteriorating economic situation was to take a good look at
the economy and propose reforms (albeit the usual fare
of the 'progressive' Left in Africa) which did not
necessarily bring immediate benefits (in the form of
wage awards) to its own sectional base. The government's handling of the situation, however, as we shall
soon see, was to force the leaders of Congress back into
their role as 'brokers' for the labour movement.

By August, there had been no reply from the government to the June memorandum. Congress therefore decided
to publish the document. Following demonstrations and
a nation-wide strike on 14th August, government responded by inviting Congress to re-submit the proposals in order of priority. A government statement

213

argued that the June memorandum was not related to
"industrial" but to "political" issues. The legality of
a general strike (vis a vis the 1971 Industrial Relations Act) was also called into question. Congress
had, moreover, published the memorandum in a foreign
newspaper (meaning West Africa) before the government
could reply.77 In response to the invitation, a new
memorandum dated 24th August was submitted by Congress
to the government. This included proposals for price
control, rent subsidies, improvement of medical facilities and "...a reduction in the exhorbitant and economi-
cally unjustifiable price of rice..."78 President
Stevens immediately responded by announcing a new control price of rice. When it was suggested to Congress
that a committee of government advisers and Congress
officials be formed to examine the other proposals,
Congress replied that this would be construed by the
workers as 'delaying tactics' on the part of government.
An indefinite general strike was called for 1st
September.79 Negotiations which were held between
labour leaders, senior APC politicians and government
officials right up to 31st August could not find a solu-
tion to the impasse.

The strike brought business activity throughout the
country to a standstill. The government responded by
declaring a state of emergency. A broadcast by
President Stevens declared also that workers who failed
to turn up for work would not be paid and hinted that
they might lose their jobs. Ministers were to be issued
with hand guns to defend themselves should they be
attacked. Labour leaders who had barricaded themselves
in the offices of Congress on Wallace-Johnson Street in
Central Freetown were rounded up, arrested, and eventually detained for a month. The government had the
situation under control within a week.80

In conversations with this author, dock workers
have argued that the strike failed because they were
faced with a government much stronger than the labour
movement as a whole. This view--and the "new mood" of
the rank and file and leadership alike--was echoed in
James Kabia's 1982 New Year Message which reflected on
events during the previous year.

> It is an undisputable fact, that in
> Sierra Leone and in the majority of
> African countries, where trade union
> rights have been wickedly trampled
> upon...the struggle between the

> governments and the central workers'
> organisations have been created by
> wide-spread corruption, financial
> mismanagement and an intolerable
> escalating prices of basic food and
> other essential commodities, which
> have stepped outside the reach of
> the average salary/wage packet. In
> Sierra Leone, rice the staple food
> became an unmentionable word...socio-
> economic problems cannot be solved by
> throwing trade unionists into prison.81

Be that as it may, the strike (and the events leading up
to it) illustrate the dynamising potential of a more
expressive labour leadership as well as, of course, the
limits of government tolerance. For much of the 1970s,
labour leaders had been content with entering clientelist relations with politicians whose influence could
be used to effect marginal improvements in wages and
working conditions during collective bargaining, as well
as, it must not be forgotten, for personal gain.
Several years of corporatist political intrigue under
the APC, declining living standards and the 'demonstration effect' of the hosting of the OAU conferences created the conditions for a radical reformulation of the
relationship between the labour leadership and the
regime.

   In its response to the June memorandum (insisting
that Congress must not get involved in 'political'
matters) the government successfully forced the leaders
of Congress back into their role as brokers for the
labour movement. Pressure from the urban work force on
government to control the price of foodstuffs means also
lower receipts for peasant farmers who respond by growing less food. Government is thus forced to import
higher levels of food (see Table 7.4) resulting in a
further discouragement of farmers.82 This of course underlines Bates' argument that to the extent there is a
rationale underlying the development process in much of
sub-Saharan Africa, it is political rather than economic
(see p. xv). Nonetheless, while there are immediate
differences between low-income rural groups (especially
those rural households producing food as opposed to cash
crops) over such issues as the official level of food
prices and in particular the importing and subsidising
of rice, it is also clear that these are really subsidiary to the major conflicts between the political and
administrative elite together with some capitalist

TABLE 7.4

Rice Imports 1968-1981

YEAR	QUANTITY (Tons)
1968	10,581
1969	12,680
1970	49,365
1971	26,929
1972	6,668
1973	43,724
1974	45,025
1975	N.A.
1976	15,000
1977	6,700
1978	22,500
1979	76,536
1980	51,054
1981	52,246

N.A. = Not Available

SOURCE: Olu Williams, "Agro-Rural Development Strategies..."

businesses on the one hand, and the low-income rural and urban work force on the other. In this sense, then, the labour leadership has demonstrated, even if belatedly, that it is fully alive to the nature of the Sierra Leonean political economy though it has yet to come to terms with the contradictions in its ideas for economic reform.

CONCLUSION

In the introduction to this book, the theoretical
problem was said to be that of 'situating' lower-paid
dockers within the political economy of Sierra Leone
when these are workers in a public corporation, which
is in turn, an integral part of a patron-clientelist
political and economic system. Several important questions were raised. These relate to (1) the rules of
operation of public corporations such as the Port
Authority and how they have been affected by the development of a system of political clientelism; (2)
whether lower-paid workers in the employ of the Authority could be said (in a Marxist sense) to be exploited;
(3) the influence that is exerted on their political
perceptions and behaviour by the role of patron-
clientelism in labour recruitment and managerial structures of control; (4) the most notable features of
their trade union organisation and action, and the extent to which they have confronted successive government over major policy issues.

These questions were systematically examined in the
three sections and seven chapters which make up this
work and point toward the following conclusions.
Firstly, the rules of operation of a public corporation
such as the Port Authority have clearly been affected by
the development of a system of political clientelism
(and associated corruption) in the post-colonial state
in Sierra Leone. One of the more easily identifiable
characteristics of British colonial public administration was its high degree of bureaucratic rigidity. This
was the means by which the British effected colonial
domination over nearly a quarter of the earth's surface.
(It was, too, the basis of the reluctance of the British
to expand the public sector or to aggressively pursue
economic development). In the individual territories,
the colonial state was therefore founded on the principle of administrative rigidity (and accountability).
Sierra Leone and the port organisation were no exception. The post-colonial state by contrast, while not
adopting (but vastly proliferating) formal procedures
of accountability is founded on a different principle.
The pattern of political competition which became established after independence is quite literally a struggle
for access to the resources of the state. The key to
understanding this form of political competition is
first to understand the role of patronage in the political sociology of neo-patrimonal leadership. In the

absence of an indigenous class of wealthy entrepreneurs
(as a result of the incipient nature of capitalist development), access to the apparatus of the state guaran-
tees access to the most important resources for distribution in political competition. Before the withdrawal
of the British, access was restricted by the rules of
accountability; afer independence (and even during decolonisation) access became relatively unrestricted. In
conditions where this form of political competition
obtains, the public sector is particularly vulnerable as
an instrument of political patronage. The vulnerability
of the Port Authority became increasingly evident after
1965 and contrasts sharply with the period of the operation of the Port Management Department as a 'quasi-commercial' enterprise when the rules worked the way they
were intended to work.

Secondly, to the extent that the rules in the post-
colonial state are not those of efficiency in profit-
maximisation such as characterises capitalist enterprises, a public corporation such as the Port Authority has
been less geared to profit-making via surplus appropriation than to providing jobs for political clients. The
provision of such political benefits via the public
sector after independence has been limited less by
financial than by political constraints and IMF pressure
to reduce public spending on over-extended public
bureaucracies. (This has not been, very clearly, in the
interest of the development of capitalism or, for that
matter, any form of economic development). There is,
therefore, a strong element of parasitism in the collective operation of such organisations and one from which
lower-paid workers might be considered in some ways to
benefit. These factors are most accurately seen,
however, as merely mitigating their 'exploitation' since
they do largely perform the labour entailed in providing
a genuine service for commerce at low rates of remuneration (even when some graft is included).

Thirdly, there can be no doubt from socio-economic
indices that they are very much a part of the urban
poor. There are immediate differences between them and
the poorer peasantry over such issues as the level of
official food prices but these are really subsidiary to
the major conflicts between the interests of the political and administrative elite together with some capitalist business on the one hand and the low-income rural
and urban work force on the other. This conflict is
reflected in their anti-pathetic attitudes towards elite
groups but which is also tampered by their keen sense of

political realism. They make their own history but they
do not make it just as they please! Hence, of course,
they resort (at times, of especial militancy) to 'populist' notions rather than to 'socialist' ideology. In
comparative terms, where in Africa has 'socialism' been
sincerely and vuluntarily adopted by the 'genuine'
working-class? Where 'socialist' ideologies have proved
to posses widespread salience, this has either been
because (a) of the severe impoverishment of what seems
to be the 'mass' of the population at the hands of
foreign imperialists, working through local 'compradors'
(as in some parts of Lusophone Africa, Latin America,
and Asia) on a scale which has not yet materialised in
Sierra Leone; or (b) because of the emergence of a
nation-wide system of social stratification in which
workers have felt themselves to occupy a central and
common position (as in Europe during the early years of
the present century). Lower-paid workers in Sierra
Leone (or Ghana or Nigeria or even Tanzania) know very
well that they are not part of a majority of the national population in essentially the same position. Consequently, a 'socialist' ideology which stresses proliter-
iat versus capitalists (or kleptocrats) as the major
issue of the times can carry little conviction with
them. Ideology does not operate in a vacuum.

Fourthly, while the opposition to the elitism and
corruption of the political and bureaucratic class by
the dockers has generally been conceived within fairly
narrow limits of economic self-protection, they have,
at least, had some success in maintaining the accountability of their union organisation against clientelist
incorporation. More recently, they have demonstrated
solidarity with other lower-paid workers in Sierra
Leone (the majority of whom are also employed in the
public sector) in the 1981 general strike (this event
being provoked by unprecedented levels of inflation and
the 'demonstration effect' of the hosting of OAU conferences). The 1981 Strike (like the 1955 one) demonstrated the power (if limited) of organised labour surely
enough. But it is only after twenty years of 'independent' government that lower-paid workers began to develop a clear political perspective, partly because
things had not seemed so hopeless before and partly
because government had only by this stage reached such
a level of irresponsibility--i.e. workers quite correctly came to identify the regime as the main source of
their exploitation and that of their rural relatives and
the country more generally.

Hence, therefore, both of the familiar positions--workers as a labour aristocracy and workers as the most exploited and potentially revolutionary class in an ostensibly capitalist system--are inapplicable. Post-colonial regimes in Sierra Leone have used the surplus appropriated from mining, peasant production, etc., to expand what is a largely parasitic public sector and thereby to provide 'jobs' for political clients. To this extent, the senior public salariat constitute a class exploitative of the peasants, mine workers, etc. To the extent that the more junior public sector employees benefit from this patron-clientelist system (e.g. through the recruitment system and through the creation of additional but largely artificial jobs), and to the extent that they benefit from policies designed to cheapen (artificially) the price of foodstuffs, they are in a relatively privileged position. This is, however, only partially the case, and there is another side to the story. To the degree that they labour in roles that contribute to production and that they are relatively poorly remunerated for such work; to the degree that they suffer from the corruption and inefficiency of the public sector managerial salariat, they are in a position of antagonism to this political-bureaucratic (kleptocratic) class. Hence, they are, objectively, in a distinct ambivalent class position, and their 'progressiveness' or otherwise depends on the line which they choose to take, e.g., the degree to which they actively oppose the 'kleptocracy' and/or identify with the interests of the poorer peasants and urban poor more generally.

LABOUR STUDIES QUESTIONNAIRE

Port Authority, May 1980

1. BACKGROUND INFORMATION

1.1	Residence-street/neighbourhood
1.2	Sex
1.3	Ethnic group
1.4	Marital Status/No. of children
1.5	Year/period born
1.6	Where born
1.7	If respondent was not born in Freetown: Town/chiefdom/district
1.7a	When did you come to live in Freetown?
1.7b	What were you doing before then?
1.7c	What made you decide to come to town?
1.8a	Education (last level)
1.8b	Other training
1.9a	Number of siblings
1.9b	Educational level of each sibling
1.9c	Occupation of each sibling
1.9d	Father's education/occupation
1.9e	Mother's education/occupation
1.10	What are your future intentions and aspirations?

2. WORK HISTORY AND WORK PLACE AND PRIVATE AFFILIATIONS

2.1	When did you first begin to work at the quay?
2.2a	How long did you have to wait to find a job there?
2.2b	How were you managing?
2.2c	How did you find and get the job?
2.2d	What are the different tasks you have done at the quay?
2.2e	Starting with first work experience, list subsequent work, including periods of unemployment and returns upline
2.3	SECONDARY EMPLOYMENT: Do you have, at the moment, any other job that brings in money or provisions? Yes/No (If yes, specify type of job/earnings/goods)
2.4	Can you list the main problem related to your job at the quay?

2.5 Does your job make you feel within your heart that you are doing something worthwhile? Yes/No Why?

2.6 Do you use the port canteen? If yes, how often? If no, why?

2.7 Have you used the medicare facilities? If yes, what is your opinion of the facilities?

2.8 Do you interact with other workers outside working hours (but including the mid-day break)? If yes, which of these groups of workers do you like to mix with:
  i Workers working in your department/section
  ii Workers in your age group
  iii Workers from your ethnic group/region
  iv Workers living in your neighbourhood
  v Cuts across the groups above
  vi Other (specify)

2.9 Do you have friends outside the port whom you mix with? If yes, do they fall into any of the groups listed above?

2.10 Do you belong to any groups or associations, for instance:
  i Religious (e.g. Church, Mosque)
  ii Mutual Aid (burial societies, osusu)
  iii Ethnic/Regional (e.g. Bo descendants, Limba Friendly Society)
  iv Social or sports club (e.g. East End Lions, Old Bo School Boys)
  v 'Societies' (e.g. Masons, Ojeh, Porroh, Hunting)
  vi Other

2.10b If so, do you hold any special position in the group?

3. TRADE UNIONISM

3.1a In any of the jobs you have had, did the workers or staff go out on strike? (If yes, specify)

3.1b Were there ever any trade unions to represent workers? (If yes, specify)

3.1c In general, what do you think of unions?

3.1d What about strikes?

3.2a Do you belong to a trade union here?

3.2b If yes, i What is the name of the union?
           ii How long have you been a member?
           iii How has the union helped you?
           iv What is the name of your shop steward?

        v   What is the name of your union
           secretary?
3.3   What do you consider to be the qualities of
        a good trade union leader?
3.4   Do you think the unions should do something
        about the decausualisation of the shore
        casual labourers and the stevedores? (If
        yes, what? If no, why?)

4.   HOUSEHOLD AND HOUSEHOLD ECONOMY

4.1a   At the place where you stay now, what other
        persons are living with you (starting with
        head of household, list all permanent
        residents sharing same dwelling unit)
4.2   Do you have (other) children not staying
        with you now? (If yes, please give sex/
        schooling/occupation)
4.3   Like anyone living in Freetown these days
        you must have a lot of expenses (e.g. rent/
        rates, school fees, food, medicare, clothes)
        Do you have to take responsibility for all
        of these yourself, or do other persons (in
        the family) contribute?
4.4   Apart from your own children, family and
        household, are there any persons you are
        helping? (If yes, specify)
4.5a   At the end of the month, do you usually find
        that (Tick one)
           You have to borrow just to make ends meet
           You have just enough to get by
           You are able to save a bit
4.5b   (If borrows): Who is it that helps you?
4.5c   (If saves): What do you plan to do with the
           money?
4.6   How does your household/family generally buy
        some of these necessities (Tick)
         i   Rice: by cup/by bag
         ii Palm Oil: by pint/bottle or by gallon
               can
        iii Cooking Oil: by pint/bottle or by
                 gallon can
         iv Sugar: by cubes/spoonfuls or by packet
         v   Coffee: by spoonfuls or by jar
         vi Tea: by bag or by packet
         vii Cigarettes: by sticks or by packet
        viii Shoes: from street hawkers or from
               shops
         ix Household repairs: Done by local

craftmen through informal arrangement
or by contractor

4.7   Compared with other people, do you think you
and your family are getting a fair share or
benefit for the work you do? Why?

4.8   In the place where you live now, (tick)
- (a) Is the house pan body/cement/board/
  mud?
- (b) Is the pump inside/outside in the
  compound/street?
- (c) Electricity (Yes/No)?
- (d) How many rooms do you have for self/
  family?
- (e) Do you rent or own?
- (f) If own,
  - i Did you (or spouse/parent)
    purchase/inherit the land only/
    the land and house together?
  - ii Are you renting any rooms or
    flats to other people?
  - iii If yes, how many units, at what
    rent?
  - iv If house purchased or built, in
    what year? Approximate cost

4.9   Consumer durables which have been acquired:
- (a) Fridge?
- (b) Radio/Tape?
- (c) TV?
- (d) Car?
- (e) Motorbike/Bicycle?

5. GENERAL QUESTIONS

5.1   In this country now, we can see that there
are some 'Big Men' or gentry people, and we
can also see that there are those who are
managing, and those who are poor. Thinking
of people like yourself, to which of the
groups do you belong? Why?

5.2a   How do you think people come to be gentry?

5.2b   How do you think people come to be poor?

5.2c   How do you think people come to be only
managing?

5.3   Apart from these differences between gentry,
poor, and people who are managing do you
know of any other differences between people
which are important?

5.4   Do you think Sierra Leone's politicians and
senior civil servants are:

          (a)   Setting an example by making a
                sacrifice?
          (b)   Capable of improving the country's
                economic position?

5.5   Thinking of people like yourself, would you
say that there are any people or groups that
are helping people like you so that you can
'go before'? (If yes, who, and how? If no,
who is making your life more difficult, and
how?

5.6   Do you agree that government's first priority
should be rural development?

NOTES

INTRODUCTION (pp. xv-xxiii)

1 Cf., e.g., Robert Bates, Markets and States in Tropical Africa: The Political Basis of Agricultural Policies, Berkeley, 1981, for a penetrating analysis of the socio-political context of policy-making in agriculture in post-colonial sub-Saharan Africa.

2 Cf., e.g., the editorial sections in Richard Sandbrook and Robin Cohen (eds.), The Development of an African Working Class, London, 1975; or Peter Waterman, Division and Unity Amongst Nigerian Workers: Lagos Port Unionism, 1940s,-1960s, The Hague, 1982

3 The most important influences here have been Franz Fanon (cf. The Wretched of the Earth, London, 1965) and John Saul (cf. Giovanni Arrighi and John Saul, Essays in the Political Ecomomy of Africa, New York, 1973). In a more recent reply to critics, Saul accepts the "danger of prematurely labelling the African Working Class" (cf. John Saul, The State and Revolution in East Africa, New York, 1979, p. 345).

4 Cf. Adrian Peace, Choice, Class and Conflict: A Study of Southern Nigerian Factory Workers, Brighton, 1979.

5 Cf. Richard Jeffries, Class, Power and Ideology: The Railwaymen of Sekondi-Takoradi, Cambridge, 1978.

6 Cf. Gavin Kitching, Class and Economic Change in Kenya, Boston, 1980, especially pp. 438-461.

7 Cf. Stanlislav Ossowski, Class Structure in the Social Consciousness, London, 1963.

8 Cf. Stephen Riley, "Sierra Leone Politics: Some Recent Assessments", Africa 52 (2), 1982, pp. 106-109. Chris Clapham's Comparative Study of Liberia and Sierra Leone, Cambridge, 1976, does implicitly, at least, rest on an understanding of the fundamentally clientelist nature of Sierra Leone politics; see now his "The Politics of Failure: Political Instability in Liberia and Sierra Leone" in Clapham (ed.), Private Patronage

and Public Power: Political Clientelism in the
Modern State, London 1982, pp. 76-92.

9   Cf. Richard Sklar, "The Nature of Class Domination
     in Africa", Journal of Modern African Studies, 17
     (4) 1979 pp. 531-552; and Crawford Young, "Patterns
     of Social Conflict: State, Class and Ethnicity",
     Daedalus, Spring, 1982, pp. 71-98.

10   Cf. Hans Gerth and C. Wright Mills (eds.), From Max
     Weber: Essays in Sociology, London, 1948 (repr.
     1977), p. 299. For a more colourful interpretation
     of Weber, cf. Robert 'Jackson and Carl Rosberg,
     Personal Rule in Black Africa: Prince, Autocrat,
     Prophet, Tyrant, Los Angeles, 1982; but see also
     John Cartwright, Political Leadership in Africa,
     London, 1982.

11   For descriptions of the sociological characteris-
     tics of neo-patrimonal regimes, cf., e.g., S.
     Gellar, "State-Building and Nation-Building in West
     Africa", in S. N. Eisenstadt and S. Rokkan (eds.),
     Building States and Nations, Beverly Hills, 1973,
     pp. 348-426. For studies of neo-patrimonal regimes,
     cf. Chris Clapham (ed.), Private Patronage and
     Public Power; Donal Cruise O'Brien, Saints and Poli-
     ticians: Essays in the Organisation of a Senegalese
     Peanut Society, Cambridge, 1975; and S. N.
     Eisenstadt and R. Lemarchand (eds.), Political
     Clientelism, Patronage and Development, Beverly
     Hills, 1981.

12   The term 'literate and educated elite' (in contra-
     distinction to notions of the 'ruling class', the
     'bourgeoisie', or 'petty bourgeoisie') seems just-
     ified because a crucial characteristic of the modern
     state in African societies is that it operates in
     a language and according to procedures which are
     largely alien and incomprehensible to a majority
     of the population. Hence a description of the
     elite in this way identifies their most essential
     qualifications. There is a further justification
     in the use of the description precisely because it
     is the state (i.e. political power) which largely
     determines class relations, both vertically and
     between different communities, rather than
     political power being merely a reflection of
     economic power or of the 'mode of production'.
     For an elaboration of this argument, cf.

Colin Leys, "The 'Over-developed' Post-Colonial
State: A Re-evaluation", The Review of African
Political Economy, 5, January - April 1976, pp. 39-
48.

13   Cf. John Lonsdale, "The State and Social Processes
in Africa: A Histriographical Survey", African
Studies Review, 24, 1981, pp. 136-226. Nonetheless, alliances may be made between communal groups
(cemented via clientelism) and much energy expended
on the assertion of platitudes relating to the
desirability of national unity. Or, indeed, a
nationwide organisation of political mobilisation
may be maintained. (Cf. Richard Jeffries, "The
Ghanaian Elections of 1979", African Affairs, 79,
July 1980, pp. 397-414). For an account of the
political fragmentation that results when there is
an erosion of the means of preventing the destabili-
sation of the nation-state, cf. Cherry Gertzel,
"Uganda after Amin", African Affairs 79, October
1980, pp. 461-489. This, of course, underlines
the fact that the legitimacy of a neo-patrimonal
regime is, at best, doubtful, and procedures for
maintaining accountability, tenuous.

14   Thus a legal and moral definition of corruption is
avoided. For a moralistic appraisal of corruption
in West Africa, cf. M. McMullen, "A Theory of Corruption", Sociological Review, IX, June 1961, pp.
181-200. While it must be acknowledged that Riggs'
model of the operation of the 'sala' in 'prismatic'
society is illuminating, it was, however, largely
anticipated by Weber's description of patrimonal authority. Moreover, it does not seem helpful, in the
interest of clarity, to adopt Riggs' neologisms (cf.
Fred Riggs, Administration in Developing Societies:
The Theory of Prismatic Society), Boston, 1964.

15   This is a relatively unexplored theme in the literature on African labour studies. For a recent review
of the field, cf. Bill Freund, "Labor and Labor History in Africa: A Review of the Literature", paper
discussed at the African Studies Association Annual
Conference, Boston, December 1983.

CHAPTER 1   (pp. 3-19)

1   Cf. Christopher Fyfe, A History of Sierra Leone,
Oxford, 1962, p. 382; p. 395.

2   London Chamber of Commerce Archives, File No. 16597
    Minutes of the Joint West African Committee of the
    London, Liverpool, and Manchester Chambers of Comm-
    erce, 19 July 1911.

3   Cf. J. Best, A History of the Sierra Leone Railway
    1899-1949, Freetown, 1949, p.35.

4   Cf. P. N. Davies, The Trade Makers: Elder Dempster
    in West Africa, 1852-1972, London, 1973, pp.
    114-116.

5   Cf. Laurens van der Laan, European Commercial Ent-
    erprise in Colonial Sierra Leone 1896-1961: A
    Preliminary Survey, Leiden, 1978, p. 8.

6   Cf. the annual Blue Book for the years between 1900
    and 1939.

7   Cf. from among the literature, M. H. Y. Kaniki,
    "Economic and Social History of Sierra Leone, 1929-
    1939", PhD thesis University of Birmingham, 1972,
    ch. 2; M.J. M. Sibanda, "Colonial Policy and Devel-
    opment in North-West Sierra Leone", PhD thesis, Univ-
    ersity of Birmingham, 1978, ch. 4; E. Frances White
    "Creole Women Traders (1792-1945)", PhD thesis,
    Boston University 1978.

8   Labour Department, Labour Report 1939-40, p. 1.

9   Cf. Chris Fyfe, A History of Sierra Leone, p. 78;
    the word 'Kroo' is also spelt 'Kru'. In this study
    the former spelling which is used by the people
    themselves in Freetown will be adopted. For a
    survey of the involvement of Kroos in West African
    shipping, cf. G. E. Brooks, The Kru Mariner in the
    Nineteenth Century: A Historical Compendium,
    Newark, 1972; for accounts of Kroo society in
    Freetown, cf. Michael Banton, West African City: A
    Study of Tribal Life in Freetown, London, 1957;
    and Barbara Harrel-Bond et al, Community Leadership
    and the Transformation of Freetown (1801-1976),
    London, 1979.

10 Banton, West African City, p. 14.

11 Ibid, p. 15.

12 Cf. F. W. H. Migeod, A View of Sierra Leone, London,
    1926, p. 13.

13 The Sierra Leone Weekly News, 4th March 1893; King
    Peter was then recognised as the leader of the Kroos
    in Freetown.

14 Banton, West African City, p. 24.

15 Interview of a small group of Kroo stevedores, 3rd
    March 1980. In this group were two Kroo men who
    had worked at the port since 1942 and 1945.

16 Cf., e.g., Graham Green, Journey Without Maps,
    London, 1937, p. 37; Katherine Fowler-Lunn, The
    Gold Missus: Journal of a Woman Gold Prospector in
    Sierra Leone, New York, 1938.

17 Throughout this study, the word Krio, which is also
    spelt Creole, will be used to describe the descen-
    dants of liberated slaves who settled in Freetown
    during the latter part of the eighteenth century.
    The former spelling which emphasises the pronuncia-
    tion of the word by the people themselves in Sierra
    Leone, carries the connotation that Krio culture is
    essentially rooted in African traditional experi-
    ence. For an elaboration of this theme, cf.
    Akintola Wyse, Searchlight on the Krio of Sierra
    Leone: An Ethnographical Study of a West African
    People, Institute of African Studies, Fourah Bay
    College, University of Sierra Leone, Occassional
    Paper No. 3, 1980.

18 Cf. Martin Kilson, Political Change in a West
    African State, New York, 1965, ch. 5.

19 Cf. R. W. Cole, Kossoh Town Boy, London, 1962,
    p. 113.

20 British Parliamentary Papers, CMND 2744, Report by
    the Hon. W. G. A. Ormsby-Gore, MP, (Parliamentary
    Under-Secretary of State for the Colonies) on His
    Visit to West Africa During the Year 1926, London,
    1926, p. 55; cf. Allister MacMillan, The Red Book
    of West Africa, London, 1920, pp. 233-234.

21 National Workshop Archives, Public Notice No. 62
    (The Defence and Control of Traffic in the Port of
    Freetown), 5th May 1942.

22 Cf. D. Meredith, "The British Government and Colo-
    nial Economic History 1919 - 1939", Economic History
    Review, 28, 1975, pp. 449-487, p. 484; A. Hopkins,

231

An Economic History of West Africa, London, 1973;
B. Niculescu, Colonial Planning: A Comparative
Study, London, 1958, pp. 60-63; and D. C. Carney,
Government and Economy in British West Africa, New
York, 1961

23 National Workshop Archives, Government Notice No.
    385, Sierra Leone Royal Gazette, 31st May 1945.

24 National Workshop Archives, Sierra Leone Royal
    Gazette, 31st December 1945, "Dissolution of Port
    Executive Committee and appointment of Port Advisory
    Committee".

25 Ibid.

26 Colonial Office, Major Capital Works in the Colonial
    Territories, Colonial No. 285, London, 1952.

27 R. R. Kuczynski, Demographic Survey of the British
    Empire, Vol. 1, London, 1948, pp. 159-161.

28 For the evolution of Colonial Office labour policy,
    cf., e.g., B. C. Roberts, Labour in the Tropical
    Territories of the Commonwealth, 1962; and M. Amolo,
    "Sierra Leone and British Colonial Labour Policy,
    1930-45", PhD thesis, Dalhousie University 1977.

29 Amolo "Sierra Leone and British Colonial Labour
    Policy", ch. 5.

30 Sierra Leone, Labour Report 1939-40, p. 1.

31 Cf. N. A. Cox-George, "An Essay on Employment and
    Unemployment", Typescript, Freetown, 1950.

32 See ch. 5 of this study which develops a 'Sociolo-
    gical profile' of the dockers using the material
    from this survey.

33 Cf., e.g., Central Statistics Office, Household
    Survey of the Western Province, Economic and Expen-
    diture, 1966-68, Final Report, Freetown, 1969;
    Central Statistics Office, Household Survey of the
    Western Province, Household Characteristics and
    Housing Conditions, 1968-69, Freetown, 1969; David
    Fowler, "The Urban Informal Sector in Sierra Leone",
    Africana Research Bulletin, 6, (3), 1976, pp. 4-34;
    Katherine Moseley, "Work, Class and Community: The
    Safroko Limba of Freetown" (forthcoming); and

Josef Gugler and William Flanagan, Urbanisation and
Social Change in West Africa, Cambridge, 1978.

34 Sierra Leone, Labour Department Annual Report 1946,
    p. 2, Freetown, 1947.

35 Cf. Kuczynski, Demographic Survey of the British
    Empire, pp. 162-163.

36 Sir Alexander Patterson, Report on Penal Administra-
    tion and Welfare Services in Sierra Leone, Sessional
    Paper No. 3., Freetown, 1944.

37 National Workshop Archives, Minutes of Extra-ordi-
    nary Meeting of the Port Advisory Committee,
    23rd September 1946.

38 National Workshop Archives, Minutes of Meeting of
    Port Advisory Committee, 11th May 1948.

39 Ibid.

40 Sierra Leone, Labour Department Annual Report 1952,
    Freetown, 1953, p. 4.

CHAPTER 2 (pp. 21-54)

1   Cf. John Lonsdale and Bruce Berman, "Coping with the
    Contradictions: The Development of the Colonial
    State in Kenya, 1895-1914", Journal of African
    History, 20, 1979, pp. 487-505; and John Lonsdale
    and Bruce Berman, "Crisis of Accumulation, Coercion
    and the Colonial State: The Development of the
    Labour Control System in Kenya, 1919-1926". Cana-
    dian Journal of African Studies, 14, 1980, pp. 55-
    81.

2   Cf. A. B. C. Sibthorpe, The History of Sierra Leone,
    London, 1906 (reprinted New York 1970), p. 115.
    Conway and Lisk (cf. Hugh Conway, "Industrial Rela-
    tions in Sierra Leone with Special Reference to the
    Development and Functioning of the Bargaining
    Machinery Since 1945", PhD thesis, London Univer-
    sity, 1968; Franklyn Lisk, "Industrial Relations in
    Sierra Leone", M.Sc. dissertation, Queens Univer-
    sity, Belfast, 1970) both mention a strike of Kroo
    seamen in 1874. A photograph of the strikers was
    featured in the London (UK) Illustrated Evening News
    of 10th January 1874.

3 Cf. The Artisan, 24th September 1884; see also Table 2.1.

4 Cf. The Sierra Leone Weekly News, 26th November 1892.

5 Ibid.

6 Ibid. Cf. A. B. C. Sibthorpe, The History of Sierra Leone, p. 116.

7 Sierra Leone Weekly News, 26th November 1892.

8 Cf. Arthur Porter, Creoledom: A Study of the Development of Freetown Society, Oxford, 1963.

9 Cf. The Artisan, 29th July 1885.

10 Cf. Best, A History of the Sierra Leone Railway, p. 30. This monograph was commissioned as the official history of the railway to mark the fiftieth anniversary of the inauguration of the first train service in Sierra Leone. A thorough and detailed work based on Railway Administration documents--but sympathetic as one would expect to the railway management--this chapter will draw on its account of action taken by the railwaymen.

11 Ibid., p. 16

12 Ibid., p. 36

13 Cf. from among the literature, M. J. Bennie, "Government and Politics in Sierra Leone with special reference to the Creole Community", M.Phil. thesis, Nottingham University, 1970; Leo Spitzer, The Creoles of Sierra Leone: Responses to Colonialism 1870-1945, Wisconsin, 1974; and Akintola Wyse, "The 1926 Railway Strike and Anglo-Krio Relations: An Interpretation", International Journal of African Historical Studies, 14, 1981, pp. 93-123.

14 Cf. N. O. Leighton, "The Lebanese Middleman in Sierra Leone: The Case of Non-indigenous Trading Minority and Their Role in Political Development", PhD thesis, Indiana University, 1971; Laurens van der Laan, The Lebanese Traders of Sierra Leone, The Hague, 1975.

234

15 Cf. Kilson, Political Change in a West African State, pp. 59-60.

16 Cf. Michael Banton, "The Origins of Tribal Administration in Freetown", Sierra Leone Studies, (New Series), June 1954, pp. 109-121.

17 For an account of economic conditions during the war, Cf. Cox-George, Finance and Development, pp. 179-195.

18 Ibid.

19 The delay, Best implies, was a result of the perennial problem of operating deficits incurred by the Railway Administration; but see also, Hugh Conway, "Labour Protest Activity in Sierra Leone During the Early Part of the Twentieth Century", Labour History (Australia) 15, 1968, pp. 49-63

20 Cf. Martin Kaniki, "Attitudes and Reactions Towards the Lebanese in Sierra Leone During the Colonial Period", Canadian Journal of African Studies, 8, 1, 1973, pp. 97-113.

21 Best, A History of the Sierra Leone Railway, 48.

22 Ibid.

23 Ibid, p. 6.

24 Interview with Pa F. B. Hamilton, 31st March 1982; Pa Hamilton's father, an artisan at the railway, was a member of the union. He joined the railway himself as a clerk in 1937 and became a union official when the Railway Workers' Union was reconstituted during the Youth League years. He is now a part-time official of the Labour Congress (the federation of Sierra Leonean trade unions).

25 Cf. Bennie, "The Government and Politics of Sierra Leone".

26 Cf. Wyse, "The 1926 Strike and Anglo-Krio Relations".

27 For details, see Kilson, Political Change in a West African State.

28 Jombul is the Krio word for a white man or European

but has the connotation that such a person is in authority. This researcher was reminded by Pa Hamilton that this word is now almost extinct in present day Krio vocabulary. (Interview with Pa Hamilton, 31st March 1982).

29 During the depression years of the 1930s by contrast, wage rates dropped to between 6d. and 9d. per diem for unskilled and skilled labour respectively. Assuming twenty-five working days a month, this becomes 12s.6d. and 18s.7d. At the end of that decade Orde-Browne opined "...the conclusion...is that for the plainest adequate living and poor accommodation, 30s. monthly is the minimum figure ... I accordingly recommend the adoption of a basic figure of 30s. monthly as the minimum wage". (Cf. Orde-Browne, Labour Conditions in West Africa, p. 120).

30 Cf. Best, A History of the Sierra Leone Railway, p. 61.

31 Ibid.

32 Ibid.

33 Ibid.

34 Ibid.

35 Ibid, p. 62.

36 Ibid.

37 Ibid.

38 Ibid.

39 Interview with Pa Hamilton, 31st March 1982.

40 Ibid, see also Best, A History of Sierra Leone Railway, p. 79.

41 For a full biography of Wallace-Johnson, cf. La Ray Denzer, "I. T. A. Wallace-Johnson and the West African Youth League: A Case Study in West African Radicalism", PhD thesis, Birmingham University, 1977. The generousity of Dr. Denzer in allowing the author to read this work which is temporarily on restricted access is acknowledged. Dr. Denzer also shared with the author during conversations at the

Sierra Leone Studies Symposium, Birmingham, 17-19th
July 1981) her personal recollections of Wallace-
Johnson whom she had met in Ghana and in Sierra
Leone. She has collaborated with a scholar of Krio
society, Dr. Leo Spitzer, in the writing of an im-
portant two-part biographical article on Wallace-
Johnson. Cf. L. Denzer and L. Spitzer, "I. T. A.
Wallace-Johnson and the West African Youth League",
Part I, International Journal of African Historical
Studies, 6, 3, 1973; part 2 Ibid., 6, 4, 1973.
This account of the influence of Wallace-Johnson on
the development of trade unionism in Sierra Leone
is indebted to these studies.

42 Cf. Kaniki, "Economic and Social History of Sierra
Leone, 1929-1939".

43 Interview with Marcus Grant, veteran trade union
leader, 10th February 1982.

44 For glimpses of working conditions in the mines,
cf. Fowler-Lunn, The Gold Missus: A Woman Prospec-
tor in Sierra Leone. Since this ground has been
extensively covered by previous writers, a rehash
of the details is not necessary. Only these facts
that are relevant to the influence of Wallace-
Johnson on the labour movement and the structure of
conflict within the movement are discussed.

45 Cf. K. Swindel, "Labour Migration and Mining in
Sierra Leone", PhD thesis, London University, 1973.

46 Cf. Denzer and Spitzer, "I. T. A. Wallace-Johnson
and the West African Youth League" (Part 2).

47 Interview with Marcus Grant, 10th February 1982.

48 Cf. Denzer and Spitzer, "I. T. A. Wallace-Johnson
and the West African Youth League" (Part 2).

49 Denzer, "A Case Study in West African Radicalism"
Appendix 2; the composition of the Youth League's
central committee in 1938 was as follows: four
lawyers, eight businessmen, seven senior clerks,
three teachers, one surveyor, one clergymen, and
two accountants including a Muslim Imam.

50 For the details relating to the reform of labour
policies, cf. especially Amolo, "Sierra Leone and
British Colonial Labour Policy 1930-45".

51 Interview with Marcus Grant, 16th February 1980;
    H. N. Georgestone, 23rd January 1980; and other
    veteran trade unionists during fieldwork in 1980 and
    1982.

52 Cf. Edgar Parry, "Colonial Trade Unions", Corona,
    August 1949, p. 21.

53 Sierra Leone, Labour Department Annual Report
    1941-2, p. 3.

54 Interview with H. N. Georgestone, 23rd January 1980.

55 Cf. Sierra Leone, Labour Department Annual Report
    1941-1942, p. 3.

56 Cf. Kilson, Political Change in a West African
    State. p. 143.

57 For details relating to the strikes, cf. Amolo,
    "Sierra Leone and British Colonial Labour Policy";
    for details relating to the economy, cf. Cox-George,
    Finance and Development, p. 255 ff.

58 Interview with Marcus Grant, 16th January 1980.

59 While in the U.K., Stevens wrote "...experience has
    shown us...that Labour Advisers and Officials of the
    right type can be of inestimable value to colonial
    trade union movements. Not by dictating to, or
    unnecessarily interfering with the unions, but by
    tactful guidance, pointing out pitfalls in trade
    union work, recommending suitable material to
    read--above all by straight dealing with the
    unions--can Labour Advisers and Officers from the
    U.K. be of help to the colonies". Cf. Siaka
    Stevens, "Trade Unionism in Sierra Leone", Empire, A
    Socialist Commentary on Colonial Affairs, Journal of
    the Fabian Colonial Bureau, 2, (3), September 1948,
    p. 5).

60 This point emerged during interviews with Marcus
    Grant and H. N. Georgestone.

61 Marcus Grant, 6th March 1947, quoted in The Shaw
    Report, p. 4. Marcus Grant, however, fully realised
    the implications of Parry's reforms. He has
    written, "It was of course easier for the govern-
    ment to keep a check on the development of the
    unions in Sierra Leone". (Marcus Grant, "Research

on Trade Unionism in Sierra Leone", Freetown, type-
script, n.d.; copy in this author's possession).

62 Rhodes House, Oxford, Parry to Hinden, Fabian Colo-
    nial Bureau 86/2/173-115, 23rd September 1945; also
    quoted in Amolo, "Sierra Leone and British Colonial
    Labour Policy".

63 The New Leader, 13th October, "What Colonial Workers
    demanded at the WFTU Conference"; also quoted in
    Amolo, "Sierra Leone and British Colonial Labour
    Policy".

64 SLTUC, "Statement on the Present Situation in
    Congress", Freetown circa June 1946. (Copy in this
    author's possession). The emphasis is in the origi-
    nal. The statement also went on to accuse Wallace-
    Johnson of dishonesty and misuse of union funds.

65 Interview with Marcus Grant, 16th January 1980;
    Marcus Grant has also said that the idea for the
    formation of a Labour Party in Sierra Leone came
    from Parry's remarks on British trade union history.
    (Interview with Marcus Grant, 10th February 1982).

66 Sierra Leone, Labour Department Annual Report 1946,
    p. 6.

67 Grant, "Research on Trade Unionism in Sierra
    Leone".

68 To term the 1955 strike a 'general' strike is in
    fact a misnomer. Although workers throughout the
    country took part in it unofficially, the action was
    taken by members of the Artisan and Transport
    Unions.

69 The literature on decolonisation in Sierra Leone is
    extensive; cf., e.g. Kilson, Political Change in a
    West African State; John Cartwright, Politics in
    Sierra Leone, 1947-67, Toronto, 1970; Dennis Austin,
    "People and Constitution in Sierra Leone" (a five-
    part article in the weekly, West Africa, 13th
    September 1952 - 11th October 1952); W. H. Kaim-
    Caudle, "Review of Economic Changes in Sierra Leone
    1930-55", Durham University Journal, December 1957,
    pp. 34-41; and H. H. Gaffney, "Administration and
    the Administrative Service in Sierra Leone", PhD
    thesis, Columbia University, 1967.

70 This author has tackled Dr. LaRay Denzer, Wallace-
    Johnson's biographer, over the question of the irony
    of his support for Dr. Bankole-Bright's parochial
    NCSL. She insisted that Wallace-Johnson could have
    only been an effective critic of the government from
    the Opposition benches and drew attention to the
    fact that his collaboration with Bankole-Bright was
    short-lived. (Conversation with Dr. Denzer, 18th
    July 1981).

71 In pursuance of the policy of parity in the condi-
    tions of service of British and Sierra Leonean
    senior civil servants, the latter and their families
    were also allowed a few months leave in Britain
    every three years, with mail boats passages being
    paid by the government.

72 Cf. Laurens van der Laan, The Sierra Leone Diamonds:
    An Economic Study Covering the Years 1952-1961,
    Oxford, 1965.

73 Interview with Marcus Grant, 16th January 1980;
    interview with H. N. Georgestone, 23rd January 1980.

74 Sierra Leone National Archives, "Chronological
    Summary of Events from November 1954 to February
    1955", p. 1.

75 Interview with Marcus Grant, 16th January 1980.

76 "Chronological Summary of Events" p. 2.

77 Ibid.

78 Ibid.

79 Interview with Marcus Grant, 16th January 1980.

80 "Chronological Summary of Events", p. 2.

81 Ibid, Appendix B, J. Akinola Wright to Comrades
    Grant and Georgestone, 21st January 1955.

82 Ibid., p. 5.

83 Ibid.

84 Ibid.

85 Ibid., p. 6 and Appendix N.

86   Ibid., p. 7.

87   Ibid., p. 8.

88   Interview with Marcus Grant, 16th January 1980;
     interview with H. N. Georgestone, 23rd January
     1980.

89   "Chronological Summary of Events", p. 9.

90   Sierra Leone National Archives, The Marke Report,
     Freetown, 1955, p. 19.

91   "Chronological Summary of Events", p. 10; on 10th
     July 1980, this author showed Marcus Grant a copy
     of the The Marke Report which had been obtained
     from the Sierra Leone National Archives at Fourah
     Bay College. Grant, who had never seen it but had
     all along rightly believed that the report was
     broadly supportive of his case, was visibly moved,
     and exclaimed, "after 25 years!".

92   "Chronological Summary of Events", p. 10; see also
     Appendix AA.

93   Sierra Leone, Annual Report of the Labour Depart-
     ment 1955, pp. 9-10.

94   The Shaw Report, p.4.

95   Ibid., p. 7.

96   Ibid., p. 48.

97   Interview with Marcus Grant, 16th January 1980;
     interview with H. N. Georgestone, 23rd January
     1980.

98   Department of Labour Annual Report 1955, p. 9.

99   Interview with Pa Hamilton, 31st March 1982; inter-
     view with C. A. Wilton-During, veteran union offi-
     cial, 13th April 1982.

100 Shortly before the strike, the Railway Workers'
     Union had attempted to organise dock workers at
     the new quay. This was aborted when the workers
     realised that the union leadership was opposed to
     the strike. (Interview with Pa Hamilton, 31st
     March 1982).

101 <u>The Shaw Report</u>, p. 31; that Marcus Grant was
    personally blamed for the violence during the
    strike is a travesty of grotesque proportions. The
    commission not only failed to situate the episode
    in the changing social structure in Sierra Leone,
    but also failed to understand, or view with any
    sympathy, the aspirations towards a reasonable
    standard of living among urban wage earners and the
    poorer sections of the peasantry. As such, the
    commission could not anticipate the peasant riots
    which occurred a year later in November 1956, when
    peasant farmers in several parts of country, but
    more particularly in the northern province, engaged
    in riots during which the homes of chiefs and public
    buildings were damaged. The immediate cause of the
    riot was the decision of the Ministry of Local
    Government headed by Albert Margai to increase tax-
    ation of peasant farmers. This, coupled with the
    regular extortionate demands of some chiefs and
    other local Big Men, spurred the peasants to riot.
    (Cf. <u>Report of the Commissioners of Enquiry into</u>
    <u>the Conduct of Certain Chiefs and Government's</u>
    <u>Statement Thereon</u>, Freetown, n.d., <u>circa</u> 1957).

102 Cf. D. J. R. Scott, "The Sierra Leone Election of
    May 1957", in W. J. M. Mackenzie and K. Robinson
    (eds.), <u>Five Elections in Africa</u>, Oxford, 1960 pp.
    181-102.

103 Cf. V. Minikin, "Local Level Politics in Kono Dist-
    trict, Sierra Leone, 1945-70", PhD thesis, Birming-
    ham University, 1971.

104 This account of the reasons for the SLPP's success
    is indebted to William Fitzjohn's autobiography,
    <u>Ambassador of Christ and Caesar</u>, Ibadan, 1975 (per-
    haps the only memoir that has been written by a
    post-war Sierra Leonean politician).

105 Property qualifications were removed but entry to
    the franchise confined to adult males who had pre-
    viously not had the vote.

106 Interview with Marcus Grant (himself a candidate of
    the Labour Party), 10th February 1982.

107 When these elections were discussed with dockers
    who had voted in them, most said they voted for the
    SLPP because of its broad base of support.

108 Interview with Marcus Grant, 10th February 1982.

109 Ibid; but it should be noted that the proportion of
     urban inhabitants employed as wage earners in
     Sierra leone is relatively small.

110 Arguably, <u>all</u> political and electoral competition
     is a struggle for access to the resources of the
     state and the institutions of state power. The
     crucial point of distinction here is that a vict-
     orious party in a western democracy, for example,
     is accountable (in the accountant's sense of the
     word) for its custody and use of the resources of
     the state. Under a neo-patrimonal regime, institu-
     tionalised means of accountability can be shown to
     have been fragile, and moreover, access to the sta-
     ate is used primarily to <u>maintain</u> the system of pa-
     tron-clientelism. As such, the legitimacy of a neo-
     patrimonal regime is tenuous in a way the legiti-
     macy of a government in a Western democracy is not.

<u>CHAPTER 3</u> (pp. 57-73)

1 Sierra Leone, Sessional Paper No. 1 of 1946,
   <u>Report of a Committee on Proposals to Build a Deep</u>
   <u>Water Quay at Freetown</u>, p. 5.

2 Interview with a retired senior official of the
   Authority, 14th January 1980.

3 Ibid.

4 Port Authority Archives, Port Manager to General
   Manager Railway Administration, 9th December 1953.
   (The new port was officially named Queen Elizabeth
   II Quay but is more popularly known in Sierra
   Leone as Deep Water Quay).

5 Ibid.

6 Port Authority Archives, Port Manager to Permanent
   Secretary, Ministry of Works and Communications,
   21st May 1953.

7 Port Authority Archives, Port Manager to General
   Manager Railway, 8th February 1954.

8 Port Authority Archives, Governor's Annual Address,
   25th January 1957; (notes on the activities of the

Port Management Department prepared by the Port Manager for the governor's annual review of the work of government at the Legislative Council).

9   Sessional Paper No. 1 of 1946, <u>Report of a Committee on Proposals to Build a Deep Water Quay at Freetown</u>, p. 5.

10 Cf. Davies, <u>The Trade Makers</u>, p. 364; Dr. Davies elaborated on this point during an interview at Liverpool on 12th February 1981.

11 Port Authority Archives, Gillespie to E. E. Pollock (of The Economist Intelligence Unit), 23rd November 1959.

12 Ibid.

13 Ibid.

14 Port Authority Archives, Memorandum by the Minister of Works and Transport and (by) the Financial Secretary (a document on the financing of the port lighterage service presented to the Executive Council), 27th July 1954.

15 Port Authority Archives, Minutes of the Port Advisory Committee, 13th August 1958.

16 Interview with Pa Karanke Limba, 28th February 1980; aged about 63, Pa Karanke had forty years behind him as a docker, and had been a member of the Works Committee.

17 Ibid.

18 Port Authority Archives, The strike and subsequent disorders in relation to the port of Freetown, n.d., <u>circa</u> March 1955.

19 Interview with a retired senior official of the Authority, 14th January 1980.

20 Interview with Pa Karanke Limba, 28th February 1980.

21 Ibid.

22 Port Authority Archives, Christmas Message from the Port Manager, E. P. C. Gillespie, 24th December 1957.

23 Port Authority Archives, Port Management Works Com-
    mittee, Minutes of Inaugural Meeting, 27th January
    1959.

24 Port Authority Archives, Port Management Works Comm-
    ittee, Objects and Constitution, n.d.

25 Ibid.

26 Interview with a retired senior official of the
    Authority, 14th January 1980.

27 Port Authority Archives, Minutes of the Port Mana-
    gement Works Committee, 15th June 1959.

28 Port Authority Archives, Minutes of the Port Manage-
    ment Works Committee, 18th February 1959.

29 Port Authority Archives, Minutes of the Port Manage-
    ment Works Committee, 10th November 1960.

30 Port Authority Archives, Minutes of the Port Manage-
    ment Works Committee, 18th February 1959.

31 Ibid; the same point was made during informal con-
    versation with dock workers during both periods of
    field work.

32 Interview with Aziz Kassim (founder member of the
    union), 6th March 1982.

33 Interview with Pa Karanke, 28th February 1980.

34 Labour Department, Annual Report 1963, p. 7.

CHAPTER 4 (pp. 75-96)

1   National Workshop Archives, memorandum by the Mini-
    ster of Communications, April 1962.

2   Sierra Leone, The Open Door Policy, Freetown, 1961.

3   Cf. Alwyn Taylor, "The Role of Financial Institu-
    tions in the Economic Development of Sierra Leone",
    PhD thesis, University of Glasgow, 1973, especially
    ch. 1 and 2.

4   The style of leadership of the two Margai brothers
    has been compared by John Cartwright, in Political

Leadership in Sierra Leone, 1978. Sir Milton is
described as a "conservation ideologue" and Sir
Albert as a "radical ideologue".

5 Cf. R. J. Bhatia et al, "Stabilisation Program in
Sierra Leone", IMF Staff Papers, November 1969,
pp. 504-525.

6 Ibid., p. 505.

7 Ibid.

8 Cf. T. Cox, Civil-Military Relations in Sierra
Leone, Camb., Mass., 1976, p. 179; see also Franklyn
Lisk, 'The Political Economy of Sierra Leone 1961-
71, with special reference to the IMF Stabilisation
Programme of 1966-69', PhD thesis, Birmingham Uni-
versity, 1974.

9 Bhatia et al, "Stabilisation Program in Sierra
Leone".

10 Ibid., p. 508-12.

11 Sierra Leone, Budget Speech Delivered by the Hon.
Dr. M. S. Fornah, Minister of Finance, 8th July 1968
Freetown, 1968.

12 Budget speech delivered by the Hon. C. A. Kamara-
Taylor, Minister of Finance on 28th June 1971, re-
produced in Sierra Leone, Twelve Years of Economic
Achievement and Political Consolidation Under the
APC and Dr. Siaka Stevens 1968-1980, pp. 104-110.
This document is an official record of the day-to-
day activities of leading members of the APC regime
from April 1968 to March 1980.

13 Cf. Budget speeches of 1968; and of 1971 and 1973,
reprinted in Ibid.

14 Cf., e.g., Bank of Sierra Leone, Annual Report 1979,
Freetown, 1979 p. 17.

15 Cf. President's Annual Address to parliament, 21st
June 1974, reprinted in Twelve Years of Economic
Achievement and Political Consolidation Under the
APC and Dr. Siaka Stevens 1968-80, pp. 35-243.

16 Bank of Sierra Leone, Annual Report 1979, p. 25.

17 Cf. Ensuring Equitable Growth: A Strategy for
    Increasing Employment, Equity and Basic Needs
    Satisfaction in Sierra Leone (Report to the Govern-
    ment of Sierra Leone by a Jobs and Skills Program-
    me for Africa Employment Advisory Mission), Addis
    Ababa, 1981, p. 290. This document will henceforth
    be referred to as The JASPA Report.

18 Budget speech delivered by the Hon. A. B. Kamara,
    Minister of Finance, on 30th June 1978 (reproduced
    in Twelve Years of Economic Achievement and Politi-
    cal Consolidation... pp. 445-453).

19 Sierra Leone, The Port Act (No. 56) 1964, Freetown,
    1964, Section 5, p. 4.

20 Cf. Gaffney, "Administration and the Administrative
    Service in Sierra Leone", ch. 6

21 Port Authority Archives, Hon. Minister of Transport
    and Communications to Acting Secretary, 16th
    February 1967.

22 Port Authority Archives, Minutes of Meeting of the
    Board, 17th June 1966.

23 Port Authority Archives, Minutes of Joint Staff and
    Finance Committees Meeting held on Thursday, 18th
    and Friday, 19th July 1966.

24 Port Authority Archives, Acting Chief Accountant to
    General Manager, 22nd February 1967.

25 Port Authority Archives, Minutes of Board Meeting
    held on 2nd August 1966.

26 Port Authority Archives, Minutes of Board Meeting
    held on 8th November 1966.

27 Cf. Cox, Civil-Military Relations in Sierra Leone,
    p. 179.

28 Port Authority Archives, Consolidated Profit and
    Loss Account for the Year Ending, 31st December
    1965.

29 Port Authority Archives, Consolidated Profit and
    Loss Account for the Year Ending, 31st December
    1966.

30 Port Authority Archives, Acting Chief Accountant to General Manager, 22nd February 1967.

31 Port Authority Archives, Brief comments on attached graphs and statistics showing revenue/cost position for the period January to June 1968.

32 Sierra Leone, Report of the Commission Appointed to Inquire into all Aspects of the Affairs of the Sierra Leone Port Authority as a Viable Economic Revenue Making Establishment Covering the Period, 1st January 1965 to 4th July 1976, Freetown, 1977, pp. 7-8. (This document will henceforth be referred to as The Forster Report).

33 Ibid., p. 25.

34 Ibid., Appendix 52, p. 156.

35 Ibid., p. 31.

36 Ibid.

37 Ibid., p. 32.

38 Ibid., p. 26.

39 Ibid., p. 3.

40 Port Authority Archives, Acting General Manager to General Manager, Sierra Leone Oil Refinery, 21st August 1975.

41 Port Authority Archives, Acting General Manager to General Manager, Sierra Leone Electricity Corporation, 31st August 1975.

42 The Forster Report, p. 13.

43 Ibid., p. 9.

44 Ibid., Appendix 8.

45 Ibid., p. 6.

46 Ibid., pp. 8-9.

47 For comparative material (with regard to Ghana) on the parastatal sector, cf., Tony Killick, Development Economics in Action, New York, 1978.

48 The Forster Report, p. iii.

CHAPTER 5 (pp. 99-138)

1 See the writings of Antonio Gramsci for an elaboration of this truism, e.g., Selections from Political Writings (edited by Quentin Hoare), London,
1977 (2 volumes). For an example of a study of
African workers inspired by Gramsci's writings, cf.,
Jane Parpart, Labor and Capital on the African
Copperbelt, Philadelphia, 1983.

2 Cf. Gavin Kitching, Class and Economic Change in
Kenya, p. 449

3 Ibid,. pp. 449-450.

4 Cf. Jeffries, Class, Power and Ideology, for the
use of just such an approach.

5 The Forster Report, Appendix 3, p. 49.

6 For an indication of the scale of elite corruption
in the public sector, cf., e.g., Sierra Leone,
Report of the Auditor-General for the Years 1974-
79, Freetown, 1980.

7 For an elaboration of this theme, cf. Bates,
Market and States in Tropical Africa, esp. pp. 30-
44. The extent to which official agricultural
policy has contributed to the discouragement of
farmers and to their low receipts has been discussed
by Olu Williams in "Agro-Rural Development Strategies: Past, Present and Future", paper presented at
the 11th Annual Conference of the Agricultural Society of Sierra Leone, held at Njala University
College, 24th - 27th March 1982.

8 Cf. Fowler, "The Urban Informal Sector in Sierra
Leone" loc. cit; and David Fowler, "The Informal
Sector in Freetown: Opportunities for Self-
Employment in E. V. Sethuraman (ed.), The Urban
Informal Sector in Developing Countries: Employ-
ment, Poverty and Environment, ILO, Geneva, 1981.

9 Cf. Kathrine Moseley, "Work, Class and Community"
(forthcoming); and J. Gugler and W. Flanagan, Urbanisation and Social Change in West Africa, pp. 138-
141 for an account of market mammies on the sub-
continent.

249

10   Fowler, "The Urban Informal Sector in Sierra
     Leone", p. 4.

11   The results of these surveys have been published by
     Central Statistics Office under the following
     titles: Household Survey of the Western Province:
     Economic and Expenditure, 1966-68; Household Survey
     of the Northern Province: Economic and Expenditure,
     1966-68; Household Survey of the Eastern Province:
     Economic and Expenditure, 1966-68; Household Survey
     of the Southern Province: Economic and Expenditure,
     1966-68; Household Survey of the Western Province:
     Household Characteristics and Housing Conditions
     1968-69; Household Survey of the Northern Province
     Urban Areas: Household Characteristics and Housing
     Conditions 1968-69; Household Survey of the Eastern
     Province Urban Areas: Household Characteristics
     and Housing Conditions 1968-69; Household Survey of
     the Southern Province Urban Areas: Household
     Characteristics and Housing Conditions 1968-69;
     Household Survey of the Rural Areas of the Provin-
     ces: Household Characteristics and Housing Condi-
     tions 1968-69. All titles were published in 1969 in
     Freetown.

12   Central Statistics Office, Household Survey of the
     Western Province: Economic and Expenditure, 1966-
     69, Final Report, p. 14.

13   Ibid., p. 3.

14   The problem of overcrowding must be apparent to even
     the most superficial observer of African cities.
     For a discussion of this phenomenon, cf. Gugler and
     Flanagan, Urbanisation and Social Change in West
     Africa, pp. 45-49.

15   Ethnicity and religious affiliation is discussed in
     some detail by Edward Fashole-Luke, "Religion in
     Freetown", in Chris Fyfe and Eldred Jones (eds.),
     Freetown: A Symposium, Oxford, 1968.

16   Cf. Harrel-Bond et al, Community, Leadership and the
     Transformation of Freetown (1801-1976), ch. 9.

17   It should be noted that none of the dockers in the
     sample were members of any of the masonic lodges.
     The membership of these lodges has been restricted
     to the elites among the Krios (cf. Abner Cohen, The
     Politics of Elite Culture, Los Angeles, 1981) but

during the last fifteen years or so, has become increasingly open to the elites of other ethnic groups including the Asian mercantile community.

18 Cf. J. I. Clarke, Sierra Leone in Maps, London, 1969, p. 36.

19 Cf. Banton, West African City, pp. 48 ff.

20 Stevedoring was taken over by the Port Authority on 1st November 1978, and the Maritime and Waterfront Workers' Union continued to represent the Stevedores. Casual store cargo-handling labourers, who have always been in the employ of the Port Authority and were members of the Dock Workers' Union accounted for 22 percent of the sample. The casuals will continue to be treated as a group in this discussion of orientation to work and to trade unionism.

21 In 1979/80 the Dock Workers' Union was negotiating a medicare package with the Authority.

22 Cf. Peter Lloyd, Power and Independence: Urban Africans' Perception of Social Inequality, London, 1974, especially p. 184 ff.; and Margaret Peil, Nigerian Politics: The People's View, London, 1976, for survey reports and discussions of ambivalence among low-income groups vis a vis inequalities in Nigerian Society.

23 Interview with a senior official of the Authority, 8th January 1980.

24 Cf. Jeffries, Class, Power and Ideology.

CHAPTER 6 (pp. 139-177)

1 Sierra Leone, Report of the Board of Inquiry into the Docks Dispute, Freetown, 1967 (henceforth referred to as The Panda Report).

2 Interview with J. T. Kanu, founder member of the union and former Union President, 26th February 1980. The same ground was covered in interviews of other founder members and in more informal conversations with dockers during the first and second periods of field research in 1979/80 and 1982. Cf. also Labour Department, Annual Report, 1963, p. 7.

3 Interview with Aziz Kassim, 6th March 1982.

4   Interview with J. T. Kanu, 26th February 1980.

5   Ibid.

6   Interview with Aziz Kassim, 6th March 1982.

7   Ibid.

8   Assuming that each of the 2,649 members of the
    union paid their subscriptions, monthly revenue of
    the union in 1963 would have been £55.1.6d.

9   In August 1964, Sierra Leone changed over to the
    decimal system and introduced new currency, Leones
    and Cents.

10 Interview with Aziz Kassim, 6th March 1982.

11 The Panda Report, p. 2.

12 Ibid.

13 Interview with Thema Conteh (former Union Shop
    Steward), 5th March 1982.

14 Interview with Aziz Kassim, 6th March 1982.

15 Ibid.

16 Interview with M. I. Mansaray, 28th April 1980; it
    should be noted that in Sierra Leone, an opportunity
    to travel abroad, particularly to the industrial-
    ised countries, is regarded with considerable excit-
    ement. This is because the individual is in effect
    presented with an opportunity to bring back consu-
    mer durables produced in these countries, which are
    scarce and extremely expensive locally.

17 Interview with M. I. Mansaray, 3rd April 1982.

18 Interview with M. I. Mansaray, 28th April 1980; the
    same point was made during the 1982 interview.

19 The Panda Report, p. 3.

20 Ibid.

21 Ibid.

22 Paid-up members of the Dock Workers' Union to the

the Registrar of Trade Union, Labour Department, 8th October 19675, quoted in The Panda Report, p. 4.

23 Interview with M. I. Mansaray, 28th April 1980.

24 The Panda Report, p. 5.

25 Interview with M. I. Mansaray, 28th April 1980.

26 Ibid; Mansaray has since said that the government was willing to appoint a commission as Sandy had become an embarassment (interview with M. I. Mansaray, 3rd April 1982).

27 Interview with M. I. Mansaray, 28th April 1980.

28 The Panda Report, p. 10.

29 The point should also be made that the union leadership have been equally eager to grab the carrot and to enter into clientelist relations with politicians whose influence could be used in bargaining with management.

30 Interview with M. I. Mansaray, 3rd April 1982.

31 Labour Department Annual Report 1967; figure includes casual stevedore labourers; cf. Table 4.1 supra.

32 Interview with M. I. Mansaray, 3rd April 1982.

33 Ibid.

34 Dock Workers' Union, M. I. Mansaray, to the General Manager, Sierra Leone Produce Marketing Board, 14th March 1968.

35 Dock Workers' Union, Minutes of a meeting held on on Thursday, 12th June 1969, between the representatives of the Dock Workers' Union and the management of the Sierra Leone Produce Marketing Board.

36 Interview with M. I. Mansaray, 3rd April 1982.

37 Ibid.

38 Interview with Mark Luseni (Shop Steward), 18th February 1980.

39 Ibid.

40 Interview with Aziz Kassim, 6th March 1982.

41 Interview with M. I. Mansaray, 3rd April 1982.

42 Dock Workers' Union, D. T. Patnelli to Secretary-General, 20th January 1970.

43 Interview with Aziz Kassim, 6th March 1982.

44 Dock Workers' Union, Minutes of the Executive Council Meeting, 17th June 1970.

45 Dock Workers' Union, Minutes of the Executive Council Meeting, 2nd July 1970.

46 Ibid.

47 Interview with Aziz Kassim, 6th March 1982.

48 Dock Workers' Union, Minutes of the Executive Council Meeting, 25th August 1971.

49 Dock Workers' Union, Minutes of the Executive Council Meeting, 3rd October 1971.

50 Dock Workers' Union, Summary of Mass Meeting, 9th October 1971.

51 Ibid.

52 Dock Workers' Union, Minutes of the Executive Council Meeting, 20th December 1971.

53 Ibid.

54 Dock Workers' Union, Minutes of the Executive Council Meeting, 13th April 1972.

55 Dock Workers' Union, Minutes of the Executive Council Meeting, 5th August 1974.

56 Dock Workers' Union, Minutes of the Executive Council Meeting, 10th May 1976.

57 Dock Workers' Union, Minutes of the Executive Council Meeting, 17th February 1978.

58 Dock Workers' Union, Minutes of the Executive Coun-

cil Meeting, 17th February 1972.

59 Dock Workers' Union, Minutes of the Executive Council Meeting, 14th March 1972.

60 Dock Workers' Union, Minutes of the Executive Council Meeting, 17th February 1972.

61 Interview with Aziz Kassim, 6th March 1982; the same ground was covered in conversations with dock workers.

62 Dock Workers' Union, Minutes of the Executive Council Meeting, 21st December 1972.

63 Dock Workers' Union, O. B. Conteh to Executive Council, 16th March 1973.

64 Dock Workers' Union, Minutes of the Executive Council Meeting, 29th May 1973.

65 Dock Workers' Union, Minutes of the Executive Council Meeting, 30th August 1973.

66 Ibid.

67 Interview with Aziz Kassim, 6th March 1982.

68 Ibid.

69 Dock Workers' Union, Minutes of the Executive Council Meeting, 17th January 1974.

70 Dock Workers' Union, Minutes of the Executive Council Meeting, 23rd December 1974; this was only a part-time appointment although Conteh did in fact act as Congress Secretary during the absence from the country of the substantive holder.

71 Dock Workers' Union, Minutes of the Executive Council Meeting, 26th March 1975.

72 Dock Workers' Union, Minutes of the Executive Council Meeting, Thursday, 28th September 1978.

73 Interview with Aziz Kassim, 6th March 1982; interview with Alfred Conteh, 23rd February 1982; the same ground was covered in informal conversations with dockers.

74 Dock Workers' Union, Minutes of the Executive Coun-
    cil Meeting, 12th April 1976.

75 Dock Workers' Union, Minutes of the Executive Coun-
    cil Meeting, 13th October 1977.

76 Interview with Aziz Kassim, 6th March 1982.

77 Dock Workers' Union, Minutes of the Executive Coun-
    cil Meeting, Thursday, 30th November 1978. (The
    medicare package was limited to workers and--not
    their families--with the condition, for casuals
    seeking treatment at the Authority's clinic, that
    they must have fallen ill while at work).

78 Dock Workers' Union, Report on Union Conference,
    Friday, 23rd March 1979.

79 Dock Workers' Union, Minutes of the Executive Coun-
    cil Meeting, 26th April 1979.

80 Ibid.

81 Interview with Aziz Kassim, 6th March 1982; the same
    ground was covered in conversations with dockers.

82 Dock Workers' Union, Minutes of the Executive Coun-
    cil Meeting, 28th May 1979.

83 Ibid.

84 Ibid.

85 Interview with Aziz Kassim, 6th March 1982.

86 Dock Workers' Union, Minutes of the Executive Coun-
    cil Meeting, 30th August 1979.

87 Ibid.

88 Interview with Aziz Kassim, 6th March 1982; the same
    ground was also covered during informal conversa-
    tions with dockers. (O. B. Conteh himself declined
    to comment on these issues; interview with O. B.
    Conteh, 21st April 1980).

89 Ibid; a letter from Mark Luseni of 25th August 1980
    brought news that O. B. had been found guilty by a
    Freetown High Court.

90 Port Authority Archives, Minutes of the Board, 12th Januaray 1965.

91 Interview with M. I. Mansaray, 3rd April 1982; it was established that Jack Sandy now lives in Liberia, and as such it was not possible to interview him during both periods of field research in Freetown.

92 Port Authority Archives, Minutes of the Board, 4th March 1965.

93 The Panda Report, p. 8.

94 Ibid., p. 5.

95 Port Authority Archives, Matters leading up to and connected with the recent work to rule called by the Sierra Leone Dock Workers' Union, 22nd November 1966.

96 The Panda Report, pp. 5-6.

97 Port Authority Archives, Matters leading up to and connected with the recent work to rule...

98 Ibid.

99 The Panda Report, p. 7.

100 Interview with M. I. Mansaray, 28th April 1980.

101 Port Authority Archives, 'Record of a meeting held on 25th June'.

102 Ibid.

103 Port Authority Archives, Record of a meeting held on 12th December 1968, between Management and the Sierra Leone Dock Workers' Union.

104 Port Authority Archives, Secretary-General, Dock Workers' Union to General Manager, Sierra Leone Port Authority, 4th May 1968; ibid, 6th January 1969.

105 Port Authority Archives, Minutes of the JIC for the Port Industry, Monday, 8th September 1969.

106 Interview with M. I. Mansaray, 3rd April 1982.

107 Port Authority Archives, Acting Secretary Dock Workers' Union to General Manager, Sierra Leone Port Authority, 18th October 1972.

108 Port Authority Archives, Personnel Manager, to Acting Secretary, Dock Workers' Union, 21st October 1972.

109 Interview with O. B. Conteh, 21st April 1980.

110 Port Authority Archives, Secretary, Dock Workers' Union to General Manager, 21st February 1973.

111 Dock Workers' Union, Minutes of the Executive Council Meeting, 17th October 1972.

112 Dock Workers' Union, Minutes of the Executive Council Meeting, 11th October 1973; according to the minutes, "...joyous sentiments were expressed by the whole meeting which regarded this as a special distinction for dock workers..."

113 Dock Workers' Union, Minutes of the Executive Council Meeting, 13th December 1974.

114 Interview with a senior official of the Port Authority, 8th January 1980.

115 Port Authority Archives, Minutes of Management-Union Meeting, 30th May 1978.

116 The Forster Report, p. 8.

117 Dock Workers' Union, Minutes of meeting held on 12th June 1969 between representatives of the Produce Marketing Board and the Dock Workers' Union.

118 Cf. H. Braverman, Labour and Monopoly Capital, New York, 1974.

119 Cf. Melson and Wolpe, Nigeria: Modernisation and the Politics of Communalism, East Lansing, 1972.

CHAPTER 7 (pp. 179-216)

1 Cf. Gershon Collier, Sierra Leone: Experiment in Democracy, New York, 1970, p. 32. But see also APC Secretariat, Red Sun: A History of the All

Peoples' Congress Party of Sierra Leone, Freetown, 1981; and Gustav Deveneaux, Power Politics in Sierra Leone, Ibadan, 1982.

2   Interview with H. N. Georgestone, 23rd January 1980.

3   Interview with Marcus Grant, 16th January 1980.

4   Interview with President Siaka Stevens, 11th July 1980.

5   Interview with C. A. Wilton-During, 13th April 1982.

6   This account of the 1962 elections has been taken from Cartwright, Politics in Sierra Leone, ch. 9. The same ground is covered in Victor King, "The Search for Political Stability in Sierra Leone 1960-72", ch. 2.

7   Cartwright, Politics in Sierra Leone, p. 166.

8   Interview with Tejan Kassim, Secretary, Artisans, Ministry of Works Employees' Union (nee Artisans and Allied Workers' Union), 26th March 1982.

9   Interview with H. N. Georgestone, 23rd January 1980.

10 Interview with Marcus Grant, 16th January 1980; cf. Labour Department, Annual Report 1962, p. 8.

11 Interview with Tejan Kassim, 26th March 1982.

12 Interview with Marcus Grant, 16th January 1980.

13 Interview with E. T. Kamara, 25th May 1982.

14 Ibid.

15 Ibid; cf. Labour Department, Annual Report 1966, p. 7.

16 Interview with a senior Labour Department official, 3rd March 1982.

17 Interview with a senior official of Selection Trust, 14th January 1981.

18 Cartwright, Politics in Sierra Leone, pp. 216-217.

19 Interview with H. N. Georgestone, 23rd January 1980;
    cf. Cartwright, Politics in Sierra Leone, p. 225.

20 Interview with M. I. Mansaray, 3rd April 1982;
    interview with E. T. Kamara, 25th May 1982.

21 Interview with E. T. Kamara, 25th May 1982; det-
    ails on the election campaign, the results and
    subsequent events are provided in Cartwright, Poli-
    tics in Sierra Leone, pp. 249-255, and in King,
    "The Search for Political Stability". In the South
    and South-east, six SLPP supporters or MPs who had
    grown dissatisfied with Sir Albert's leadership
    stood as 'independents' and were successful. For a
    detailed account of the cleavages within the SLPP
    in the South-east, cf. Walter Barrows, Grassroots
    Politics in an African State, New York, 1976.

22 A comprehensive study of the intervention of the
    army has been undertaken by Cox, Civil-Military
    Relations in Sierra Leone.

23 Labour Congress, E. T. Kamara to H. A. Tulatz,
    Assistant General Secretary ICFTU, 11th April 1967.

24 Interview with H. N. Georgestone, 23rd January 1980.

25 Labour Department, Annual Report 1969, Freetown,
    1969.

26 Statement on the Budget for 1967/68 Broadcast by
    Col. A. T. Juxon-Smith, Chairman National Reforma-
    tion Council on 30th June 1967, p. 6.

27 Ibid., p. 8.

28 Interview with E. T. Kamara, 25th May 1982.

29 Labour Congress, Item for inclusion in the agenda
    for consideration of the Advisory Committee, sub-
    mitted by E. T. Kamara, n.d., circa August 1967.

30 Ibid.

31 Cf. Twelve Years of Economic Achievement and Poli-
    tical Consolidation Under the APC and Dr. Siaka
    Stevens (1968-80), p. 9).

32 Ibid., p. 13.

33 Ibid., p. 17.

34 Ibid; Labour Congress, E. T. Kamara to General Sec-
    retaries of all registered trade unions of Sierra
    Leone, 10 November 1968.

35 Artisans, Ministry of Works Employees' Union, Archi-
    ives, Report of ad hoc Committee on Centralisation,
    5th March 1969.

36 Interview with Uriah Davies, formerly Assistant Sec-
    retary of the Clerical Union, and currently Secre-
    tary of the Hotels, Foods, Drinks, Tobacco, and
    Entertainment and Services Workers' Union, 19th June
    1980. The same point was made with further elabora-
    tion in second interview with Davies on 5th April
    1982.

37 Artisans, Ministry of Works Employees' Union, Sec-
    retary-General Labour Congress to all Secretaries of
    affiliated unions, 18th February 1970.

38 Labour Congress, An Agreement between the Sierra
    Leone Labour Congress and the Sierra Leone Employ-
    ers' Federation, 13th March 1970.

39 Labour Congress, Shop Steward Manual (produced in
    conjunction with the AALC), n.d.

40 Chris Allen, 'Sierra Leone' p. 205.

41 The author is obliged to Abdul Salami Williams, a
    former aide of Ibrahim Bash-Taqi, for bringing this
    to my attention.

42 Artisan, Ministry of Works Employees' Union, Minutes
    of the Extraordinary Meeting of the Sierra Leone
    Labour Congress held on Tuesday, 26th March 1971.

43 Twelve Years of Economic Achievement and Political
    Consolidation Under the APC and Dr. Siaka Stevens,
    p. 85.

44 Interview with H. N. Georgestone, 23rd January 1980.
    Around the time of Georgestone's public statements
    of reservation on trends in the conduct of the APC,
    he was informed that his union, Transport and
    General Workers', was to be investigated by a public
    inquiry for corruption and other malpractices.
    There is evidence that some sections of the rank and

file demanded the inquiry. Georgestone and other
union officials were found guilty of misusing union
funds and other instances of maladministration.
(Cf. Report of the Faulkner Commission of Inquiry
into the Finance and Administration of the Transport
and General Workers' Union and Government Statement
Thereon, Freetown, 1970, pp. 74-77).

45 Interview with H. N. Georgestone, 23rd January
    1980; Georgestone's reservations and his disagree-
    ment with George Palmer over this issue have been
    corroborated by Uriah Davies. (Interview with
    U. O. H. Davies, 5th April 1982).

46 Labour Congress, Minutes of Extraordinary Meeting
    held on 23rd September 1971.

47 Labour Congress, AALC Budget Provision--1972 to
    Sierra Leone Labour Congress, 2nd December 1972.
    According to this document, the contribution of the
    AALC to salaries and other organisational expendi-
    ture of Congress was Le15,786.80.

48 It should be noted that the Industrial Relations
    Court has never been constituted in view of success-
    ful interventions of the Minister, and indeed senior
    politicians in settling disputes.

49 Sierra Leone House of Representatives, Parliamentary
    Debates, 13th October 1971.

50 Ibid.

51 Sierra Leone Employers' Federation, Newsletter No.
    52 January/February 1972. The statement was repro-
    duced in full in the newsletter.

52 Labour Congress, Minutes of Executive Meeting held
    on 8th January 1972.

53 Labour Congress, Resolutions adopted on Tuesday, 2nd
    April 1974 on the persistent inflationary trend in
    the economy of Sierra Leone.

54 Cf. President's Annual Address to Parliament, 21st
    June 1974 (reproduced in Twelve Years of Economic
    Achievement and Political consolidation..., pp.
    235-243.

55 Cf. Budget Speech delivered to Parliament by the

Hon. Minister of Finance, C. A. Kamara-Taylor, 29th June 29 1973 (reproduced in ibid, pp. 200-210).

56 Interview with U. O. H. Davies, 5th April 1982.

57 Ibid.

58 Interview with a senior official of Congress.

59 Labour Congress, Report of the Eighteen-man Committee of the Sierra Leone Labour Congress and the Sierra Leone Council of Labour to seek ways and means for the merger of the two organisations, n.d., circa December 1975.

60 Interview with Pios Foray and Samuel Tumoi (two of the leaders of the students) 14th June 1980; cf. Pios Foray, "The Students' Crisis of January 1977", B.A. dissertation, Fourah Bay College, University of Sierra Leone, 1977.

61 Cf. Chris Clapham, Liberia and Sierra Leone, p. 94.

62 Labour Congress, first Press Release, 31st January 1977.

63 Labour Congress, Press Release, 31st January 1977.

64 Interview with a senior official of Congress, 26th February 1982.

65 Interviews, Pios Foray and Samuel Tumoi, 14th June 1980.

66 Labour Congress, Proposals of the Sierra Leone Labour Congress to Government in connection with the pending general elections...and for the economic reconstruction of our beloved Sierra Leone, 28th February 1977.

67 Ibid.

68 Cf. The Path to One Party System of Government p. 14.

69 Cf. Twelve Years of Economic Achievement and Political Consolidation..., p. 434 for the details relating to the organisation of the referendum and the results.

70 Sierra Leone Teachers' Union, Suggested Topics of Discussions, presented to the delegates conference, 28th October 1977.

71 Interview with a senior official of Congress, 26th February 1982.

72 Cf. Bank of Sierra Leone, Economic Review, January-June 1980, p. 13.

73 Informal conversations held by this researcher with the rank and file of the Dock Workers' Union and with Congress leaders during the months preceding the conference and during the conference itself.

74 Since the wage rates of other lower-paid workers in Sierra Leone are comparable to those of the dockers, and since the 1980 awards were also comparable, the decline in the real value of wages must also be comparable. The actual figures, however, have not been obtained and computed.

75 West Africa, 10th August 1981, p. 1822.

76 Ibid., cf. Report of the Taju-Deen Commission of Inquiry (into the strike), Freetown, Government Printers, 1982, pp. 28-29; cf. Richard Jeffries, "Revolution in Black Africa" in C. Dodd and N. O'Sullivan (eds.), Revolutionary Theory and Political Reality, London, (forthcoming) for a discussion of theories of development prevalent on the Left.

77. Cf. West Africa, 24th August 1981, p. 1911 and p. 1913.

78 Cf. Report of the Taju-Deen Commission of Inquiry, p. 31; and West Africa, 7th September 1981, p. 2030-2031.

79 Cf. Report of the Taju-Deen Commission of Inquiry, pp. 31-32; and West Africa, 31st August 1981, pp. 2019-2020.

80 Cf. West Africa, 14th September 1981, pp. 2089-2090.

81 Cf. Report of the Taju-Deen Commission of Inquiry, pp. 36-37.

82 Cf. Olu Williams, "Agro-Rural Development Strategies: Past, Present and Future".

BIBLIOGRAPHY OF SOURCES CITED

ARCHIVES

Artisan, Ministry of Works Employees' Union, Freetown.
London Chamber of Commerce, The Guildhall, City of
   London.
National Workshop Corporation, Freetown.
Ocean Transport Limited (Elder Dempster Lines),
   Liverpool.
Rhodes House, Oxford.
Sierra Leone Dock Workers' Union, Freetown.
Sierra Leone Employers' Federation, Freetown.
Sierra Leone House of Representatives, Freetown.
Sierra Leone Labour Congress, Freetown.
Sierra Leone National Archive, Freetown.
Sierra Leone Port Authority, Freetown.
Sierra Leone Teachers' Union, Freetown.

NEWSPAPERS

The Artisan, Freetown.
The Illustrated London Evening News, London.
The New Leader, London.
The Sierra Leone Weekly News, Freetown.
We Yone, Freetown.
West Africa, London.

OFFICIAL

(a) Report of Committees or Commissions.
        Sir Alexander Paterson, Report on Penal Admini-
        stration and Welfare Services in Sierra Leone,
        Sessional Paper No. 3 of 1944, Freetown, 1944.
     Report of a Committee on Proposals to Build a Deep
        Water Quay at Freetown, Sessional Paper No. 1 of
        1946.
     The Marke Report, Freetown, 1955.
     Report of the Commission of Inquiry Into the
        Strikes and Riots in Freetown During February
        1955 (The Shaw Report), Freetown, 1955.
     Report of the Commissioners of Enquiry into the
        Conduct of Certain Chiefs and Government State-
        ment Thereon, Freetown, n.d., circa 1957.
     Report of the Board of Inquiry into the Docks Dis-
        pute (The Panda Report), Freetown, 1967.

265

Report of the Faulkner Commission of Inquiry into the Finance and Administration of the Transport and General Workers' Union and Government Statement Thereon (The Faulkner Report), Freetown, 1970.

Report of the Commission Appointed to Inquire into all Aspects of the Affairs of the Sierra Leone Port Authority as a Viable Economic Revenue Making Establishment Covering the Period 1st January 1965 to 4th July 1976 (The Forster Report), Freetown, 1977.

Report of the Auditor-General for the Years 1974-79, Freetown, 1980.

Ensuring Equitable Growth: A Strategy for Increasing Employment, Equity and Basic Needs Satisfaction in Sierra Leone (Report to the Government of Sierra Leone by a Jobs and Skills Programme for Africa Advisory Mission), (The JASPA Report), ILO, Addis Abba, 1981.

Report of the Taju-Deen Commission of Inquiry, Freetown, 1982.

(b) Sierra Leone Government, (all titles published in Freetown).

Blue Book of Sierra Leone, (cf. various years between 1900 and 1939).

Government Statement on Africanisation, Sessional Paper No. 4 of 1959.

The Laws of Sierra Leone, 1960.

The Port Act (No. 56) 1964.

Statement on the Budget for 1967/68 Broadcast by Col. A. T. Juxon-Smith, Chairman, National Reformation Council, on 30th June 1967.

Budget Speech Delivered by the Hon. Dr. M. S. Fornah, Minister of Finance, on 8th July 1968.

Budget Speech Delivered by the Hon. Dr. M. S. Fornah, Minister of Finance, on 25th June, 1969.

The Path to a One-Party System of Government, 1978.

Twelve Years of Economic Achievement and Political Consolidation Under the APC and Dr. Siaka Stevens 1968-1980.

The Sierra Leone Gazette, 6th June 1980.

OTHER BODIES

(c) Bank of Sierra Leone, (all titles published in Freetown).

Annual Report 1969; Annual Report 1979; Economic Review Jan-June 1980; Economic Review July-Dec 1981.

266

Central Statistics Office, (all titles published in
    Freetown in 1969).
Household Survey of the Western Province: Economic
    and Expenditure 1966-68.
Household Survey of the Southern Province: Econo-
    mic and Expenditure 1966-68.
Household Survey of the Eastern Province: Econo-
    mic and expenditure 1966-68.
Household Survey of the Northern Province: Econo-
    mic and Expenditure 1966-68.
Household Survey of the Western Province: House-
    hold Characteristics and Housing Conditions.
Household Survey of the Urban Areas of the Southern
    Province: Household Characteristics and Housing
    Conditions.
Household Survey of the Urban Areas of the Eastern
    Province: Household Characteristics and Housing
    Conditions.
Household Survey of the Urban Areas of the Northern
    Province: Household Characteristics and Housing
    Conditions.
Household Survey of the Rural Areas of the Pro-
    vinces: Household Characteristics and Housing
    Conditions.

Colonial Office, Major Capital Works in the Colo-
    nial Territories.
Colonial No. 285, HMSO, London, 1952.

House of Commons, (Britain), CMND 2744, Report by
    the Hon. W. G. A. Ormsby-Gore, MP (Parliamentary
    Under-Secretary of State for the Colonies), on
    his Visit to West Africa During the Year 1962,
    HMSO, London, 1926.
House of Commons, (Britain), CMND 6277, G. St. J.
    Orde-Brown, Labour Conditions in West Africa,
    HMSO, London, 1941.

Labour Department (Sierra Leone), Annual Reports
    for various years between 1939 and 1969 (pub-
    lished in Freetown).

UNPUBLISHED

Theses and Dissertations

    Amolo, M., "Sierra Leone and British Colonial
        Labour Policy 1930-45", PhD thesis, Dalhousie
        University, 1977.

Bennie, M. J., "Government and Politics of Sierra Leone with Special Reference to the Creole Community", M.Phil. thesis, Nottingham University, 1970.

Conway, H. A., "Industrial Relations in Sierra Leone with Special Reference to the Functioning of the Bargaining Machinery Since 1945", PhD thesis, London University, 1968.

Denzer, L., "I. T. A. Wallace-Johnson and the West African Youth League: A Case Study in West African Radicalism", PhD thesis, Birmingham University, 1977.

Foray, P., "The Students' Crisis of January 1977", B.A. dissertation, Fourah Bay College, University of Sierra Leone, 1977.

Gaffney, H. H., "Administration and the Administrative Service in Sierra Leone", PhD thesis, University of Colombia, 1967.

Kaniki, M. H. Y., "Economic and Social History of Sierra Leone 1929-1939", PhD thesis, Birmingham University, 1972.

King, V., "The Search for Political Stability in Sierra Leone 1960-1972", PhD thesis, Manchester University, 1975.

Leighton, N. O., "The Lebanese Middleman in Sierra Leone: The Case of a Non-indigenous Trading Minority and Their Role in Political Development", PhD thesis, Indiana University, 1971.

Lisk, F. A. N., "Industrial Relations in Sierra Leone", M.Sc. dissertation, Queens University, Belfast, 1970.

Lisk, F. A. N., "The Political Economy of Sierra Leone 1960-71 with Special Reference to the IMF Stabilisation Programme of 1966-69", PhD thesis, Birmingham University, 1974.

Minikin, V., "Local Level Politics in Kono District, Sierra Leone", PhD thesis, Birmingham University, 1971.

Sibanda, M. J. M., "Colonial Policy and Development in North-west Sierra Leone", PhD thesis, Birmingham University, 1978.

Swindel, K., "Labour Migration and Mining in Sierra Leone", PhD thesis, London University, 1973.

Taylor, A. B., "The Role of Financial Institutions in the Economic Development of Sierra Leone", PhD thesis, Glasgow University, 1973.

White, E. F., "Creole Women Traders (1792-1945)", PhD thesis, Boston University, 1978.

Others

Cox-George, N. A., "An Essay on Employment and Un-
employment", Freetown, 1950
Grant, M., "Research on Trade Unions in Sierra
Leone", Freetown, Mimeo, n.d.
Sierra Leone Trade Union Congress, "Statement on
the Present Crisis in Congress", Freetown, Mimeo,
n.d.
Williams, O., "Agro-Rural Development Strategies:
Past, Present and Future", paper presented to
the 11th Annual Conference of the Agricultural
Society of Sierra Leone, at Njala University
College, University of Sierra Leone, 24th-27th
March, 1982.

PUBLISHED

Articles

Allen, C., "Sierra Leone", in Dunn, J., West Africa
States, Cambridge University Press, Cambridge,
1979, pp. 189-210.
Banton, M., "The Origins of Tribal Administration
in Freetown", in Sierra Leone Studies (New
Series), No. 2, June 1954, pp. 109-121.
Bhatia, R. J., et al, "Stabilisation Program in
Sierra Leone", in IMF Staff Papers, November
1969, pp. 504-525.
Clapham, C., "The Politics of Failure: Political
Instability and National Integration in Liberia
and Sierra Leone", in Clapham, C., (ed.), Private
Patronage and Public Power: Political Cliente-
lism in the Modern State, Frances Pinter, London,
1982, pp. 76-92.
Cox-George, N. A., "The System of Public Financial
Control in Sierra Leone", in Bank of Sierra
Leone, Economic Review, 5, 3, 1970, pp. 1-11.
Denzer, L. and Spitzer, L., "I. T. A. Wallace-
Johnson and the West African Youth League", (2
parts), in International Journal of African
Historical Studies, 6, 3, 1973; 6, 4, 1973.
Fashole-Luke, E., "Religion in Freetown", in Fyfe,
C., and Jones, E., (eds.), Freetown: A Symposium,
Oxford University Press, Oxford, 1968.
Fowler, D., "The Urban Informal Sector in Sierra
Leone", in Africana Research Bulletin, 6, 3,
1976, pp. 4-34.

269

Fowler, D., "The Urban Informal Sector in
Freetown: Opportunities for Self-Employment",
in Sethuramam, E. V., The Urban Informal Sector
in Developing Countries: Employment, Poverty
and Environment, ILO, Geneva, 1981.
Freund, B., "Labor and Labor History in Africa: A
Review of the Literature", discussed at African
Studies Association Annual Conference, Boston,
1983, (African Studies Review, forthcoming).
Geller, S., "State-Building and Nation-Building in
West Africa", in S. N. Eisenstadt and S. Rokkan
(eds.), Building States and Nations, Sage,
Beverly Hills and London, pp. 348-426.
Gertzel, G., "Uganda After Amin", in African
Affairs, 79, October 1980, pp. 461-489.
Hopkins, A. G., "The Lagos Strike of 1897: An
Exploration in Nigerian Labour History", in Past
Present, 35, 1966, pp. 135-155.
Illife, J., "The Creation of Group Consciousness
Among Dock Workers of Dar es Salaam 1929-50", in
Sandbrook, R. and Cohen, R., The Development of
an African Working Class, Longman, London, 1975.
Jeffries, R., "The Ghanaian Elections of 1979", in
African Affairs, 79, July 1980, pp. 397-414.
Jeffries, R., "Revolution in Black Africa", in
Dodd, C., and O'Sullivan, N., (eds.), Revolution-
ary Theory and Political Reality, Harvester,
London (forthcoming).
Kaim-Caudle, P. R., "Review of Economic Changes in
Sierra Leone 1930-55", in Durham University
Journal, December 1957, pp. 34-41.
Kaniki, M. H. Y., "Attitudes and Reactions Towards
the Lebanese in Sierra Leone During the Colonial
Period", Canadian Journal of African Studies, 8,
1973, pp. 97-113.
Lonsdale, J., "The State and Social Processes in
Africa: A Histriographical Survey", African
Studies Review, 24, 1981, pp. 136-226.
Lonsdale, J., and Berman, B., "Coping with the Con-
tradictions: The Development of the Colonial
State in Kenya, 1895-1914", Journal of African
History, 20, 1979, pp. 487-505.
Lonsdale, J., and Berman, B., "Crisis of Accumula-
tion, Coercion and the Colonial State: The Deve-
lopment of the Labour Control System in Kenya,
1919-1926", Canadian Journal of African Studies,
14, 1980, pp. 55-81.
McMullen, M., "A Theory of Corruption", in Sociological Review, IX, June 1961, pp.181-200.

Meredith, D., "The British Government and Colonial
Economic History 1919-1939", in Economic History
Review, 28, 1975, pp. 449-487.
Moseley, K., "Work, Class and Community: The
Safroko-Limba of Freetown", (forthcoming).
Parry, E., "Colonial Trade Unions", in Corona,
August 1949, pp. 19-21.
Riley, S., "Sierra Leone Politics: Some Recent
Assessments", Africa, 52, (2), 1982, pp. 106-109.
Scott, D. J. R., "The Sierra Leone Election of May
1957", in Mackenzie, W. J. M., and Robinson, R.,
(eds.) Five Elections in Africa, Oxford Univer-
sity Press, Oxford, 1960, pp. 181-192.
Sklar, R., "The Nature of Class Domination in
Africa", Journal of Modern African Studies, 17,
(4), 1979, pp. 531-552.
Stevens, S., "Trade Unionism in Sierra Leone", in
Empire: A Socialist Commentary on Colonial
Affairs, Journal of the Fabian Colonial Bureau,
11, 3, September 1948, p. 5.
Wyse, A., "Searchlight on the Krio in Sierra Leone:
an Ethnographical Study of a West African
People", Institute of African Studies, Fourah Bay
College, Occasional Paper, 3, 1980.
Wyse, A., "The 1926 Railway Strike and Anglo-Krio
Relations: An Interpretation", International
Journal of African Historical Studies, 14, 1981,
pp. 93-123.
Young, C., "Patterns of Social Conflict: State,
Class and Ethnicity", Daedalus, spring, 1982,
pp. 71-98.

Books

APC Secretariat, Red Sun: A History of the All
People's Congress Party of Sierra Leone,
Freetown, APC Secretariat, 1981.
Arrighi, G., and Saul, J., Essays in the Political
Economy of Africa, Monthly Review, New York, 1973.
Banton, M., West African City, Oxford University
Press, Oxford, 1957.
Barrows, J., Grassroots Politics in a West African
State, Africana Publishing Co., New York, 1976.
Bates, R., Markets and States in Tropical Africa:
The Political Basis of Agricultural Policies,
University of California Press, Berkeley, 1981.
Best, R., A History of the Sierra Leone Railway
1899-1949, Railway Admininistration, Freetown,
1949.

Braverman, H., Labor and Monopoly Capital, Monthly
    Review, New York, 1974.
Brooks, G. E., The Kru Mariner, Liberian Studies
    Association, Newark, 1972.
Carney, D. C., Government and Economy in British
    West Africa, Bookman, New York, 1961.
Cartwright, J., Politics in Sierra Leone 1947-67,
    University of Toronto Press, Toronto, 1970.
Cartwright, J., Political Leadership in Sierra
    Leone, Croom Helm, London, 1978.
Cartwright, J., Political Leadership in Africa,
    Croom Helm, London, 1982.
Clapham, C., Liberia and Sierra Leone, Cambridge
    University Press, Cambridge, 1976.
Clarke, J. I., Sierra Leone in Maps, University of
    London Press, London, 1969.
Cohen, A., The Politics of Elite Culture, Univer-
    sity of California Press, Los Angeles, 1981.
Cole, R. W., Kossoh Town Boy, Cambridge University
    Press, Cambridge, 1960.
Collier, G., Sierra Leone: Experiment in Democra-
    cy, University of London Press, London and New
    York, 1970.
Cox-George, N. A., Finance and Development in West
    Africa: The Sierra Leone Experience, Oxford
    University Press, Oxford, 1959.
Cox, T., Civil-Military Relations in Sierra Leone,
    Harvard University Press, Cambridge, Mass., 1976.
Davies, P. N., The Trade Makers: Elder Dempster in
    West Africa, 1952-1972, Longman, London, 1973.
Deveneaux, G., Power Politics in Sierra Leone,
    African Universities Press, Ibadan, 1981.
Eisenstadt, S. N. and Lemarchand, R., (eds.), Pol-
    itical Clientelism Patronage and Development,
    Sage, Beverly Hills, 1981.
Fanon, F., Wretched of the Earth, MacGibbon and
    Kee, London, 1965.
Fitzjohn, W. H., Ambassador of Christ and Caesar,
    Daystar, Ibadan, 1975.
Fowler-Lunn, K., The Gold Missus: Journal of a
    Woman Gold Prospector in Sierra Leone, Allen and
    Unwin, 1938.
Fyfe, C., A History of Sierra Leone, Oxford Univer-
    sity Press, Oxford, 1962.
Gerth, H., and Wright Mills, C. W., (eds.) From Max
    Weber, Routledge Kegan Paul, London, 1977.
Green, G., Journey Without Maps, Allen Lane,
    London, 1937.

Gramsci, A., Selections from Political Writings, (2 volumes), Hoare, Q., (ed.), Laurence and Wischart, London, 1977.

Gugler, J., and Flanagan, W., Urbanisation and Social Change in West Africa, Cambridge University Press, Cambridge, 1979.

Harrel-Bond B., et al, Community, Leadership, and the Transformation of Freetown (1801-1976), Mouton, The Hague, 1977.

Hopkins, A., An Economic History of West Africa, Longman, London, 1973.

Jackson, R., and Rosberg, C., Personal Rule in Black Africa: Prince, Autocrat, Prophet, Tyrant, California University Press, Los Angeles, 1982.

Jeffries, R., Class, Power and Ideology: The Railwaymen of Sekondi-Takoradi, Cambridge University Press, Cambridge, 1978.

Killick, T., Development Economics in Action, St. Martin's Press, New York, 1978.

Kitching, G., Class and Economic Change in Kenya, Yale University Press, New Haven and London, 1980.

Kilson, M., Political Change in a West African State, Atheneum, New York, 1965.

Kucznski, R. R., Demographic Survey of the British Empire, 1, Royal Institute of International Affairs, London, 1948.

Laan, L. van der, The Sierra Leone Diamonds, Oxford University Press, Oxford, 1965.

Laan, L. van der, The Lebanese Traders of Sierra Leone, Mouton, The Hague, 1975.

Laan, L. van der, European Commercial Enterprises in Colonial Sierra Leone 1896-1961: A Preliminary Survey, Leiden University, Leiden, 1978.

Lloyd, P. C., Power and Independence: Urban Africans' Perception of Social Inequality, Routledge Kegan Paul, 1974.

MacMillan, A., The Red Book of West Africa, Frank Cass, London, 1938.

Melson and Wolpe (eds.), Nigerian: Modernisation and the Politics of Communalism, Michigan State University Press, East Lansing, 1972.

Migeod, F. W. H., A View of Sierra Leone, Kegan Paul, London 1926.

Niculescu, B., Colonial Planning: A Comprehensive Study, Allen and Unwin, London, 1968.

O'Brien, D. C., Saint and Politicians, Cambridge University Press, Cambridge, 1975.

Ossowski, S., Class Structure in the Social Consciousness, Routeledge Kegan Paul, London, 1963.

Parpart, J., Labor and Capital on the African
     Cooperbelt, Temple University Press, Philadel-
     phia, 1983.
Peace, A., Choice, Class and Conflict: A Study of
     Southern Nigerian Factory Workers, Harvester,
     Brighton, 1979.
Peil, M., Nigerian Politics: The People's View,
     Cassell, London 1976.
Porter, A. T., Creoledom: A Study of the Develop-
     ment of Freetown Society, Oxford University
     Press, Oxford, 1963.
Riggs, F., Administration in Developing Societies:
     The Theory of Prismatic Society, Houghton
     Mifflin, Boston, 1964.
Roberts, B. C., Labour in the Tropical Territories
     of the Commonwealth, Bell, London, 1962.
Saul, J., The State and Revolution in East Africa,
     Monthly Review, New York, 1979.
Sibthorpe, A. B. C., A History of Sierra Leone,
     (3rd Edition), Frank Cass, London, 1970.
Spitzer, L., The Creoles of Sierra Leone: Res-
     ponses to Colonialism 1870-1975, University of
     Wisconsin Press, Madison, 1974.
Waterman, P., Division and Unity Amongst Nigerian
     Workers: Lagos Port Unionism 1940s-1960s Insti-
     tute of Social Studies, The Hauge, 1982.